MONETARY PLANNING
FOR INDIA

SURAJ B. GUPTA

DELHI
OXFORD UNIVERSITY PRESS
BOMBAY CALCUTTA MADRAS

Oxford University Press, Walton Street, Oxford OX2 6DP
Oxford New York
Athens Auckland Bangkok Bombay
Calcutta Cape Town Dar es Salaam Delhi
Florence Hong Kong Istanbul Karachi
Kuala Lumpur Madras Madrid Melbourne
Mexico City Nairobi Paris Singapore
Taipei Tokyo Toronto
and associates in
Berlin Ibadan

ISBN 0 19 563746 1

Printed by Saurab Print-O-Pack, Noida
and published by Neil O'Brien, Oxford University Press
YMCA Library Building, Jai Singh Road, New Delhi 110001

To my teachers and students—with
gratitude and hope

PREFACE

Money-supply changes have wide-ranging economic effects. Yet, in India, the planning of such changes has not received the kind and amount of attention it deserves. Monetary authorities have paid only lip service to it, and books on monetary policy have generally ignored the issue. They offer only descriptive accounts of the control measures of the Reserve Bank of India.

The present book marks a strong departure from this tradition. The greater part of it is devoted to a discussion of what monetary planning should aim at and why, how changes in the supply of money come about, and the sources of change in high-powered money, the key factor responsible for changes in money supply. It is after this discussion that traditional and new measures of monetary control are brought into the picture. The discussion combines theory with empirical evidence, and a critical evaluation of the conduct of monetary policy and uses of monetary-control measures with positive suggestions regarding what can and should be done to attain well-specified goals. Monetary institutions and practices as they have operated over the period covered (1950-1 to 1976-7) have been explained, evaluated, and woven into the discussion at all steps.

Policy-making is the art of the feasible. Simple ideas in this field are more useful and powerful than complex ones. Therefore, I have postulated simple relations which are true to a first order of approximation and which yield simple policy rules that minimize the information needs of policy-making. As our understanding of the monetary system and its working in the country improves and more reliable information on its various aspects becomes available, more complicated policy models can be designed which take note of several interactions within the system and its lag structure.

The book is addressed to both policy makers, and teachers and students of monetary economics. For the former, I have tried my best to keep the main text free from technical discussions and placed them in the appendices. Yet, a full appreciation of the main argument running through the book will require careful reading and serious thinking on their part. Teachers and students of monetary economics should, of course, pay full attention to the appendices, too.

Researchers in this field will find Appendix G, which gives at one place annual average data on several commonly-used variables for the period 1950–1 to 1975–6/1976–7, particularly helpful. The book has grown out of the lectures on monetary theory and policy that I have been delivering to M.A. (Economics) students at the Delhi School of Economics for several years. The lectures have given me an excellent opportunity to formulate and experiment with my analysis and arguments relating to the subject of this book.

The teaching of monetary policy in most Indian universities has been carried on for too long at an uncritical descriptive level. It is high time for it to be updated and made more meaningful. Students need to be exposed systematically to the theory and empirical evidence on the demand for and the supply of money, and their relation to the theory, problems, and limitations of monetary planning. This alone can help them appreciate the working and importance of several monetary control measures. This book should serve as an appropriate text on the subject.

Parts of this book have been published as articles in the *Indian Economic Journal* and the *Economic and Political Weekly*. They appear in a revised and extended form as Chapters 2 and 3.

Several persons have helped me, directly or indirectly, in writing this book: S. N. Kapoor and Satya Paul with their computational assistance; Dr V. N. Pandit with useful suggestions; several officers of the Reserve Bank of India, in particular, Dr A. K. Banerjee, Dr A. Hasib, Meenakshi Tyagarajan, Dr A. Vasudevan, and, most of all, my younger brother O. P. Aggarwal, with clarifications of certain institutional practices and with the provision of data. My grateful thanks to each one of them. My debt to my predecessors and co-workers in the field is too great to be acknowledged fully.

Despite all the generous help that I have been fortunate enough to receive from the officers of the Reserve Bank of India, there are still numerous areas of darkness which deserve to be illuminated by the Bank with appropriate data and explanations. At several places in the book I have taken pains to point them out explicitly. I hope the Bank will take early measures to remedy these. I also hope that the Bank will give serious consideration to several policy suggestions that have come out of the analysis in the book.

SURAJ B. GUPTA

Delhi School of Economics

CONTENTS

LIST OF TABLES

LIST OF ABBREVIATIONS

C.S.O.	Central Statistical Organization
G.O.I.	Government of India
I.D.B.I.	Industrial Development Bank of India
I.M.F.	International Monetary Fund
N.L.R.	Net Liquidity Ratio
N.N.M.L.	Net Non-Monetary Liabilities
R.B.C.	Reserve Bank Credit
R.B.I.	Reserve Bank of India
R.B.M.	Reserve Bank Money
S.I.R. (G.S.)	Statutory Investment Ratio (Government Securities)
S.L.R.	Statutory Liquidity Ratio

CHAPTER 1

OBJECTIVES OF MONETARY PLANNING

1.1 What is Monetary Planning?

By monetary planning we mean controlled changes in the stock of money to subserve well-defined social objectives. In this definition three key terms are involved: (1) stock of money, (2) controlled changes, and (3) social objectives. The first term tells us what monetary planning is about—that it is about the stock of money. At the very outset it is essential to grasp this point because, at times, monetary planning is confused with credit planning. No doubt, at the aggregate level, money and bank credit are highly correlated, in generation as well as extinction. But money is not credit, nor *vice versa*. Money is an asset of the holding public. Credit is the asset of the lending institutions and the liability of the borrowing public. Also, credit is a much broader category than mere bank credit. Several non-bank financial institutions as well as individuals are also engaged in the provision of credit. The analytical constructs and theories explaining the role and working of money are different from those concerned with the role and working of credit. With money, the problem is only one of its *total* stock and changes in it. With credit, the problem is not merely one of its total and changes in it, but also of its allocation—sectoral, inter-industry, inter-party, regional—, cost and other terms and conditions, duration, renewal, of various sources (kinds), etc. Therefore, monetary planning should not be confused with credit planning.

All planning must be purposive—for the attainment of well-defined objectives. We shall discuss very briefly this problem of the objectives in the present chapter.

The formulation and execution of monetary planning requires a thorough understanding of the working of the monetary system and the instruments of monetary control. A major part of the book will be concerned with a discussion of these concrete issues.

1.2 Objectives of Monetary Planning

Generally, some combination of the following objectives of economic policy is specified:

1. maximum feasible output,
2. a high rate of growth,
3. fuller employment,
4. price stability,
5. reduction in inequalities in the distribution of income and wealth, and
6. healthy balance in the balance of payments.

A brief discussion of the relations between monetary policy and each of these objectives is offered below. We shall argue that monetary planning for price stability at maximum feasible output will best subserve the attainment of other objectives as well, so far as monetary planning alone is concerned.

1.3 Monetary Policy and Output

Monetary policy acts primarily through the management of *aggregate* demand. The emphasis on the word aggregate is important. Any allocational or sectoral problems are beyond its domain. They lie within the sphere of credit policy.

Monetary policy can be conducive to the attainment of the goal of maximum feasible output by ensuring sufficiency of aggregate demand for output, or, at least, by ensuring that any deficiency of aggregate demand does not emerge from forces operating in the money market. In terms of the 'Quantity Theory of Money' model this can be done by supplying the amount of money that will be demanded by the public at the maximum feasible output and at the socially-planned (or expected) values of such other variables as enter the demand function for money. This whole problem will be discussed in detail in Chapter 2. At this point, we may note that, besides money, fiscal-policy variables and other exogenous factors also affect aggregate demand. The sufficiency of aggregate demand is only a necessary condition for the realization of the maximum feasible output. It is not a sufficient condition. The composition of aggregate demand in relation to capacity to produce is also important. Then, there can be hurdles or serious bottlenecks on the supply side which militate against the realization of the potential, as given by (say) the installed capacity, land and labour resources.

There is very little that monetary policy can do on the supply front. Excessive reliance on this tool by pumping more and more money into the system can only spell disaster through inflation. A proper allocation of credit for realizing capacity output is a different matter —again, a question of credit planning.

1.4 Monetary Policy and Price Stability

This brings us to another policy objective—that of price stability. Since the beginning of the forties the danger to price stability has been mainly from inflation; and for several years now, inflation has been one of the chief economic problems in most countries of the world. There is an erroneous belief in some quarters that inflation is a necessary cost of having a high rate of economic development and for full employment. We shall discuss this issue in detail later in this chapter. At this point we shall merely deny the validity of this view for the Indian economy. In our opinion, price stability is not only compatible with, but also essential for, the realization of the other objectives listed above. This will become clear from the following paragraphs.

In the Indian context, for monetary planning, there is no serious conflict between the objective of price stability and that of maximum feasible (or 'full capacity') output, for the cost–push phenomena are still relatively weak in India. (There is, however, no guarantee that they will continue to be so for long.) This issue will be discussed in Chapter 2. There, it will be shown that the twin objectives can be best served by planning a rate of growth in the supply of money which equals the expected rate of growth in the demand for money at stable prices when the economy is moving along its 'maximum feasible output' path. Price stability with 'full capacity' output will, then, serve as the best guiding principle for monetary planning in India.

1.5 Monetary Policy and Employment

Monetary policy affects employment by influencing its proximate determinants. In a static system, the level of employment is largely a function of total output, its composition, and the labour-intensity of industries and techniques of production employed. In a growing system, given the institutional structure, what matters most for employment expansion is the rate of investment and the distribution of this investment among economic activities of differing labour-intensities.

For total output, over any short period, the best that can be done is to exploit to the full the given productive capacity in the economy. We have already seen above what (limited) role monetary policy can play in this regard by ensuring sufficiency of aggregate demand (at stable prices).

The composition of output, on the demand side, is determined largely by the prevailing highly skewed distribution of income and wealth. Much of the larger part of output and expenditure, in the public sector, too, caters to the demands of the more affluent sections of society. The implied common (but untested) assumption is that the richer households, on average, demand less labour-intensive products than do the poor households. Thus, economic inequalities hamper growth in the demand for labour. Among other things, inflation is an important factor that accentuates income and wealth inequalities. And 'excess' increases in the quantity of money are the most important single source of continued inflation. Thus, the indirect contribution of monetary policy for fuller employment via price stability needs to be recognized.

On the supply side, the allocation of credit can influence the allocation of real resources among economic activities, considered from the angle of their labour-intensity. But, as pointed out already, this is the role of credit policy and not monetary policy, which is intrinsically aggregative.

The rates of interest charged on loans by financial institutions are generally sticky. They adjust not only slowly, but also incompletely to the actual or expected rate of inflation. In an inflationary climate, this often results in very low real rates of interest, when money rates have been adjusted for the realized rates of inflation. Even in a capital-scarce country like India, this (along with other factors) makes capital seem cheaper (relative to labour) than it actually is. This encourages the growth of capital-intensive industries and technology, and hampers the expansion of employment.

Price stability at maximum feasible output is also the best contribution monetary policy can make to the promotion of investment and saving in the economy. Investment is encouraged because price stability reduces market uncertainties and makes financial planning less hazardous and more reliable. Savings and their institutionalization are encouraged because financial assets fixed in nominal terms (such as deposits of various kinds, bonds, insurance policies, etc.) as forms of holding wealth do not depreciate in real value owing to inflation. Later in the chapter we shall examine in depth a counter-hypothesis that inflation raises the saving ratio of the community by generating forced saving. We shall also discuss more fully the role of monetary policy in promoting voluntary saving and its institutionalization.

1.6 Price Stability and External Balance

The policy of price stability is also possibly the best policy for a healthy balance of payments. On capital account of the balance of payments, we leave out net foreign aid and foreign investment as independent policy variables. Recently a new source of foreign exchange receipts has come into prominence—the inward remittances of Indians residing abroad, sent to their dependents living in India. A relatively stable domestic price level by keeping the Indian rupee strong in the foreign exchange market encourages the flow of these remittances (and other foreign exchange receipts) through regular banking channels. This brings foreign exchange earnings into official hands. But, if domestic inflation causes an overvaluation of the rupee, a black market in foreign exchange will be encouraged.

On trade account, other things being the same, our exports will have a better chance for promotion if the domestic price level remains stable, though, to be more exact, what would matter is the rate of inflation (in the prices of exportables) in India as compared to the rates of inflation in other countries, especially in India's main export markets. A relatively higher rate of domestic inflation will tend to encourage imports. In a competitive world system no single country can choose autonomously its own rate of inflation. Trade barriers of various kinds do protect national economies against external economic influences—though not fully. Even from the point of view of foreign trade, too, domestic price stability still remains the best policy. Any fundamental disequilibrium in the balance of payments must, of course, be corrected by suitable changes in exchange rates rather than merely through domestic policies.

1.7 Inflationary Monetary Policy and Redistributions of Income and Wealth

It is well known that inflation causes a large-scale redistribution of income and wealth in a society. The losers are the fixed-income people (most wage-earners and rentiers) and monetary creditors (bond-holders, pensioners, depositors, holders of cash balances, etc).

6 Monetary Planning for India

The gainers are the variable-income people (profit-earners) and monetary debtors. The gains and losses from inflation arise because all prices and nominal values do not rise equiproportionately: some rise more or faster while others remain fixed for a long period. In most cases, the redistribution of income and wealth caused by inflation changes in favour of the richer sections of the population. Thus, inflation is inequality-enhancing and highly iniquitous. This reinforces further the case for price stability and against inflationary monetary policy.

In some quarters it is argued that it is only unanticipated inflation which causes redistribution of income and wealth; that, after a time, continuing inflation is anticipated, and that fully anticipated inflation ceases to cause redistribution except when it arises through inflation as a tax on cash balances. Strictly speaking, full anticipation of inflation is only a necessary and not a sufficient safeguard against the inflation-generated redistribution. What is also required is that the potential losers from inflation should be in a position to protect themselves against the losses from anticipated inflation by forcing appropriate measures (full escalation clauses) on the contracting parties (potential gainers). This condition is not easily satisfied in actual life, especially for a large mass of unorganized workers. Then, generally, inflation is rarely fully (or exactly) anticipated. For both reasons, inflation does result in redistribution of income and wealth.

1.8.1 Inflation and Forced Saving[1]

Now we come to the very important issue of the relation between inflation and forced saving (see also Chandler, 1962). In all poor countries the domestic-saving ratio is very low. This acts as a constraint on stepping up the rate of capital accumulation and so of growth. Therefore, it is sometimes recommended that if such countries desire a higher saving ratio they should follow an inflationary monetary policy, for it is believed that the redistribution of income and wealth caused by inflation will generate forced saving and thereby raise the aggregate saving ratio. Thus inflationary finance is considered one of the necessary evils and mechanisms through which a higher rate of capital accumulation and consequently of economic growth and employment expansion can be forced on the economy.

The doctrine of forced saving has had a long history in monetary

[1] The discussion in this and the next three sub-sections is largely a reproduction of Gupta (1978b).

theory. It crops up time and again, implicitly or explicitly, in con-temporary policy prescriptions. We evaluate this doctrine in relation to the inflation-induced intra-private-sector redistribution of income and wealth, not touching upon such redistribution between the private sector and the government.

1.8.2 The True Nature of Forced Saving

The doctrine of forced saving through inflation rests on two hypo-theses: (1) that inflation results in redistribution of real income and wealth, and (2) that the marginal propensity to save of the gainers from inflation is higher than that of the losers from inflation. The first hypothesis is generally well established and has already been discussed in the previous section. The second hypothesis locates some virtue in the socially iniquitous result of inflation for a poor develop-ing economy, namely, that the resultant redistribution increases the over-all saving ratio by generating forced saving. This hypothesis is widely accepted, though it is neither necessarily correct theoretically, nor empirically valid for a variety of countries that have had infla-tionary experience over long periods (see Tun Wai, 1959-60). We first examine the true nature of forced saving.

Firstly, it is worth noting that as between the gainers and the losers from inflation, the *true* savers from the social point of view are the losers and not the gainers. The latter are only *apparent savers*. This becomes obvious as soon as we ask ourselves the question: wherein lies the element of force associated with the concept of forced saving, if the true savers are the gainers from inflation? For, don't they save voluntarily whatever they save? Any answer to this question must admit that the element of force, truly speaking, is involved at a stage *prior* to the act of apparent voluntary saving by the gainers from inflation. It lies in the forced transfer of real income and wealth under the *force majeure* of inflation, against which in-dividual losers from inflation have no protection, and in the resulting forced reduction in real consumption of these losers. This line of argument reveals a very important aspect of the nature of forced saving, totally obfuscated by the traditional doctrine—that it is the forced reduction in real consumption of the losers which, from the social point of view, yields forced saving. For the society as a whole, given total real income, the only way to achieve extra (domestic) saving is by sacrificing real consumption on the part of some or all members of the community. There is no second way.

Secondly, it follows from the previous conclusion that a distinction must be made between gross forced saving and net forced saving. The cut in the real consumption of the losers from inflation represents gross fixed saving. All of it, however, is not available to the system as saving. A large part of it is frittered away in the extra consumption of the gainers from inflation, which is induced by the latter's real income and wealth gains from inflation. Thus, it is only the excess of the cut in the real consumption of the losers over the additional consumption of the gainers which constitutes net forced saving. The forced saving in common usage refers to this.

As a corollary, we note that inflation transfers far more income from the losers to the gainers of inflation than actually gets saved. More important, inflation reduces far more real consumption of the losers than the increase in net saving of the community (which may as well be negative), because a sizeable part of it is consumed on the way by the gainers from inflation. Thus, as a mechanism for promoting savings, it is not only highly iniquitous, it is also highly inefficient. The leakage of gross forced saving into the consumption of the gainers is much too high.

Thirdly, the ownership of forced saving does not rest in the hands of the true savers (in the social sense), i.e. the losers from inflation. Instead, this ownership comes to reside in the hands of the gainers from inflation, who have not sacrificed their consumption (in the social sense) to generate the extra (forced) saving.

These two considerations would suggest that any policy of forced saving through compulsory deposits is vastly superior, both in terms of efficiency and equity, to a policy of forced saving through inflation. (They do not, however, establish that a policy of forced saving through compulsory deposits is also superior to a policy of voluntary saving through appropriate incentives.)

Finally, there is *no theoretical necessity for the net forced saving through inflation to be always positive*. The proof of positive forced saving from inflation under the traditional theory rests on the simple hypothesis that the marginal propensity to save of the gainers from inflation (profit-earners) is much higher than that of the losers from inflation (especially wage-earners). But this is too simplistic an argument. We must analyse the consumption/saving behaviour of the losers from inflation more carefully before coming to any conclusion.

1.8.3 Forced Saving of the Poor

Let us divide all the losers from inflation into two sub-classes: (1) those with zero voluntary-saving potential and (2) those with positive voluntary-saving potential. The former are those who are living at or near the minimum subsistence level and consume whatever they are able to earn. They do not have any accumulated saving to draw upon in time of need. Steeped in debt, their fresh borrowing potential is also negligible. Therefore, when their real incomes are eroded by inflation, they are forced to cut down their real consumption. They simply sink below the subsistence level and suffer slow death.[2] The proportion of the population falling into this sub-class is very large. It is broadly estimated that by the mid-seventies about 60 per cent of the total population in India was living below the poverty line (defined as the minimum subsistence level, measured by Rs 20 per head per month at 1961–2 prices). Any reduction in the real income of such people means an automatic reduction in their real consumption and so the generation of forced saving.[3] They are *forced to save, that is, consume less*, because there is no way whereby they can maintain their real consumption. In aggregate analysis, the plight of such below-the-poverty-line families is neglected. In a just society, the additional burden which inflation places on the survival of such families must be borne in mind while adopting inflationary policy.

1.8.4 Forced Saving of the Not-Poor

How would the real consumption of higher-income households with positive saving potential be affected when the households lose real income through inflation? We know the traditional answer

---

[2] Some are driven to begging or petty theft. Others may try to augment their subsistence earnings by working extra hours or by making other members of their families (young children and non-working womenfolk) do all sorts of odd jobs. Technically, this means that inflation extracts greater work effort from the latter group of workers. But the net addition to national income from this additional effort is usually a mere pittance on account of the very low marginal productivity of such work. For our discussion, which is concerned only with the effects of the redistribution of real income and wealth generated by inflation, the size effects on national income have been ignored.

[3] What is saved, in real terms, are the basic wage goods, which these people would have otherwise consumed. This has obvious implications for the real demand for such goods as foodgrains, coarse cloth, etc. in the country.

embodied in the forced saving hypothesis—that their real consumption will fall and that this fall will be measured by the fall in their real income times their marginal propensity to consume (M.P.C.). The answer is based on the well-known Absolute Income Hypothesis, that the real consumption expenditure is a linear function of current real disposable income, with a positive intercept. The hypothesis implies that consumption standards are fully reversible—that they are adjusted up or down with equal ease. In other words, the traditional theory assumes that the consumption response is symmetrical to changes in current income in either direction: that, starting from a given consumption standard, the marginal propensity of a household to consume would be the same, whether it is confronted with a rise or a fall of an equal amount in real income.

This is not generally true, as it assumes too much flexibility (reversibility) of consumption standards, not found in actual life. Two features of the short-run behaviour of households are worthy of note: (1) their consumption standards are slow to change and (2) they are much slower to change in the downward than in the upward direction. There is enough empirical evidence to support (1). And it is now universally admitted that the short-run M.P.C. is lower than the long-run M.P.C.

Hypothesis (2) has not been explicitly tested. But it is built into the Relative Income Hypothesis of Duesenberry (1949). Therefore, any empirical support of the latter is also a support of hypothesis (2). It will be discussed later in this section.

Various explanations have been offered for the observed slowness of adjustment of consumption standards to changes in income. Some are based on purely intuitive reasoning and common observation, such as those of Duesenberry (1949) and Brown (1952). They emphasize social-status consciousness, psychological attitudes, and the persistence of consumption habits among households. Others are derived at the micro level, from the theory of rational choice of a utility-maximizing consumer on the simplifying (and unrealistic) assumptions of perfect knowledge about the future, perfect capital markets, and independent utility functions. They are, then, extended to the aggregate behaviour on further heroic assumptions concerning the conditions of aggregation and the conversion of certain unobservables into observables (such as the derivation of expected average or 'permanent' income from 'measured' or observed incomes).

The first kind of explanation resorts to the statistical device of

introducing lags in adjustment of consumption in one form or the
other. The second kind, by making current consumption (saving) a
problem of inter-temporal choice, introduces a time horizon into
consumption-saving decision-making, and makes consumption a
function of 'expected life-time resources' ('Life Cycle' hypothesis of
Ando and Modigliani, 1963) or of expected average, or normal, or
'permanent income' (Friedman, 1957). Current income, y_t, then, is
seen to affect current consumption, c_t, only through and insofar as it
affects W_t^* (expected wealth at time t) in one case, or y_t^p (permanent
real income for time period t) in the other case. Either approach
provides much greater stability to the c/y ratio than does the absolute
income hypothesis. Both the approaches can be combined to ration-
alize the observed greater value of long-run M.P.C. as compared
to that for the short-run M.P.C.: the speed of consumption
adjustment to changes in income may be slow partly because of the
inertia and persistence of consumption habits, and partly because the
perceived change in y^p or W^* is less than the change in 'measured' y.

The exact formulation, implications, and empirical tests of various
consumption hypotheses differ in detail, and our objective here is not
to survey the field (see Johnson, 1971, and Evans, 1969, Chapters 2
and 3). We only wish to draw selectively upon these developments to
analyse the consequences of the inflation-induced redistribution of
income and wealth for household saving and consumption. To the
best of our knowledge, the question has not been re-examined.

We concentrate on the short-run reactions of households to a
given change in current real income. A single short-run need not
necessarily be a period of only a few months. It may well span a few
years. Therefore, from a practical policy point of view (as distinct
from the purely theoretical formulation), this reaction will be of more
than transitory or passing interest.

We come now to the second feature of the short-run behaviour of
households—that their consumption standards are much slower to
change in the downward than in the upward direction. This is crucial
to the revision of the forced saving hypothesis. It has not been derived
rigorously from any utility theory or the theory of rational choice
under certainty or uncertainty, but has only an intuitive foundation.
It is based on nothing more than the common experience that downward adjustments in consumption standards are harder to make than
adjustments upwards. When faced with a reduction in current income, households in the short run try to protect their current con-

sumption standards by cutting down their voluntary savings, by postponing some of their planned purchases of consumer durables, and even by dissaving. Apart from persistence of habit, reluctance to cut consumption and status-consciousness, a further reason for this kind of slow adjustment can be the hope of the loser households that the fall in their absolute real incomes is 'transitory'—that they will 'soon' gain compensating increases in money income, and that their real incomes will grow due to the over-all growth in the economy. Only when they realize that their real incomes have gone down 'permanently' do they begin adjusting their real consumption downward.

The upward adjustments of consumption, even over a short run, are relatively easier to make. They are always more welcome, too. In a world of imperfect capital markets, there are severe penalties or even restrictions on deficit spending. Therefore, an increase in current income, by making available more owned funds, both induces and permits larger consumption expenditure than that predicted by the assumption of perfect capital markets.

We, thus, get a ratchet effect in consumption: when income falls, consumption drops less than it rises when income increases by a given amount. The consumption behaviour is asymmetrical: the downward marginal propensity to consume (given by the fall in consumption due to a small fall in real income) is much less than the upward marginal propensity to consume (given by the increase in consumption due to a small increase in real income). This runs counter to the traditional theory which assumes symmetrical consumption behaviour.

This argument is fully consistent with the Permanent Income Hypothesis as well as the Life Cycle Hypothesis, even though neither refers to such asymmetry. The reason is the particular definition of consumption adopted in these theories. By consumption is meant only the consumption of non-durables and services plus the use value of the services of consumer durables. The expenditure on consumer durables is treated as a kind of investment and hence equivalent to saving. This (less, of course, the use value of the services of such durables) is not the national-income-accounting definition of consumption or saving, which adopts the expenditure, rather than the use, approach. Accordingly, consumption (*expenditure*) is defined inclusive of household expenditure on consumer durables. We also take the national-income-accounting view of this definition. Under the Permanent Income Hypothesis all windfalls and other transitory incomes are saved. But since, in this theory, saving is defined to include purchase of consumer durables (less the current use value of their services) as forms of wealth, it is consistent with it to say that the gainers from inflation tend to *spend* a large part of their gains from inflation, howsoever transitory, on consumption. For a part of this expenditure will be on consumer durables. The gainers from inflation do so, both to catch up and to keep up with the Joneses. This is specially true of a good many first-time gainers from inflation —the newly rich. This explanation also throws light on the changing composition of the basket of consumer goods demanded under inflation and some period after.

Our explanation is akin to that of the Relative Income Hypothesis of Duesenberry (1949). In order to explain the observed pro-cyclical variability, but long-run constancy, of the saving ratio, Duesenberry hypothesized a savings function which yields the following consumption function:

$$\left(\frac{c}{y}\right)_t = a - b\,\frac{y_t}{y_0} \tag{1.1}$$

where

c = private (real) consumption expenditure,
y = personal (real) disposable income,
y_0 = past peak (real) disposable income,
a and b are positive constants, and t is a time subscript.

y_0 was chosen only as a proxy for 'a weighted average of all the incomes from the previous peak year to the current year'. It would be a constant so long as $y_t < y_0$. For $y_t > y_0$ and rising, y_0, too, will become a variable. Thus, the presence of y_0 in (1.1) introduces a variable lag in the consumption function—it is a fixed one-period lag when y_t is rising above y_0; it is a variable lag when $y_t < y_0$.

The implied marginal propensity to consume (M.P.C.) in Duesenberry (1949) is not a constant, as in a linear consumption function, but a declining function of y_t. The rate of decline of the M.P.C. is not always constant as it is an inverse function of y_0 which becomes a variable for $y_t > y_0$ and rising. Thus, M.P.C. is not symmetrical for falling and rising y_t. To reach this, we may rewrite equation (1.1) as

$$c_t = a\,y_t - b\,\frac{y_t^2}{y_0} \tag{1.2}$$

Differentiating the above equation with respect to y_t, we have

$$\frac{\partial c_t}{\partial y_t} = a - 2b \frac{y_t}{y_0}. \tag{1.3}$$

This, then, is the implied equation for the M.P.C. and what we have said above about the M.P.C. follows.

Duesenberry's consumption function (1.1) is mentioned here as a way of capturing the assumed (short-run) asymmetry and slow reversibility in consumption behaviour.

In explanation of his hypothesis, Duesenberry has said: 'If a family has a certain income y_0 and this income is higher than any previously attained, it will save some amount: $s_0 = f(y_0)$. If its income increases, the same function will hold. But, if after an increase, income declines to the original level, its saving will be less than $f(y_0)$. Some saving will be sacrificed to protect its standard of living' (Duesenberry, 1949, p. 85).

If the 'asymmetry hypothesis' is accepted, we can have net forced dissaving in place of net forced saving from inflation. This can happen because in our model, it is perfectly possible for the induced incremental consumption of the gainers from inflation to exceed the forced gross saving (or reduction in consumption) of the losers from inflation. Under the traditional theory this possibility is completely ruled out by the assumption of differences in the marginal propensities to consume of different income classes, strengthened by the implicit assumption of symmetrical consumption behaviour. We have now shown that the former assumption alone is not sufficient to generate positive forced saving. Asymmetrical consumption behaviour can upset the traditional doctrine of forced saving.

The above conclusion is not necessarily changed if we take the wealth effect on consumption into account. Inflation causes not only real-income transfers but also real-wealth transfers. The wealth-gainers are net monetary debtors and wealth-losers are net monetary creditors. Net monetary debtors are economic units whose monetary debts exceed their monetary credits. Inflation favours the former against the latter by lowering the real value of their debts. Profit-earners are, generally, net monetary debtors. Therefore, they are not only real-income gainers from inflation, but also real-wealth gainers. On the other hand, rentiers and better-off workers, being net monetary creditors, are real-wealth losers from inflation. We have already noted above that they are also real-income losers.

What effect will this inflation-generated real-wealth transfer have on aggregate consumption/saving? Even in terms of the traditional theory, the gain in real wealth of the profit-earners, other things being the same, will encourage greater consumption (and lower saving) out of the same level of real income. By parity of reasoning, this theory predicts lowered consumption of real-wealth losers. But the hypothesis of the downward stickiness of consumption standards comes in the way again. If the latter hypothesis is correct, dissaving may result via the inflation-induced wealth transfers as well.

In the absence of well-tested empirical evidence it is not advisable to claim anything more than its plausibility for our counter-hypothesis.[4] What even this result accomplishes, however, is not unimportant. For it raises a serious doubt about the empirical validity of a venerable doctrine which is treated as almost axiomatically true.

What about the long-run behaviour of consumption and saving? The asymmetrical behaviour hypothesized above is, admittedly, a short-run phenomenon. The *static* long-run M.P.C. will be the same, upward as well as downward. Then, is the traditional forced saving hypothesis true, if only in the long run?

The answer will depend upon two important considerations. One concerns the long-run character of the inflation-induced redistributions of income. Are these redistributions permanent or temporary? If the latter (say, because of the operation of some market or non-market correcting mechanism), then any hypothesized forced saving, too, can, at most, arise only in the short run, and will disappear in the long run. Related to this is another consideration—whether the economy is stationary or growing. Only for a stationary economy will the long-run redistribution of income through inflation generate

---

[4] The difficulties in the empirical testing of the counter-hypothesis for India relate to the non-availability of the relevant data. For the hypothesis (in the case of India) is not applicable to the aggregate consumption, but only to the consumption of households with positive saving or wealth, and reliable data on the consumption and real disposable income of such households are not available. At the aggregate level, the efforts of Singh and Kumar (1971) and of Singh, Drost and Kumar (1978) to fit the consumption functions of Duesenberry (1949), Davis (1952), or their modifications as given by Duesenberry, Eckstein and Fromm (1960) or by Singh and Kumar (1971) did not produce good results. The $\bar{R}^2$ turned out to be too low and the slope co-efficients statistically insignificant. However, this cannot be considered a refutation of our analysis, as the hypothesis of the downward stickiness of consumption is applicable only to households with positive saving or wealth.

forced saving in the long run. In an economy with growing per capita incomes, the real-income loss from inflation will be made good through the sharing of gains from growth. The loser households will therefore not be under pressure even in the long run to consume less in absolute terms. And the hypothesized forced saving in the long run may not materialize at all. Much will, of course, depend upon the relative strength of the two opposite forces operating on the real incomes of loser households—the negative effect of inflation and the positive effect of real income growth. But, at the same time, we do not also fully know how long it takes for the so-called long-run forced saving to materialize.

1.9 Inflation and Government Revenues

One of the major sources of inflation is the continuous 'excess' deficit financing by the government (see Chapters 4 and 5). The 'excess' deficit financing is undertaken in the belief that by it the government gains real resources from the public. This is, undoubtedly, true insofar as the direct real yield of resources from excess deficit financing is concerned. But it may or may not be true if all the effects—direct as well as indirect—are taken into account. Even from the narrow government (as distinct from the social) point of view, the government budget is affected in several ways by inflation. For example, the government gains or loses resources from/to the private sector in at least six different capacities:

1. as the ultimate currency authority,
2. as tax-transfer authority,
3. as net monetary debtor,
4. as employer,
5. as purchaser of goods, and
6. as producer.

I have discussed these individually elsewhere (see Gupta, 1975a). *A priori*, it cannot be said that the government would be a gainer on every front, and, therefore, a net gainer. The issue can only be decided empirically. But as yet we do not have the requisite empirical evidence, one way or the other.

1.10 Social Costs of Inflation

The harmful social effects of inflation are both grave and wideranging. Yet they tend to be easily ignored. We sum them up very briefly below.

1. Inflation accentuates inequalities in the distribution of income and wealth. It imposes a heavy burden on the already poor for the benefit of the rich.

2. The composition of the consumption-goods basket, whether produced domestically, imported legally, or smuggled into the country, becomes more and more socially inoptimal as the production of luxuries and socially less-essential goods and services is encouraged at the cost of necessities and other wage goods. The encouragement comes from the demand side, from the growing inequalities in the distribution of income and wealth caused by inflation. This shift in the commodity structure of consumer goods output represents a misallocation of resources from the social point of view.

3. Inflationary expectations, which are a necessary accompaniment of any inflation which has lasted for some time, encourage speculative trading and hoarding (of goods) activities at the cost of production activities by making the former excessively more profitable privately than the latter. This diverts more and more real resources, especially very scarce entrepreneurial services and capital, from the latter to the former. This distorts the structure of economic activity by over-encouraging purely trading–speculative activities. Consequently, production in the economy suffers.

4. Employment expansion suffers as capital-intensive industries and techniques of production are over-encouraged in comparison with the labour-intensive industries and methods of production. This happens because the money rates of interest do not rise fully to neutralize inflation. This makes capital look cheaper to its users than it truly is in the capital-scarce labour-surplus economy that India is.

5. Investment also suffers when inflation squeezes profit margins too much in some industries, because, at industry level, prices of capital goods, intermediates and labour may rise more than product prices. For inflation is never balanced; different prices vary at different rates. When such a phenomenon threatens profit margins, firms under weak managements easily 'go under' or fall 'sick'. Plant replacement and modernization of industry suffer. Backward and forward linkages make the sickness of some industries affect the health of others adversely. Unutilized capacity grows, production suffers in the face of rising prices, and inflation turns into stagflation.

6. Inflation renders all planning (rolling or fixed-term) fruitless, as it makes nonsense of all estimates of financial resources, allocations,

2

and project costs. Mid-plan revisions, cuts, throwing overboard of some projects, partly halting further work on some others, saving the so-called core projects, rescheduling priorities, the scramble for more foreign aid and tax revenues, etc. create chaos in place of planning, impose much unwanted waste of precious real resources on the economy, and have harmful external effects on the plans and functioning of the private sector of the economy, whose fate is crucially linked with that of the public sector. How the only two-year inflation period of 1973 and 1974 made the Fifth Five Year Plan virtually still-born, is now well known.

7. Inflation (more correctly speaking, a higher rate of domestic inflation in relation to inflation abroad) creates balance-of-payments problems in a regime of fixed exchange rates by reducing the competitiveness of exports abroad and encouraging imports into the country.

8. Inflation as a tax on cash balances imposes welfare costs on the public by discouraging the demand for real money. It hurts voluntary savings and their institutionalization by lowering the real rates of return on all kinds of monetary assets, which are otherwise important vehicles for the promotion and mobilization of savings. This point is discussed independently in the next section.

9. The most important social cost of inflation is the large-scale social unrest that it breeds in the country. It should be obvious to social scientists that losers from inflation are unlikely to take their losses calmly, especially when these losses arise through no fault of theirs and the same losses reappear as private gains to the already-rich members of the community. The dispossessed interpret it as a grand conspiracy between the government and the private gainers from inflation. The unrest is especially high among the vocal and organized sections of the population. It expresses itself in periodic demands for compensatory increases in money wages, strikes, lock-outs, protest marches, *dharnas, gheraos*, work-to-rule and other go-slow tactics, sabotage, damage to public property, and other kinds of labour trouble. Fixed-income earners are forced to accept bribes and adopt other corrupt methods of earning a living and fighting inflation. Moral and social values deteriorate. The polity becomes increasingly susceptible to violence and sudden collapse.

All these are very important social costs of inflation, though most economists tend to ignore them in their discussion of the subject. Several regimes in various countries have fallen because the very high rates of inflation there had made the lives of the masses of losers from inflation unbearable and thereby eroded completely the legitimacy of the ruling elites. No government can nurse inflation without a grave risk to itself and the whole political regime it represents.

The ruling elites in India have not shown a full understanding of the nature and working of inflationary forces in the country and its evil consequences. They have therefore tried to fight the battle against inflation in most cases by imposing price controls, leaving unchecked its causes. This is like trying to cure a disease by suppressing its symptoms rather than eradicating its cause.

In monetary economics this is called the policy of 'repressed inflation'. It has two planks—one of general inflation, the other of price controls. The government has pursued such a policy in the naïve belief that it represents the best of both worlds. Through inflationary deficit financing the government gains extra real resources and through price controls it tries to maintain the façade of price stability of some 'essential' goods.

But this represents a gross over-estimate of the government's ability to keep even the so-called controlled prices truly fixed for long. The policy of repressed inflation can have some chance of success if adopted with vigour, honesty, and competence to meet a short-term situation of aggregate or sectoral excess demand. But it is doomed to failure and sure to generate its own antithesis in the form of black markets and corruption if continued too long and too extensively.

What happens is simply this. In the absence of total control on all product prices, uncontrolled product prices rise freely under the cumulating inflationary pressures. This creates a two-way pressure on controlled prices, one from the side of demand, the other from the side of supply or cost. Excess monetary demand for goods becomes all the more excessive at controlled prices. On the other hand, many of the cost components of goods with controlled prices go up. This generates pressure from the side of the producers of these products for the upward revision of controlled prices, so that their incomes are protected. Otherwise they may be forced to cut back the output of such goods to the extent that it is feasible for them to switch over to other (uncontrolled) lines of production. The cut-back in output or slow-down in the growth of productive capacity of essential goods with controlled prices further aggravates their scarcity. Black markets in them develop and grow rapidly as the gap between the market-clearing price and the controlled price widens and the rate of return on black marketing soars. Productive activity suffers and corruption becomes the normal mode of operation in every field. The people suffer at the hands of the corrupt, inefficient, and spendthrift government on the one hand and plundering black-marketeers on the other hand. When pressures build up to an excessively high level, the government is forced to revise upwards controlled prices one after the other. There is then a temporary calm in the markets till pressures build up once again, and the same process recurs. In this fashion, as explained above, the whole wage–price structure, the output structure (the commodity-composition of output) and the structure of economic activity (trading, hoarding and speculation *vis-à-vis* activities producing goods) are distorted.

In view of these heavy social costs of inflation, the case for forced saving through inflation is indeed very weak. Yet government after government, due to short-sightedness, lack of political will and competence to manage the affairs of the state in the larger interest of the people, corruption of the ruling elite, and the class interest of their support structure, succumbs to this apparently easy but socially rapacious method of inflationary finance to raise funds, rather than adopt politically harder but socially more desirable methods of managing the government budget and the banking system.

1.11 Price Stability and Voluntary Savings

Inflation, as we have seen above, besides entailing heavy social costs, is not likely to increase the savings ratio. It thus imposes unrequited social loss. This is sufficient ground for pursuing a policy of price stability. Besides, a climate of price stability will encourage financial progress, greater savings, and their increased institutionalization. This claim can be explained briefly.

Inflation causes real value depreciation of all 'monetary assets'. Thereby it reduces their real rates of return (given by the money rates of return minus the realized rate of inflation) to even negative values. Monetary assets are financial assets with nominally-fixed maturity values and nominally-fixed returns. These values/returns are not adjusted with changes in the price level. Examples of such assets are money, deposits of all kinds, bonds, life insurance, etc. As opposed to them are real assets, which include all tangible (or physical) assets and equities among financial assets. These assets are called real assets, because, on average, their real values do not change with changes in the general price level. They act as guards against inflation.

Financial assets and markets play an important role in promoting as well as mobilizing savings of the public. This is because, as stores of value, financial assets enjoy several advantages over tangible assets, such as greater divisibility, greater liquidity, lower risk, easy storability, etc. (see Moore, 1968, Chapter 1). Most important, financial assets do not require any direct managerial work of the kind tangible assets require to be productive of income (or services). Therefore, the non-entrepreneural classes find it extremely convenient to hold their wealth in the form of financial assets. Firms also, of course, hold money and other financial assets.

Among financial assets we are presently concerned with only the monetary assets. Equities, as yet, are not an important medium of holding wealth in India, because, on the demand side, a large majority of wealth-holders do not fully understand the intricacies of equity investment, and, on the supply side, the limited growth of the private corporate sector is both a cause and an effect of the limited growth of the equity market in India. This suggests that, for quite some time to come, equities will continue to occupy a minor position in the asset portfolios of the public. This also means that monetary assets of the simplest variety will have to play a major role in the promotion as well as mobilization of savings. In addition, their growth will be the main vehicle of financial progress in the country.

Since the bulk of monetary assets in India are the liabilities of public financial institutions, any risk of their default can be easily ruled out. In recent times, the great depressant in the growth of *real* demand for them has been the factor of expected inflation, since, as said earlier, inflation causes real value depreciation of all monetary assets, which reduces their real rates of return even to negative values. Continued price stability is essential for generating confidence in the stability of the purchasing power of their nominal values. This will make the holding of monetary assets more attractive than before and encourage greater savings on the part of the large proportion of potential savers who have nothing better than monetary assets to hold their savings in, since, in the absence of real-value depreciation from inflation, the real rates of return from monetary assets will improve substantially.

Price stability will encourage greater institutionalization of savings, too, because the rates of interest paid by financial institutions to their 'depositors' will compete favourably with what the savers can get elsewhere—in the unorganized sector of the market for loanable funds. It is well known that the rates of interest paid by financial institutions to their depositors are relatively sticky. In an on-going inflation, they are not adjusted upward fast and far enough to compensate their depositors for the expected rates of inflation. In the unorganized market, on the other hand, the rates of interest are much more flexible. They adjust reasonably fast to changes in the expected rate of inflation as well as to other market changes. Consequently, during periods of inflation, funds get transferred from financial institutions to the unorganized market. In a regime of price stability this would halt. Initially, there would be a reverse flow of funds to the financial institutions. Thereafter, these institutions will attract a larger and growing proportion of real savings, which can themselves be expected to constitute a higher proportion of national income. In other words, in a regime of price stability, the demand for monetary assets of all kinds—money, time deposits of banks, post office savings deposits, life insurance, bonds, small savings certificates, etc.—in real terms will grow faster than has been the case under inflation. The resulting growing institutionalization of savings will provide greater scope for a more socially-optimal allocation of resources.

We may, then, conclude that, taking all the relevant factors into consideration, monetary policy should be so conducted as to attain and maintain (long-run) price stability along the maximum feasible output path. Price stability, far from being at variance with other social objectives, is essential for the realization of these objectives.

CHAPTER 2

PLANNING FOR NEUTRAL MONEY

2.1 Introduction

All monetary planning must rest on appropriate changes in the stock of money. This stock is the key variable in the whole financial superstructure. Any continued mismanagement on this score will have far-reaching and all-pervasive economic and social consequences. For several years, increases in the stock of money in India have been allowed to be determined residually or passively by the deficit-financing decisions of the government and the commercial sector without any regard for the real money-absorptive capacity of the economy. This has resulted in rampant inflation in the country—a negation of monetary planning.

How can one determine the socially-desirable rate of growth of the stock of money? Should the stock of money be varied with a view to ensuring long-run monetary stability or should it be varied primarily to correct short-run fluctuations in the economy? These are practical questions of policy formulation which must be faced squarely. The answers we offer are not new in any way—they are based on well-worked-out ideas in the field of monetary theory and policy. We have simply adapted them to the Indian situation.

2.2 Why Control Changes in the Stock of Money?

Changes in the stock of money deserve to be carefully watched and controlled, because such changes exert a powerful influence on changes in money income, prices, output, employment, distribution of income and wealth, balance of payments, etc. Therefore, if the monetary authority has definite policy objectives with respect to these variables, it cannot afford to be unconcerned about changes in the stock of money.

Such changes affect the level of economic activity and its various

A large part of this chapter is based on Gupta (1975b).

correlates by affecting primarily the monetary demand for output, or, which is the same thing, the money expenditure or money income. A large amount of theoretical literature as well as empirical evidence accumulating around this proposition (see Bhattacharya, 1975) holds the key to much of monetary policy and planning. We build our arguments on this foundation. The ultimate rationale for controlling changes in the quantity of money is to control changes in the aggregate monetary demand for output. Thus conceived, monetary management is essentially a part of aggregate demand management.

We have argued in the previous chapter that monetary management should be so conducted as to ensure long-run price stability along full-capacity output path. The pursuit of such an objective is not merely fully consistent with other social objectives; it is essential for their attainment. Given the present socio-economic structure, in the absence of price stability there cannot be much sustained growth, with or without social justice, though it is equally true to say that there cannot be long-run price stability and social justice without growth.

How can socially desirable year-to-year changes in the stock of money be determined? This is the main question we discuss now, together with practical difficulties in pursuing a more ambitious objective of short-run economic stability (in contrast with the rather modest but important objective of long-run monetary stability) through monetary policy.

Three kinds of increase in the stock of money in the context of a growing economy are distinguished: (*a*) neutral, (*b*) excess, and (*c*) deficient. The crucial concept in this classification is the concept of neutral increases in the stock of money. For, once we have settled on what constitutes a neutral increase, we can define the other terms very easily by simply saying that an excess increase is an increase in excess of the neutral increase and a deficient increase (including decrease as negative increase) is an increase which falls short of the neutral increase.

The concept of neutrality we have in mind is one of long-run neutrality and not of short-run (or year-to-year) neutrality. We shall call increases in the stock of money long-run neutral if they leave the price level, on an average of several years, unchanged (or approximately unchanged), while the economy operates at or near the level of maximum feasible output.

For price-level stability it is necessary to avoid both inflationary and deflationary pressures. We shall define the two kinds of pressures in terms of the relation of aggregate demand to aggregate supply. For this, we posit a benchmark of maximum feasible output, which we define as 'full-capacity' output. In the Indian context, given the structural imbalance between the supply of labour and the supply of the co-operating factors of production, such as land and capital, full employment of labour in the near future is usually treated as structurally infeasible. Without going into the normative aspect of this view, we accept it as a binding policy constraint in the present socio-political framework and economic organization[1] so far as the employment-generating aspect of output management is concerned. Accordingly, in the Indian context, full-capacity output is the appropriate counterpart of the concept of full-employment output used in western economies.

What is the analytical significance of the concept of full-capacity output? It flows from our earlier assumption that we view it as the short-run maximum feasible output, as some kind of a (short-run) ceiling on total output—a ceiling which is independent of the demand side or the average price of output. The hypothesis here is that, at the aggregate level, any increase in the demand for output beyond the ceiling level of output results in pure inflation of prices. And we shall identify inflation as such—as the excess of aggregate demand over the ceiling output. At the opposite end, when aggregate demand (at prevailing prices) falls short of ceiling output, we shall have deflation. Under deflation both output and prices will fall. That is, deflation will cause some loss of potential output.

The policy objective should be to avoid both inflationary and deflationary situations, i.e. the price-level stability that we seek is not the stability at any level of output but the stability at the level of maximum feasible output, which would be growing over time in a growing economy.

A serious problem arises here. How can we be sure that in a position of maximum feasible output we can successfully keep prices stable at their initial level (even, on an average, over a long period of several years)? A difficulty may arise from what is known as the Phillips-curve phenomenon (see Phillips, 1958). If at the level of

---

[1] Under a different politico-economic organization, however, it should be possible to provide gainful employment to all able-bodied persons in a medium run, if not immediately.

maximum feasible output, workers insist on a rate of increase in money wages in excess of the rate of increase in labour productivity (and other factor-owners insist on, and are capable of, protecting their relative shares in the national income), ceiling output can be realized only at a positive rate of inflation, or inflation can be avoided only at the cost of some feasible output. In other words, there may be a short-run trade-off between price stability and full-capacity output and not mutual harmony between the two.[2] What can be done then?

In our judgement, whatever the validity of the Phillips-curve hypothesis in the developed countries of the West, the phenomenon is not an important feature of the Indian labour market.[3] This is primarily because in India a large part of the output in agriculture, cottage industries, retail trade, and transport is produced with the help of family labour, and even within wage-labour, a large proportion of it is unorganized. Then, even at full-capacity output we shall have huge unemployment and underemployment of labour. Therefore, any presumed danger to price stability at ceiling output coming from the labour market in India in the present or near future can be only a result of an unwarranted and blind application of western results to the Indian situation.

However, a parallel danger coming from the side of profit-earners cannot be ruled out equally easily. The profit-earners as entrepreneur-producers can insist on a higher relative share in the national cake as a price for producing maximum feasible output. The high profit margins may be realized in diverse ways, including easy and cheap supply of institutional credit, cheap and subsidized supply of inputs routed through the public sector, or upward revision of officially-fixed prices on the basis of inflated costs. And all this has been done in recent years in the name of increasing production and investment in the economy. If the inflated claims of this entrepreneural class are continuously met and the other classes cannot be squeezed any further, there is no escape from inflation, whether the economy operates at full-capacity output or not. Our monetary policy should surely be not a surrender to this kind of

---

[2] For a brief survey of the Phillips curve, see Turnovsky (1977, Chapter 5).

[3] We are making this statement in spite of the increases in money wages gained in recent years by employees in banks, insurance companies, airlines, the government, etc.

pressure, but form a defence against it. For designing such a policy, it is necessary to build on the assumption that price-level stability is fully consistent with the objective of producing maximum feasible output. If we yield on this point, the profit-earners will call the tune and determine the rate of inflation in the economy.

2.3 The Money-Supply Growth Rule

We have said above that monetary management is a part of the aggregate demand management. The objective is to so manage variations in the stock of money that no inflationary or deflationary pressures in the commodity market originate from the money market or get validated by the money market. This requires that the money market is kept in (long-run) equilibrium at stable prices and maximum feasible output. Since the demand for money cannot be controlled directly by the monetary authority, though it can be influenced to some extent by it, whereas the supply of money is very much under its control, the aforesaid equilibrium in the money market is to be arrived at and maintained primarily by adapting suitably the supply of money to the demand for it. More specifically, what is required is to keep the stock of money equal to the amount of money demanded at constant prices and maximum feasible output over each long period. When stated in terms of the rate of growth of the stock of money, this rule would require that, starting with a position of monetary equilibrium, the stock of money over a period is increased at the same proportionate rate at which the demand for money at constant prices grows when the economy grows along its maximum feasible output path.

This prescription makes the following minimal assumptions, which also determine some of the information requirements for a successful policy execution:

1. that the demand for money is a stable function of a few specifiable variables, so that changes in it can be predicted with a reasonable degree of confidence; and

2. that, if the authorities so desire, they can successfully control actual changes in the stock of money within narrow limits.

Various problems of empirically estimating the demand function for money in India will be considered in Appendix A. Here, we report only one 'best-fitting' regression equation for money in India for the period 1950-1 to 1975-6.

$$\text{Log} \left(\frac{M}{P}\right)^d = -1.680 + 1.019 \text{ Log } y - 0.119 \text{ Log } P$$
$$(-1.390) \quad (7.620) \qquad (-1.697)$$

$$-0.026 \ r_{12}; \qquad \bar{R}^2 = 0.939$$
$$(-1.077) \qquad \qquad d = 1.455 \qquad (2.1)$$

In the equation above, M/P stands for real money balances, y for real national income (at market prices), P for wholesale price index number, r_{12} for 12-month time-deposit rate of commercial banks, $\bar{R}^2$ for the co-efficient of determination adjusted for degrees of freedom, and d for the Durbin–Watson statistic as a measure of the first-order serial correlation among residuals. Figures within parentheses are t values of the co-efficients directly above them. The data used are annual values—annual averages in the case of stock magnitudes. The equation gives a very good fit, explaining about 94 per cent of the observed variation in the log of M/P ($\bar{R}^2 = 0.939$) and without any serial correlation among its residuals at only one per cent level of significance. (The last result is not very strong, for if we had chosen 5 per cent level of significance, the alternative hypothesis of positive autocorrelation could not be rejected.) The income co-efficient is very highly significant. The co-efficient of log P is significant at only 10 per cent level of significance. The co-efficient of r_{12} fails to be significant even at the 10 per cent level (also see Appendix A, Section 7).

On the basis of statistical criteria currently in vogue, the following tentative conclusions about the demand for money in India may be drawn from the above fixed-coefficient regression equation:

1. that the demand for money in India is highly stable;

2. that real income is the major statistically-significant determinant of it;

3. that income-elasticity of demand for money is unity or not different from it (see Appendix A, Section 7 for explanation); and

4. that the rate of interest on non-money assets (r_{12} as the sole representative of such rates) is not statistically significant in explaining observed variations in real money balances of the public.

In addition, as a matter of casual empiricism, most of the observed increase in r_{12} and other money rates of interest over the sample period can be attributed to continuous inflation. In a regime of price stability, such rates can therefore be expected to remain nearly stable, or at least so over every long period of a few (say, five) years.

This will further reduce the influence of the rate of interest on the demand for money.

The above evidence and judgements, if broadly true, simplify substantially the task of monetary planning for India. They suggest that, for a target regime of price stability, we can start with the working hypothesis of a very simple demand for money function of the following form:

$$\left(\frac{M}{P}\right)^d = k \cdot y \qquad (2.1.1)$$

where k may be treated either as a time-constant or as a behaviourally stable time-variate, and other symbols are as defined above. We start with the simple assumption of k as a time-constant. We shall take up the other case later in this section.

If equation (2.1.1) is assumed to hold well over time, we can say that the demand for money at constant prices will grow at the same proportionate rate at which real income grows. Since we want to plan our monetary policy for realizing the maximum feasible output with price stability, the supply of money, in terms of the principle stated above, should be increased at the same rate at which the maximum feasible output grows, i.e. the rate at which the demand for money at constant prices will also grow.

Symbolically, the simple money-supply–growth rule may be stated thus:

$$g_M = g_{yf} \qquad (2.2)$$

where g_M = the rate of growth of the supply of money and g_{yf} = the rate of growth of full-capacity output.

In steady-growth equilibrium, the realized rate of growth of output will be equal to the expected rate of growth of output. Therefore, in steady-growth situations, g_{yf} in equation (2.2) can be interpreted as both the realized rate and the expected rate. The problem of interpreting as well as estimating g_{yf} in the real-life context of the Indian economy will be discussed in a later section.

It will be noted that equation (2.1.1) makes the demand for real money a proportional function of real income, yielding unitary (real) income elasticity of demand for (real) money.[4] Therefore, the

[4] Because of the proportional form of the demand relation in equation (2.1.1), the statement in the text holds equally well when both the amount of money demanded and income are measured in nominal terms. This can be seen simply by multiplying both the sides of equation (2.1.1) by p.

demand for money at constant prices is expected to grow at the same rate at which real income grows. And hence our simple policy-prescription of equation (2.2).

Suppose our demand function for money was different in only one respect—that it gave income elasticity of demand for money different from unity. Let us denote this elasticity by α. Then, equation (2.1.1) would be replaced by

$$\frac{M^d}{P} = k \cdot y^\alpha. \tag{2.1.2}$$

In a growing system this would give the rate of growth of the demand for real money equal to α times the rate of growth of real income.[5] The logic of the money-supply growth rule stated above would, then, require that

$$g_M = \alpha \cdot g_{yf}. \tag{2.3}$$

It is easily seen that the rule of equation (2.2) is a special case of the rule in equation (2.3) when $\alpha = 1$.

Now we take up another possibility concerning the demand for money function (2.1.1)—that the co-efficient k in it is a time-variate, and not a time-constant. We consider the simplest possibility first—that k is subject to a predictable time trend: that it tends to grow at the rate of $100h$ per cent per year. As one of the possibilities, we may associate this time trend in k with the hypothesis of growing monetization of the Indian economy. We shall examine the latter in the next section. The possibility of cyclical variations in k and its implications for monetary planning will be discussed in Section 2.5. In a growing system, the above assumption about k would yield yet another money-supply growth rule:

$$g_M = g_k + g_{yf}. \tag{2.4}$$

where g_k is the postulated (or estimated) rate of growth of k per year.

If the hypothesis of k being subject to a predictable time-trend were

[5] Differentiating (2.1.2) logarithmically with respect to time, treating k and α as time constants, would give

$$\frac{\frac{M^d}{P}}{dt} \cdot \frac{P}{M^d} = \alpha \cdot \frac{dy}{dt} \cdot \frac{1}{y}$$

which is the same thing as the statement in the text.

to be combined with that of α being different from unity, we would get a very general money-supply growth rule:

$$g_M = g_k + \alpha \cdot g_{yf} \tag{2.5}$$

All the other rules given earlier can be seen to be special cases of this general rule. We operate with it in our theoretical discussion.

2.4 The R.B.I. and the Money-Supply Growth Rule

The money-supply growth rule suggested (but not followed) by the R.B.I. (1970, p. 34) is, broadly speaking, the same as that given by our equation (2.5). The R.B.I. has said that, 'as a working rule', the g_M should be 'somewhat higher than the projected rate of growth of real national income'. Two reasons have been offered in favour of this prescription. 'First, as incomes grow the demand for money as one of the components of savings tends to grow.' (It is not clear from the statement what value of the income elasticity of demand for money the R.B.I. has in mind.) Second, other things being the same, 'the gradual reduction of the non-monetized sector in the economy' leads to increases in the demand for money.

The first reason corresponds to the factor $\alpha \cdot g_{yf}$ in our equation (2.5); the second to g_k. On comparison, it should be clear that our derivation as well as specification of the rule are much more systematic and precise. They also lay bare the underlying assumptions and objectives.

While deriving equation (2.5), we have already admitted that it is plausible to attribute the presumed time trend in k to the hypothesis that the Indian economy is getting more and more monetized at a steady rate. Direct reliable estimates of the rates of monetization of the Indian economy are hard to come by, though sporadic attempts have been made from time to time to estimate, or simply guess, the level of monetization and its rate of growth. Thus, for example, the (First) Working Group on Money Supply of the R.B.I. (1961a, p. 1046, para 5) had surmised that 'the rate of [growth of] monetization in the Indian economy may be assumed to be one per cent per annum on the basis of the results of successive rounds of the National Sample Survey and other relevant data'. Prasad (1969) estimated that in 1950–1 about 61.4 per cent of national income was monetized. For subsequent years, he simply applied a 1 per cent annual compound growth rate to arrive at his estimates of the monetized portion of national income. For various periods, Mukherjee (1967) and

Bhattacharya (1975, pp. 31–4) have separately produced their own estimates of the annual rates of monetization. Bhattacharya's figures show that starting from the 64.98 per cent rate of monetization of national income in 1948–9, the monetization level grew to 75.29 per cent in 1967–8, giving a compound rate of growth of 0.77 per cent (of monetized income) per year.

Some other researchers have a different story to tell. Rangarajan (1965) found no evidence of growth in monetization during the period 1951–9. Madalgi (1976), too, has found no evidence of growth in monetization over the period 1960–1 to 1974–5. For 1961–2, he has estimated 83.8 per cent of national income to be monetized.

We do not consider it a worthwhile exercise to evaluate critically methods of measuring monetization used by individual researchers or to try to produce our own alternative estimates, as for our purposes the issue is not of much practical importance. To the best of our knowledge, no one has suggested a rate of growth of monetization of more than 1 per cent per year. Suppose we accept the lowest among the estimates of the level of monetization—that of 61.4 per cent of national income for 1950–1 given by Prasad (1969). Then, at the compound rate of 1 per cent per year, by 1977–8, 81 per cent of national income would have been monetized. Given the continued predominance of the subsistence form of agriculture in India and very high weight of agriculture in the national economy, there is very limited scope left for increased monetization in the foreseeable future (see Madalgi, 1976). Therefore, 'much' cannot be gained for the neutral rate of growth of money supply by way of presumed increases in the monetization of the economy.

So far we had assumed that variations in monetization affect only the multiplicative factor k in the demand for money function (2.1.1). But it can also or alternatively affect the income elasticity of demand for money α. Statistically, we only estimate the value of α. We do not know for sure what factors impart that value to it, or bring about changes in it over time, and what their respective contributions are. Surely, a large number of factors may matter here, such as innovations in the payments mechanism, variations in the relative volume of purely financial transactions, changes in the spatial distribution of economic activity and in the use of trade credit, growth in the number of households and offices of firms, etc. Increased monetization is only one among several factors affecting the value of α and the measured income velocity of money. If reliable annual estimates of the degree of monetization are available and one is interested in estimating the independent contribution of this factor in the observed variations in the demand for money, the index of monetization should be entered as an independent variable in the demand function for money, along with income and other variables. The results would then decide the issue of the degree of importance of the monetization factor. Unfortunately, we cannot perform the experiment as reliable data on monetization are not available. For reasons given in the previous paragraph, we consider the quantitative importance of this factor in determining the neutral rate of growth of money supply pretty low in any case.

2.5 Other Suggestions for Monetary Planning

Before proceeding further, we shall look briefly at two more suggestions for regulating money-supply changes.

2.5.1 Food Output and Money Supply

It is sometimes suggested that the growth of money supply should be linked positively with the growth of food output rather than with the growth of total real output in the country. The underlying theory of this alternative suggestion has never been carefully spelled out. The argument, however, seems to run along these lines: since new money represents extra purchasing power and food represents the major item of consumption in India, extra food output represents extra capacity to absorb additional purchasing power. Therefore, so long as the extra purchasing power generated by new money creation matches the extra absorptive capacity represented by additional food output, food prices, and therefore prices in general, will remain stable. A direct outcome of this kind of argument is the popular suggestion made during 1977–8 that in view of the large buffer stock of foodgrains with the government, 'excess' deficit financing leading to 'excess' supply of money could be resorted to by the government without any fear of inflation.

This is a rather crude, but telling, way of putting the alternative proposition. We examine it very briefly here. The last part of the proposition, viz. the leading role of food prices in determining the course of prices in general, has been discussed in detail elsewhere (see Gupta, 1974c). The main part of the proposition neglects the basic fact about money—that it is general purchasing power: that, therefore, increases in it lead to spending all around, that is, in all markets, and not just in the one market of food. Therefore, what matters is not only the output of food, but also the output of non-food items, i.e. of all kinds of goods and services which make up the national income of a country. Of course, in the Indian context, food output is specially important, because its weight both in the total output of the country and the various price index numbers is very high. Also, increase in food prices may have some cost–push impact on other prices. But this does not justify the suggestion that food output should replace total output in the determination of neutral changes in the stock of money.

The alternative proposition can be recast in the framework of our theory. It amounts to saying that the real demand for money is essentially a function of food output and a more stable function of it than of real income, so that as the output of food grows, the real demand for money will also grow and, for price stability, there should be an appropriate increase in the nominal quantity of money. Such a proposition has, however, never been stated theoretically and no sound theoretical support for it can be easily mustered. A purely empirical basis for it is also likely to be very weak. Therefore, it must be rejected in favour of our proposition stated above.

2.5.2 Credit Needs and Money Supply

Another indirect suggestion regarding money-supply growth which is perennially made in influential business quarters is that the monetary-credit policy of the R.B.I. should be so conducted as to meet all the legitimate (bank) credit needs of industry and trade. That is, at increasing prices, at least proportionately increasing bank credit should also be provided to meet fully the real credit needs of industry and trade (e.g., see Parekh, 1974; also see Gupta, 1974b for a critique). Since, given the government's proportionate share in total bank credit, banks can provide more credit to the private sector only if they have more deposits and since the demand-deposit portion of these deposits is a part of money, normally, increased bank credit is accompanied by an increased supply of money too. Therefore, the policy recommendation clearly says that the supply of money, instead of being an autonomous policy constraint on the price level, should become a function of it and increase in step with it.

It can be easily seen what this kind of monetary rule would lead us to. Theoretically, outside of a regime of fully-administered prices, this would make the price level indeterminate (see Patinkin, 1965,

p. 303). In practice, it would open the flood-gates of hyper-inflation. The economy would get caught in a vicious inflationary spiral: higher prices would lead to higher nominal demand for credit. The creation of a larger amount of credit, both directly and indirectly through the creation of bank deposits, would result in larger excess demand for output, which would lead to still higher prices and a still larger demand for nominal credit. The world is full of instances of countries running into hyper-inflation when they followed a policy of validating increases in the supply of money and credit to meet the increasing demand for credit at higher and higher price levels.

What representatives of industry and trade must recognize is that the capacity of any banking system to provide *real* credit at any time is limited by the asset preferences of the public—by the latter's readiness to hold the real deposit liabilities of banks, given the total real wealth of the public. For the same reason, the incremental amount of real credit that the banking system can provide is determined by the portion of real savings the public is willing to deposit with banks. The banks with the active support of the R.B.I. can, no doubt, expand total *nominal* credit to any extent they like. But this does not mean that the banking system can also generate corresponding real credit as well. Time and again, it has been experienced in country after country that any attempt to force larger real credit through nominal credit expansion is a sure road to inflation. The Indian experience also amply bears out the truth of this statement. This can be easily seen when we compare nominal and real values of 'aggregate monetary resources' (i.e. money 'broadly' defined to include time deposits of banks) for each year since 1960–1 (for evidence, see Gupta, 1978a, pp. 66–7).

2.6 Fixed versus Flexible Rule for the Growth of Money Supply

There are two competing ways in which the money-supply growth rule of equation (2.5) can be applied in actual practice. One gives us a fixed (trend) rule; the other a flexible rule.

Under the former, the supply of money should be increased at a fixed (proportionate) rate year after year. Having estimated the value of α, the fixed rate is derived by using trend values of g_{yf} and g_k in equation (2.5). Therefore, the fixed rule can be alternatively called the trend rule (see Friedman, 1959, Chapter 4).

Under the flexible rule, the rate of growth of money supply is supposed to be varied from year to year, according to the expected values of g_{yf} and g_k for that year and not the trend values of these rates. Apart from the trend, both y_f and k (or its reciprocal $V \equiv$ income velocity of money) may be subject to regular cycles or other changes. A flexible monetary policy is expected to iron out these fluctuations so as to make the economy move along its y_f path. This will require a contra-cyclical monetary policy so far as cycles in k (or V) are concerned. Thus, the supply of money would be required to be increased at a rate faster than the trend rate when k is rising (V is falling) faster than its own trend rate g_k (which may as well be zero) and would be required to be increased at a rate lower than the trend rate when k is falling (V is rising) faster than its own trend rate. In either case, the counter-cycle variation in g_M from its trend value should exactly match the cyclical variation in g_k around its own trend value, i.e. should exactly counter the cyclical variation in V around its own trend value.

The objective of the contra-cyclical monetary management of the above kind is to stabilize the economy against fluctuations arising from aggregate demand—from inflationary or deflationary pressures emerging from the cyclical behaviour of V, so characteristic of developed economies. But that is not enough, especially for the Indian economy. What about the autonomous supply-side cycles (or other changes) in real output, originating, say, in agriculture? Aggregate demand management through contra-cyclical monetary management cannot counteract them. On the other hand, it can aggravate the resulting price situation. For example, in a year of bumper food crops, a lower-than-trend growth-rate of money supply will cause a virtual crash in food prices and in a year of drought, a higher-than-trend growth-rate of money supply will make prices rise very high. So, apart from supply-side remedial measures, what will be advisable in such situations are pro-cyclical rather than contra-cyclical money-supply changes.

The case for a flexible monetary policy is very simple: it will lead to greater monetary stability than the trend rule policy by giving a better match between the demand and supply of money. Since the real demand for money is subject not only to trend changes but also to cyclical and other non-trend changes, whether arising from non-trend changes in g_k or g_{yf}, the supply of money should also be varied similarly to meet fully the varying demand for money at stable prices.

Theoretically, this case for a flexible monetary policy is unexceptionable. Maintaining continuous monetary equilibrium in the economy is, surely, a laudable objective. But the odds in the path of its attainment in actual life are really very great. The danger is that in the pursuit of such a perfect equilibrium we may not even realize the relatively modest but more feasible objective of long-run average monetary stability. Sound monetary management can suffer as much from its over-enthusiastic supporters as from neglect or under-estimation of its potential. We discuss below the major practical difficulties and dangers of a truly flexible monetary policy.

Let us first evaluate the flexible monetary policy in the context of the simple g_M rule of equation (2.2). This will marry g_M for a particular year to the g_{yf} for that year. Therefore, if the g_{yf} is expected to vary from year to year, so should the g_M. Paradoxically, this variability in g_M is derived from too rigid an assumption: that the demand for money equation (2.1.1) holds exactly (with constant k) and between contemporaneous values of M/P and y. This condition is too rigid, because it does not always hold well for individual short periods. On the other hand, the trend rule requires only a milder and more flexible underlying condition to be satisfied: that the demand for money equation (2.1.1) hold on an average of a long period of several years. This would only ensure that the errors of money-supply variations will not accumulate, but be corrected automatically through mutual cancellation, on an average, over any long period.

Secondly, the information needs of a flexible monetary policy are quite heavy. To decide about the current year g_M, the monetary authority must know well before the year is out what the current year g_{yf} is going to be. Any error in this prediction will cause a corresponding error in g_M.

But the required true information about the g_{yf} is hard to come by. True, some estimate can always be made, and is perforce actually made, for making other policy decisions. The problem is that the degree of reliability of such predictive or 'quick' estimates is very low. For example, for food production for 1972–3, the quick estimate was 102 million tons; later on, it was revised down to 96 million tons. Similarly, for 1973–4, starting with an estimated figure of 111 million tons, foodgrain production was scaled down to 108 million tons, then to between 106 and 108 million tons, and finally to only 103 million tons. Similar errors are committed in estimating non-food agricultural output and non-agricultural output. Thus, quick estimates of national income suffer from a large margin of error, and mostly these errors stem from over-estimation.

The trend rule also makes errors of prediction if the trend value of g_{yf} is interpreted as the best estimate of the expected rate of growth of output of the current or the next year. But this interpretation is necessary only in the case of a flexible monetary policy, not under the confines of the trend rule. Under the latter, the matching between g_M and g_{yf} has to be done only on an average of a number of years, and not for each individual year.

The information needs of the flexible monetary policy variant of equation (2.5) are heavier still. This equation, when applied flexibly, would require that the monetary authority should be in a position not only to anticipate correctly the true value of g_{yf} but also of g_k for the current year. The latter is even harder to predict: it is very difficult to say what proportionate change in the desired income velocity of money will take place over a current or future year. Again, the trend rule obviates the need for such exact and exacting information, because its modest goal of long-run monetary stability can be easily satisfied so long as k or V shows a steady long-run trend with only mild fluctuations. This condition is satisfied substantially for the period under observation (1950-1 to 1975-6). A detailed statistical analysis of the empirical evidence on V is given in Appendix B.

The short-run variability as well as unpredictability of V lies at the root of Friedman's hypothesis of long and variable lags in the effects of monetary policy (see Friedman, 1959, 1961; Culbertson, 1960; and Kareken and Solow, 1963). Friedman's basic argument is that due to the presence of such lags, a flexible monetary policy runs the danger of increasing rather than decreasing the amplitudes of cyclical fluctuations. In addition, they increase the over-all uncertainty in the economy. Also, in the absence of a fixed or well-defined indicator or criterion of the correctness of monetary policy (such as that provided by the trend rule), we cannot easily know the errors committed by the monetary authority in its conduct of monetary policy.

We do not have any systematic information about the dynamic working of monetary policy or its lag structure in India. And, on the basis of casual empiricism, we cannot reject outright the hypothesis of long and variable lags for India. Therefore we are likely to be much better off if the monetary policy is conducted mainly so as to generate conditions of long-run monetary stability and, most of the time, short-term fluctuations are mostly either left alone or to other instruments of government policy. The main job which needs to be tackled urgently and on which continued caution is to be maintained by the monetary authority is avoiding inflationary pressures arising on account of monetary policy.

And this brings us to an even greater danger arising from flexible monetary policy—that it will tend to be highly inflationary. This danger arises for two reasons. Firstly, every year it is likely to over-expand the money supply by over-estimating the expected rate of growth of output. The latter phenomenon is almost unavoidable if we commence each year with substantial excess capacity, shortfalls in target output, and heavy public pressures to increase output fast through increase in public expenditure, whatever the structural difficulties on the side of supply. This has been our experience year after year. Secondly and more important, under the present-day paper-currency regime, an indigent government is always tempted to interpret flexible monetary policy to mean that it can run to the Central Bank of the country for help at the slightest excuse, rather than raise revenue from additional taxes or cut or postpone some less urgent expenditures. And, in the Indian case, it is not purely an imaginary fear, but something real. We have been reaping the fruits of such flexibility, or 'controlled expansion' of money supply in the language of the R.B.I. (1970, p. 34), in the form of very high rates of inflation for some time.

The chief merit of a fixed monetary rule will be that it will put a check on over-expansion of money supply. And this is the most important task of monetary policy both in the present and foreseeable circumstances.

2.7 What Trend Rate of Growth of Money Supply for India?

For the practical application of the trend variant of the g_M rule of equation (2.5), we have to choose the 'best' values of g_k, g_{yf}, and α. We have already seen in Section 2.3 that the best estimate of α (for the Indian economy) is unity. On the basis of statistical evidence on V presented in Appendix B and the expected behaviour of its chief determinants (12-month time-deposit rate of interest and the ratio of agricultural income to total national income), the 'best' trend value of g_k can be assumed to be zero. This leaves us with the problem of deciding upon the trend value of g_{yf}.

Two practical methods are open to us. One is to adopt straight-away the target rate of growth of output as embodied in the Five Year Plans, e.g. the 4.7 per cent per annum adopted in the Sixth Plan.

If the past performance of these plans is any guide, this is likely to be an over-estimate of the trend value of g_{yf}.

The other alternative is to use the average annual rate of growth of output realized in the past. Over the 26-year period 1950–76, taking good years with bad, real national income at market prices increased at the rate of 3.8 per cent per annum on the average. Barring the year 1952–3 when in the aftermath of the Korean War wholesale prices fell steeply by 15 per cent over their average level of the previous year, the years 1954–5 and 1955–6 when prices fell by 7 per cent and 5 per cent, respectively, and the years 1968–9 and 1974–5 when prices fell by 1 per cent each time, all other years have been marked by price rise. During some of the latter years, the rate of rise has been very high. This suggests that, broadly speaking, the sample period has been one of excess, and not of deficient, aggregate demand in money terms, because, over this period in the Indian economy, autonomous cost–push phenomena or large-scale monopolistic manipulation of prices cannot be claimed to be important determinants of price behaviour. On the other hand, the economy has increasingly suffered from much avoidable excess capacity and shortfalls of output due to all-round bad planning, governmental mismanagement, corruption, and the resultant supply bottlenecks and hurdles. The latter are no transient phenomena. Rather, they have become an established part of the very structure of the economy as well as policy. *Given such a structure*, the economy does not seem to be capable of doing anything better, on average, than what it had accomplished on average over the 26-year period 1950–76. An optimistic estimate of the trend value of g_{yf} may put it at 4 per cent per annum. On this reckoning, the trend value of g_M should also be fixed at 4 per cent per annum.

A liberal alternative will be a compromise between the two competing trend values for g_{yf} and so for g_M, and between the fixed rule and the flexible rule. This may be stated in the form of a flexible trend rule: the annual growth-rate of money supply should be allowed to vary between 4 per cent and 5 per cent so that the long-run average rate comes to 4.5 per cent.

To help appreciate that this suggestion gives a liberal specification of the trend value for the g_M, we may point out that in the past (since 1950–1) the economy has not absorbed real money growing even at the annual trend rate of 4 per cent per annum. This can easily be checked by looking at the time series of real money supply (M/P)

(Appendix G). The realized annual compound rate-of-growth of *real* money supply for the period 1960–1 to 1976–7 was only 3 per cent, though the authorities allowed *nominal* money supply to grow at an annual compound rate of 10.8 per cent. This also shows how futile it is for the authorities to force an appreciably higher growth rate of real money supply on the public via excess expansion of money supply in nominal terms than the public is willing to absorb.

2.8 Actual Behaviour of g_M (*1950–1 to 1975–6*)

The actual course of the annual values of g_M for the period 1950–1 to 1975–6 is given in Appendix G. We may sum up briefly the broad features of this course:

1. During the 1950s the average annual value of g_M was 3.65 per cent. It rose to about 9 per cent during the sixties and 12.5 per cent during the first six years of the seventies. The average value of g_M for 1976–7 was 14.8 per cent. This shows continued acceleration in the value of g_M over the period.

Only for the period of the fifties can the average value of g_M be claimed to be non-inflationary. For the later period, it has been increasingly on the 'excess' side (as compared to the neutral trend value of 4 per cent per annum); and

2. There has been too much year-to-year variation in the value of g_M (see Gupta, 1974a).

Both the features of the actual behaviour of g_M can be traced to the following: 'The stock of money (M) has been (and is still) treated as a residual quantity of no major significance, variations in which are allowed to be the outcome of several other policy decisions, autonomous developments, and random changes' (Gupta, 1974a, p. 265).

Recent evidence gives us no reason to revise this observation made more than four years ago. This runs counter to the claim of the R.B.I. that it follows a monetary policy of 'controlled expansion' (R.B.I., 1970, p. 34).

2.9 Relation between g_M and g_P (*The Rate of Change of Prices*)

The concept of neutral increases in the quantity of money used in this chapter necessarily implies that 'excess increases' in the quantity of money are inflationary. On the assumption (supported by empirical evidence) that the real income elasticity of demand for real money is unity, the excess rate of increase in money supply in a growing economy is given by $g_M - g_{yf}$. Then, will

$$g_P = g_M - g_{yf} \qquad (2.6)$$

be true?

This hypothesis can be empirically tested provided reliable estimates of g_{yf} are available (for we do have reliable measures of both g_P and g_M). In the absence of such estimates, the substitution of g_{yf} by g_y (for which we do have estimates) can be justified if we are willing to assume that the realized g_y was not adversely affected by any deficiency of aggregate demand during any year of the sample period, or that the realized g_y was purely the product of supply-side factors. Making this substitution, we set up equation (2.6) in a simple testable form:

$$(g_P)_t = a_0 + a_1 (g_M - g_y)_t + \epsilon_t \qquad (2.7)$$

where ϵ is an error term and $a_1 > 0$.

We have fitted this equation to the annual data (measured in percentages) for the period 1949–50 to 1975–6. The results are given below:

$$(g_P)_t = \ 3.43 \ + \ 0.602 \, (g_M - g_y)_t,$$
$$\qquad\quad (2.28) \quad (2.99)$$

$$\bar{R}^2 = 0.233; \qquad d = 2.178 \qquad (2.8)$$

The fit is very poor as the equation can explain only 23.3 per cent of the observed variation in g_P. However, the regression coefficient of $(g_M - g_y)$ has the right sign and is highly significant. The equation does not suffer from first-order autocorrelation among residuals.

What possible reasons can there be for the poor fit? Substitution of g_y for g_{yf} is one. More important, the regression equation (2.7) fitted to annual values of g_P and $(g_M - g_y)$ implies a rather strong assumption that the underlying Quantity Theory of Money holds good for each short period of a year—that the income velocity of money V (or its reciprocal the Cambridge k) does not change from year to year. The empirical evidence given in Appendix B runs counter to this assumption. For the time-path of V does show cyclical and other fluctuations in it. This suggests that the kind of relation hypothesized in equation (2.7) can, at best, hold for individual periods much longer than a year. In order to conserve degrees of freedom and yet remove much of short-run cyclical and other fluctuations from the data, we took 5-year moving averages of the annual observations on g_P and $(g_M - g_y)$ separately. When equation (2.7) was fitted to these averages, we obtained the following result:

$$(g_P)_5 = 1.713 + 0.886 \ (g_M - g_y)_5$$
$$\quad\quad (2.864) \quad (8.221)$$

$$\bar{R}^2 = 0.752; \quad d = 1.121 \quad\quad\quad\quad (2.9)$$

where the subscript $_5$ indicates that the associated variable is a 5-year moving average of its annual observations.

Equation (2.9) clearly marks a substantial improvement over equation (2.8). The fit is much better. The t value of the regression coefficient of the only explanatory variable in the equation is very high. It is more than 2.5 times the t value of the regression coefficient of the explanatory variable in equation (2.8). The d statistic has gone down in value indicating positive first-order autocorrelation at 5 per cent level of significance (but no such correlation at 1 per cent level of significance). This is perfectly understandable, for the method of moving averages tends to introduce such correlation where none exists. Therefore, we need not worry about this result. Equation (2.9), on the whole, is quite good. It shows that, on a five-year average, excess increases in the quantity of money at the rate of 1 per cent per annum have led to a 0.886 per cent rate of inflation over the sample period.

A comparison of equations (2.8) and (2.9) also supports our view emphasized in this chapter that the Quantity Theory of Money as a theory of the relation between changes in the quantity of money and rates of inflation in a growing economy is better interpreted as a theory of a longer-term relation between the two variables. It should not be expected to hold good for short periods. Therefore, if a particular year's excess increase in the quantity of money does not result in an equal (or substantially equal) proportionate increase in the general price level of that very year, it should not be held against the Quantity Theory of Money properly interpreted. Nor should it be interpreted to mean that, in the event of a much smaller rate of inflation in that year, all the excess increase in the quantity of money has somehow been fully and permanently absorbed in the system, and that nothing need be feared on this account regarding the rates of inflation in future years.

CHAPTER 3

MONEY SUPPLY ANALYSIS

3.1 Introduction

All sensible monetary planning must be based on a dependable theory of money supply determination. In the past, while most discussions of monetary control have been conducted without any explicit foundation of a theory of money supply, these discussions, as well as the actual use of monetary control measures by the authorities, have always drawn upon some implicit theory of money supply, howsoever crudely conceived. With increased theoretical as well as empirical attention being paid to the problem of money supply determination since the early sixties, we are now in a much better position than before to lay down a highly reliable theory of money supply, which can serve as a suitable basis as well as framework for monetary planning in India. This will also serve to highlight institutional and other difficulties of successful monetary planning in the country and the areas and problems of useful monetary research.

3.2 Empirical Definitions of Money (M) and High-Powered Money (H)

Before we begin a substantive discussion of the analysis of money supply, it is essential to be clear about what we mean empirically by each of these key terms.

Empirically, money is usually defined in two ways, one broader than the other; accordingly, in the literature, one is called the 'narrow' definition of money and the other the 'broader' definition of money. Of the two definitions, the former is more widely accepted. Till March 1977 the R.B.I. also used to define money narrowly and used the term 'aggregate monetary resources' for money defined in a broader sense. Since April 1977 the R.B.I. has adopted four alternative empirical definitions or measures of money supply, denoted by

A large part of this chapter is based on two papers: Gupta (1976a) and (1976b).

M_1, M_2, M_3 and M_4 (discussed in Appendix C). The major attention, however, continues to be devoted to money narrowly defined and denoted by M_1. *In this book also we shall use the term money in its narrow sense but denote it simply by M.*

Further, money is always viewed as money held by the public. The public includes all economic units (households, firms and institutions) except the banking system and the government. For our purposes, 'banking system' denotes the R.B.I. plus all banks which accept demand deposits; 'government' means the Central Government plus all state governments. This means that the word public is inclusive of all local authorities, non-bank financial institutions, and non-departmental public-sector undertakings (such as Hindustan Steel, Indian Airlines, etc.) and even the foreign central banks and governments and the International Monetary Fund, who hold a part of Indian money in India in the form of 'other deposits' of the R.B.I. (see below). In other words, in the standard measures of money, money or cash held by the government and the banking system is not included.

The rationale for defining money as only 'money held by the public' (and the public as defined above) is that this separates the producers or the suppliers of money from the holders or the demanders of it. For both monetary analysis and policy formulation, such a separation is essential.

Empirically, then, money (M) is defined as currency (C) plus demand deposits of banks (DD) plus 'other deposits' of the R.B.I. (OD) which are of the nature of demand deposits—all held by the public:

$$M \equiv C + DD + OD. \tag{3.1}$$

More simply, money comprises currency and demand deposits of the banking system (including the R.B.I.) held by the public. The latter is also called deposit money.

Currency consists of paper currency or currency notes as well as coins. Paper currency is predominantly in the form of Reserve Bank of India currency notes of the denomination of two rupees and above. In addition, we also have small amounts of Government of India one-rupee notes. One-rupee notes and small coins also are the liability of the Government of India. But all notes and coins are issued to the public through the R.B.I.

The demand deposits of banks held by the public are self-explanatory: they comprise *net* demand deposits of all commercial banks (scheduled and non-scheduled), i.e. net of inter-bank demand deposits, and net demand liabilities of the state co-operative banks. (For recent revisions, see Appendix C and R.B.I., 1977.) The figures are inclusive of the 'demand deposit portion of saving deposits' of banks.

'Other deposits' of the R.B.I. included under money are its deposits other than those held by the government (central as well as state governments), banks, the International Monetary Fund in its Account No. 1, and a few others.[1] They are the demand deposits of quasi-government institutions, like the Industrial Finance Corporation of India, State Financial Corporations, Industrial Development Bank of India, Agricultural Refinance and Development Corporation, etc., deposits of the Reserve Bank of India Employees' Co-operative Credit Society, demand balances of foreign central banks and governments, the International Monetary Fund (Account No. 2) and the World Bank, etc.

The structural composition of money supply on the last Friday of March 1977 is given in Table 3.1.

TABLE 3.1

	Rs. crores	Percentage of total money supply
1. Currency	7,903	52.1
2. Deposit money (a + b)	7,256	47.9
a) Net demand deposits of banks	7,156	47.2
b) 'Other deposits' of the R.B.I.	100	0.7
3. Total money supply (1 + 2)	15,159	100.0

Source: Reserve Bank of India Bulletin, March 1977, Table No. 17.
Note: All figures are preliminary.

Thus, we find (1) that currency constitutes a little more than half of money supply in India and (2) that the 'other deposits' of the R.B.I. are a negligible part of the money supply, and even as a proportion of deposit money of very small value. Both these structural features

[1] The other important exclusions are 'compulsory deposits' of the public with the R.B.I. and the R.B.I. Employees' Pension Fund, Provident Fund, and Co-operative Guarantee Fund.

are important. We shall appreciate the importance of the first structural feature when we come to discuss the money-multiplier process of money-supply changes. The second feature allows us some simplification. Since 'other deposits' of the R.B.I. are a very small proportion of *M*, we shall not go into their behavioural analysis as a separate category.

High-Powered Money (H)

High-powered money is money produced by the R.B.I. and the government and held by the public and banks. More simply, it is 'government money' held by the public and banks. It comprises (*i*) currency held by the public (*C*), (*ii*) cash reserves of banks (*R*), and (*iii*) 'other deposits' of the R.B.I. (*OD*).

Thus,

$$H \equiv C + R + OD. \tag{3.2}$$

On comparing the empirical definitions of *M* and *H* as given in equations (3.1) and (3.2) respectively, we find (*a*) that *C* and *OD* are common in both *M* and *H*, and (*b*) that the only difference between *M* and *H* is that whereas the former includes *DD* (net demand deposits of banks), the latter includes *R* (reserves of banks) in place of *DD*. And this difference is of crucial importance. The quality of *H* which makes it high-powered as compared to ordinary money (*M*) is that *H* can serve as the base for the generation of *DD* in a fractional reserve system.

We shall understand the full import of the last statement in the previous paragraph when we study in the next section the multiplier process of the secondary expansion of deposit money. At this point, we may simply note that at any time only *R* serves as the actual base for the total deposit structure of banks. Yet, the whole of *H* is called high-powered money, because other components of *H* (*C* and *OD*) held by the non-bank public also have the potential of becoming *R* without any further intervention of the monetary authority, if the public moves out of currency or 'other deposits' of the R.B.I. into bank deposits. This emphasizes, once again, that *H* is government money (treating the R.B.I. as an agency of the government). The R.B.I. calls *H* 'reserve money'. Some others call it 'base money'. Both these additional appellations for *H* highlight the fact that *H* has the capacity to serve as the reserve base for the creation of deposits. This fact lies at the bottom of the money-multiplier theory of money supply as well as of the deposit and credit creation by banks.

The structural composition of H on the last Friday of March 1977 is given in Table 3.2.

TABLE 3.2

	Rs. crores	Percentage of total H
1. Currency held by the public	7,903	82.8
2. Bank reserves	1,539	16.2
3. 'Other deposits' of the R.B.I.	100	1.0
Total H	9,542	100.0

Source: Reserve Bank of India Bulletin, March 1977.

Note: All figures are preliminary.

Thus, we find that currency held by the public constitutes the bulk of H. It will be seen that the structural composition of H is of great practical importance for money-supply generation. *Ordinarily*, the higher the proportion of reserves in H, the greater also the high-poweredness of H in that the same H, other things being the same, will come to be associated with a larger amount of money (as well as deposits).

3.3 A Simple Theory of Money Supply

Our objective here is not to enter into a theoretically sophisticated discussion of money-supply determination, but to present very briefly a widely-held theory of it in its simplest form. This is the well-known money-multiplier theory of money supply or the high-powered-money theory of money supply. The two alternative designations of the theory will automatically become clear from the structure of the theory discussed below.

In its simplest form, the theory says that the supply of money (M^S) is a highly stable increasing function of high-powered money (H).[2] In other words, it says (1) that as H changes M also changes in the same direction; and (2) that most of the change in M is due to

[2] To be correct, of adjusted H. The meaning and rationale of the concept of adjusted H are discussed in Appendix E. As a first approximation, other variables, such as market rates of interest, are considered unimportant and hence neglected.

the change in H. Mathematically, this may be represented by the following equation:

$$M^S = f(H), \frac{dM^S}{dH} > 0. \tag{3.3}$$

Two particular forms of the general relationship in equation (3.3) may be noted specially:

$$M^S = mH \tag{3.4}$$

and $\quad M^S = a + bH,$ (3.5)

where m and b are positive constants and a may be positive or negative.

Equation (3.4) makes M^S a proportional function of H; equation (3.5) a non-proportional function of H. Of the two, equation (3.4) is more popular. In it, m is the money multiplier and H is the multiplicand, because m multiplies H up to yield M^S. In equation (3.5) b also is a multiplier; but it is only a marginal multiplier, whereas m is both the average and the marginal multiplier. (For an empirical analysis of money supply in India, see Appendix F.1.)

A slightly more sophisticated and flexible, yet simple, form of the monetarist theory of money supply is given by the following equation:

$$M^S = m(\quad)H. \tag{3.6}$$

In the above equation, the money multiplier m is assumed to be a function of a few unspecified variables (indicated by the empty parentheses after m), and not a constant. (For the determinants of m, see Appendix D.)

On the analytical plane, equation (3.6) can be interpreted to mean that, *broadly speaking*, the determinants of the supply of money can be meaningfully classified under two heads: (*a*) those that affect H and (*b*) those that affect m. That is, in the first instance, the equation serves one of the useful functions of a theory—that of providing a filing or classificatory device for various factors affecting a dependent variable, as, for example, is done by the well-known theory of demand and supply of price determination under perfect competition. Whether the classificatory device suggested by the theory of equation (3.6) is empirically meaningful or not can be known only after a detailed examination of the factors governing H and the

4

factors governing m and the extent to which the former can be meaningfully separated from the latter.

The factors governing H and changes in H will be discussed at length in Chapter 4, and the factors governing m are analysed in Appendix D. Anticipating these discussions, we may say that the factors governing H and changes in H are *largely* policy-controlled, whereas the factors governing m and changes in m are *largely* endogenous, i.e. are such as depend on the behavioural choices of the public and banks. Policy changes do have some effect on the value of m, but, usually, this effect is relatively small. This knowledge makes the simple theory of money supply embodied in equation (3.6) empirically highly meaningful and very useful for the purpose of monetary planning. It implies that, for policy purposes, the authorities will do well if they take the behaviour of m as, more or less, 'autonomously' given, i.e. outside their control (unless a specific policy change can be seen to affect m). For controlling changes in M, they should, therefore, concentrate their efforts on controlling changes in H.

Money-Multiplier Process

Since a technical discussion of the money multiplier will be offered in Appendix D, only a simple heuristic explanation of the money-multiplier process is offered here. As a prelude to such a discussion, we begin with the uses of high-powered money (H) or with the demand for it. H is held partly by the 'public' (as defined in Section 3.2) and partly by banks. The public holds it in the form of currency and other deposits of the R.B.I. Banks hold H as cash reserves (R), partly in the form of 'cash on hand' or vault cash to meet the currency drains from the public and partly in the form of balances with the R.B.I. to meet the statutory reserve requirement of the R.B.I. and a part of their clearing drains.

Earlier we had observed that the division of H between C and R is of great importance for the determination of money supply. We shall now elaborate on our remark.

C and OD are directly a part of M. How much of M the public wants to hold in the form of C and OD is decided by the public. So, how much of H is held in the form of C and OD becomes a decision-variable of the public. The rest of H, i.e. R, stays with banks and serves as the base for the secondary creation of deposits by banks through their interaction with the public and the government. This results in multiple expansion of money, bank deposits, and bank credit and constitutes the heart of the money-multiplier process.

The money-multiplier process can be explained heuristically thus. Suppose there is a one-rupee injection of new H in the form of new demand deposit with banks. This increases their reserves by one full rupee. Banks keep a part of this increase in reserves (ΔR) at the rate of their usual or desired reserve ratio (r) in the form of reserves (including required reserves) and lend or invest the rest in earning assets. The recipients of bank credit spend it in the market. Those who receive payments retain a part of it in the form of currency and deposit the rest with banks, partly in the form of demand (and saving) deposits and partly in the form of time deposits. The division into currency, demand deposits, and time deposits will be made according to the desired currency–demand deposit (C/DD) ratio and time-deposit – demand-deposit (TD/DD) ratio. This causes a further increase in the deposits—both demand and time. The return flow of a part of bank reserves induces banks to enter into a second round of creation of credit and deposits as their actual reserves would be higher than the desired reserves. The process continues till banks have re-attained their desired reserve ratio and the public its desired C/DD and TD/DD ratios. The process leads to multiple creation of bank credit, bank deposits, and money. Hence it is called the money-multiplier process and also the credit-multiplier process.

Since in the multiplier process one extra rupee of reserves serves as the base for the multiple creation of bank money (DD), the reserve money becomes high-powered money. Since reserves are drawn from H, C and OD being the other components of H, which, if transferred to banks, will form part of their reserves, the sum of C, OD, and R (i.e. H as a whole) is called high-powered money in monetary literature.

3.4 Reserve Bank's Analysis of Money Supply

The R.B.I.'s analysis of money supply is published every month in its *Bulletin*. From March 1968 to March 1977 it used to be published in a table captioned 'Factors Affecting Money Supply'. Since then the table (with a few additional details) has been retitled 'Analysis of Sources of Change in M_1 (New Series)', following the recommendations of the Second Working Group (on Money Supply) of the R.B.I. (1977).

The R.B.I.'s analysis is not based on the theory of money supply spelled out briefly in the previous section or on any other theory. The elements of the former were, in fact, published in the R.B.I. *Bulletin* (R.B.I., 1961b) as 'Analysis of Money Supply in India—II', but unfortunately this analysis was not adopted as the basis of the subsequent publications on the subject. Instead, 'Analysis of Money Supply in India—I' in the July 1961 issue of the *Bulletin* (R.B.I., 1961a) has since served as the basis of the R.B.I.'s analysis of money supply variations.

The factors affecting money supply or the sources of change in money supply are derived in the following easy steps:

First, definitionally,

$$M \equiv ML + GC, \tag{3.7}$$

where $ML \equiv$ monetary liabilities of the banking sector as a whole (comprising the R.B.I. and banks) and

$GC \equiv$ government currency with the public.

Next, the balance-sheet identity of the banking sector can be written as

$$\begin{matrix} \text{monetary liabilities} \\ + \text{ non-monetary liabilities} \end{matrix} \equiv \begin{matrix} \text{financial assets} \\ + \text{ other assets.} \end{matrix}$$

By transposing non-monetary liabilities on the right-hand side of the above identity and defining

$$\begin{matrix} \text{net non-monetary} \\ \text{liabilities} \end{matrix} \equiv \begin{matrix} \text{non-monetary liabilities} \\ - \text{other assets,} \end{matrix}$$

we have

$$\begin{matrix} \text{monetary liabilities} \equiv \text{financial assets} - \text{net} \\ \text{non-monetary liabilities.} \end{matrix} \tag{3.8}$$

Using (3.8) in (3.7), we have

$$\begin{matrix} M \equiv \text{'financial assets} - \text{net non-monetary} \\ \text{liabilities' of the banking system} + GC. \end{matrix} \tag{3.9}$$

Finally, the financial assets of the banking sector are divided under the following three heads:

1. net bank credit to the government,
2. bank credit to the commercial sector, and
3. net foreign exchange assets of the banking sector.

Using this information in (3.9), the R.B.I. finally arrives at its analysis of the Factors Affecting Money Supply or of the Sources of Change in Money Supply. The relevant R.B.I. table (called the table hereafter) gives the following break-down of the main factors or sources (e.g. see R.B.I., *Bulletin*, July 1977, Table No. 11).

1. *Net bank credit to government* (A + B)
   A. R.B.I.'s net credit to government (*i*—*ii*)
      (*i*) Claims on government
      (*ii*) Government deposits with R.B.I.
   B. Other banks' credit to government

2. *Bank credit to commercial sector* (A + B)
   A. R.B.I.'s credit to commercial sector
   B. Other banks' credit to commercial sector

3. *Net foreign exchange assets of banking sector* (A + B)
   A. R.B.I.'s net foreign exchange assets
   B. Other banks' net foreign exchange assets

4. *Government's currency liabilities to the public*

5. *Net non-monetary liabilities of banking sector* (A + B + C)
   A. Time deposits with banks
   B. Net non-monetary liabilities of R.B.I.
   C. Other net non-monetary liabilities of banks (derived)[2]

In terms of the above factors, then,

$$M \equiv 1 + 2 + 3 + 4 - 5.$$

3.5 A Critical Evaluation of the R.B.I.'s Analysis

The main property of this analysis is that it is a purely accounting or *ex-post* one. After much protracted debate over this point in the *Economic and Political Weekly* in 1976, the R.B.I. has also finally admitted that the analytical frame of its money-supply analysis is, in fact, an accounting identity (R.B.I., 1977, p. 87).

It immediately follows that the R.B.I.'s analysis is meaningless. It has no substantive content, or explanatory power, of its own. These characterizations have well-accepted scientific meanings, which cannot be faulted. In simple words, they mean that the R.B.I.'s analysis does not 'explain' the consequences (for money supply) of

---

[2] Comprises mainly capital and reserves of banks, other liabilities (like bills payable) over other assets (like premises, furniture) of banks, errors and omissions, etc.

various policy and non-policy autonomous changes, such as the open market operations of the R.B.I., or changes in the statutory reserve requirement for banks, or changes in net foreign aid, etc., much less explain how and why such autonomous changes come to affect the supply of money. All that it does is measure changes in the stock of money after they have occurred (not predict them before-hand) and allocate the measured change to different sectors, factors, or sources according to a particular scheme of classification.

But a mere classification of the data provides no explanation. Nor is a particular accounting scheme of data presentation any substitute for theory. Nor does it obviate the need for a theory, however crude, both for understanding the money-supply mechanism or the way several forces operate to bring about changes in the supply of money, and for monetary planning. For example, before the R.B.I. uses a particular monetary control measure, it must know how this measure is likely to function and its likely effect on the quantum of money supply. Obviously, the R.B.I.'s analysis, being only an accounting analysis, cannot answer such questions. It is important to stress this point, because apart from recognizing that the R.B.I.'s analysis is purely an accounting analysis, we must also understand its true nature as well as limitations.[3]

The distinction between accounting (tautological, empirically meaningless, or *ex post*) analysis and theoretical (substantive, empirically meaningful, or *ex ante*) analysis, to which attention has been drawn in the previous paragraph, is so fundamental and yet so easily lost sight of in several quarters that it is best illustrated with the help of an analogy from the well-known fields of national income accounting and determination. Since income and expenditure are circular flows, or since *ex post* total income is identically equal to total expenditure in a closed economy, one way to measure the national income (Y) is to measure total national expenditure. The latter can be taken as the sum of private consumption expenditure (C), private investment expenditure (I), and government expenditure (G). This gives us $Y \equiv C + I + G$. Thus, income is measured in terms of the components of expenditure. From the income-expenditure identity it follows arithmetically that increase in any one of the component expenditures, $C, I,$ or G, will be matched by an equal increase in Y.

[3] A careful reading of R.B.I., 1977, Section 4 should convince the reader that this point has not been fully grasped by the authors of the *Report*.

But this is a purely tautological statement, and thus devoid of any substantive or explanatory content. In other words, it is true by definition that *ex post* an increase in *C*, other things being the same, will be identically equal to the increase in *Y*. The aforesaid identity does not tell us whether it is the increase in *C* which leads to the increase in *Y*, or *vice versa*, or it is the variation in some other factor (or factors) which lies at the root of the increase in both *C* and *Y*. And this is what a genuine theory should explain.

In general terms we may say that though it is always open to us to divide any aggregate into any number of component parts and say tautologically that the value of the change in the aggregate will always be equal to the sum of the changes in the component parts, we are not explaining anything new, for we are only stating what is true by definition. This is true of all accounting equations.

On the other hand, the Keynesian theory of national-income determination explains what factors lead to changes in income (*Y*) and how. In its simplest version, both *I* and *G* are assumed to be autonomous of *Y*. Together, they are called autonomous expenditure (*A*), *C* is assumed to be an increasing function of *Y*. Then, since *A* is assumed to be autonomous of *Y*, changes in *A* can occur independently of *Y*. It is these changes in *A* which bring about induced changes in *Y* and *C* via the well-known multiplier process. Thus, changes in both *C* and *Y* are explained by autonomous changes in *A*.

These arguments are fully applicable to the analysis of factors affecting money supply. We have stated earlier that the R.B.I. analysis is only an exercise in *ex post* measurement and, therefore, it cannot serve the purpose of a theory. But if we are genuinely interested in explaining changes in money supply, we must have recourse to some theory of money supply. One such theory has been spelt out in Section 3.3. In the first instance, such a theory attempts to explain changes in *M* in terms of changes in *H* and in *m*. In addition, it tells us what lies behind changes in *m* and how to explain them in terms of their determinants—proximate and ultimate. A fuller use of the theory would also require that changes in *H* are traced to their several sources in a systematic manner. Though this will involve only an accounting analysis, it will not detract from the explanatory power of the money-multiplier theory as a theory of money supply (see Gupta, 1976b). Nor will it mean the end of the matter on the *H* front. After the individual sources of changes in

H have been identified and measured, the nature of each source can be (and should be) examined and explained either as a policy variable, as an endogenous variable, or as an exogenous variable (see Chapter 4).

Not only does the R.B.I.'s analysis, being only an accounting identity, offer no explanation of money-supply changes, but also the particular accounting identity used by the R.B.I. has been highly misleading—it has been the source of some very serious errors concerning money-supply analysis. And all these errors inhere in the consolidation of the balance sheet of the R.B.I. with those of other banks, which obliterates the distinction between *H* and *M*, so fundamental to any money-supply analysis. The major errors are discussed below:

1. The R.B.I.'s accounting adds up components of *H* and *M*, ignoring the dependence of the latter on the former. Without taking any position on the appropriate theory of money supply, this could have been (and can still be) avoided by separating the 'sources of change in *H*' from the 'sectoral distribution of bank credit' (this will be discussed in greater detail later). But this was not done. The result has been a total denial of any money-multiplier process or of the 'secondary' expansion of money and credit by banks induced by reserves accretion—something which no monetary economist or even the R.B.I. has ever seriously denied. This has further resulted in a large number of untenable derivations, all traceable to the R.B.I.'s accounting table and the associated explanations and interpretations. Consider a few examples:

(*i*) 'The government sector's total impact on money supply ... would be equal to its total budget deficit minus its net purchases of foreign exchange from the Reserve Bank' (R.B.I., 1961a, para 8). This is not correct. For, what the latter measures is the effect on *H*, not on *M*. The latter would increase by a certain multiple of the increase in *H*, depending upon the value of the money multiplier, *m*.

(*ii*) 'Bank credit to the government sector ... leads to an equivalent increase in money supply' (R.B.I., 1961a, para 33). The term bank credit includes both the net R.B.I. credit and banks' credit. The effects of these two kinds of bank credit on money supply are very different from each other. The increase in the net R.B.I. credit increases *H* and thereby *M*, which is a certain multiple of the increase in *H*. Therefore, it is wrong to say that the increase in the net R.B.I. credit 'leads to an equivalent increase in money supply'. Increase in banks' credit to the government sector, on the other hand, leaves *M* as well as banks' total credit more or less unchanged.[4] It simply reallocates banks' credit in favour of the government at the cost of the commercial sector.

(*iii*) '. . . Bank credit to the commercial sector was the most important factor contributing to the expansion of money supply' (GOI, 1973–4, p. 32). 'Bank credit' in such statements also usually includes both the R.B.I. credit and the credit from banks. The causal role of the former in the expansion of money supply is understandable, but not so the role of the credit from banks. The latter is as much a dependent variable as the total money supply. Therefore, to say that money supply increased *because* banks' credit (whether to the government or the commercial sector) increased is not correct. Nor does it explain anything. It only moves the enquiry (about the money-supply increase) one step backward. For, then, the question must be asked: how could the banks increase their credit? Do they have unlimited power to increase credit or isn't it limited by something? To say that banks could increase their credit because their deposits grew, clearly contradicts the earlier assertion that an increase in bank credit causes an increase in money supply (which includes demand deposits of banks). Also, it is no solution to say so, because, then, we have only to re-word our previous question and ask: why did the bank deposits grow?[5] Either way we must locate some autonomous change which induces banks to increase their credit and, in the process, deposits as well. The answer is provided by the theory of money supply (Section 3.3).

2. The R.B.I.'s accounting analysis in the table suppresses completely the 'R.B.I. credit to banks' as a 'factor affecting money supply'. In the words of the 1961 Working Group, '[a] The transactions between the Reserve Bank and the banks, by themselves, would not give rise to any variation in money supply; [b] as, in consolidating the assets and liabilities of the banking system, such transactions

[4] 'More or less', because we are assuming that a change in the asset composition of banks (resulting from increased government borrowing from them) leaves the value of the money-multiplier unchanged, and this may not be strictly true always. Also see Gupta (1976a).

[5] 'Do loans make deposits or deposits make loans?' is a well-known puzzle in banking theory. The answer is also well known. At the level of an individual small bank, it would be broadly true to say that 'deposits make loans'. But at the macro level both deposits and credit are jointly-determined (or interdependent) variables. Neither is a cause or effect.

would cancel out' (R.B.I., 1961a, para 28).[6] [*a*] is a necessary consequence of [*b*]. But [*a*] is patently wrong, for the borrowings of banks from the R.B.I. do increase *H* and thereby *M*. In the very next paragraph (29), this fact is explicitly recognized: 'This does not, however, mean that when banks borrow from the Reserve Bank, this borrowing would not result in an increase in money supply. This borrowing would increase banks' reserves and enable them to add to their financial assets and thus to increase money supply.' This makes the two paragraphs 28 and 29 contradictory,[7] which the R.B.I. has not done anything to resolve. A little thought would have indicated that the contradiction is inherent in the *ex post* approach adopted in adding up the R.B.I. credit, which generates *H*, with banks' credit, which is not *H* but some function of *H*. *Ex ante* this is wholly wrong: the R.B.I. credit is fundamentally different from banks' credit.

The R.B.I., however, does not see any merit in these arguments. For, even after being presented with them (see Gupta, 1976a, 1976b), it has decided to continue with its old (accounting) framework of money-supply analysis only altering the title to 'Sources of Change in Money Supply' from 'Factors Affecting Money Supply' (see R.B.I., 1977, Section 4). In defence the R.B.I. has offered several arguments, which, since the issue is of fundamental importance to the whole approach of this book, we must examine carefully.

The arguments offered by the R.B.I. in favour of its accounting analysis are:

1. It provides an 'analytical' [accounting] frame for the presentation of 'primary' monetary data in terms of a 'broad sectoral distribution of total domestic credit'. This is stated to be the basic function of the table.

2. Since it is the transactions of the non-bank sectors with the banking sector which 'cause' variations in the financial assets and the net non-monetary liabilities of the banking sector, and, therefore, money (see equation (3.9)), the accounting table giving the sectoral distribution of total bank credit 'traces the origin of the money supply variations to specific sectors, which draw upon the credit from the banking system. In this sense, the frame [the table] is designed to indicate the sources of change in money supply' (R.B.I., 1977, p. 87).

[6] The second Working Group (R.B.I., 1977) is silent on the issue.
[7] On this point, see Shetty, Avadhani, and Menon (1976) and Gupta (1976b).

3. The R.B.I.'s schema of data presentation (the table) 'facilitates credit planning and forecasting', as it gives 'the disaggregation of total domestic credit into major user sectors' (R.B.I., 1977, p. 87). In defence of this claim it is asserted that this is so in India because the R.B.I. 'determines both the total stock of credit and its sectoral allocation through a system of credit planning and credit rationing.' Each of these arguments is examined below.

1. The R.B.I. is undoubtedly the only source of monetary data on India. As such, it is one of its important functions to publish such data regularly. The question is how best to present them. At the least, such presentation must not mislead readers about monetary phenomena. It is our strong contention that the present form of data presentation in the table does not fulfil this desideratum—that ever since its first appearance in July 1961 it has been instrumental in spreading false ideas about the 'factors affecting money supply'.

The table has a definite origin and a history of its own from which, in its present form, it cannot be disassociated. As pointed out earlier, it is the product of the R.B.I.'s first Working Group on Money Supply (1961), which had designed it to 'explain' changes in money supply in terms of the components of bank credit derived from a balance-sheet identity, and, perhaps unwittingly, christened these components 'the factors affecting money supply' (now renamed the 'sources of change in money supply'). Following this, almost all official and unofficial publications on money supply 'explain' money-supply changes religiously in terms of these accounting components. Thus, the accounting analysis of money supply embodied in the table has already usurped the status of a theory of money supply and of a reigning orthodoxy, whether we like it or not.

Against this background it cannot be claimed that the table merely presents monetary data—that it is 'explanation or theory neutral'. It is not. The table was explicitly designed to carry a definite message about the factors affecting money supply, and ever since it has been widely interpreted in that manner. Even the R.B.I.'s Second Working Group on Money Supply (1977), after deep deliberation, could not rid itself from this impression, as is exemplified by its recommendation for the continued publication of the table with only minor alterations and a changed name, 'Analysis of Sources of Change in M_1 (New Series),' which is equally misleading.

The presentation of monetary data in the same old form cannot but be interpreted in the old faulty way. If the faulty notions about the determinants of the supply of money have to be dispelled, the minimum the R.B.I. must do is stop publication of the table in its present form. All the data can be rearranged and published under two separate tables, entitled (1) Analysis of Sources of Change in High-Powered Money (or Reserve Money); and (2) Sectoral Allocation (or Composition) of Bank Credit.[8] From the April–May 1977 issue of its monthly *Bulletin*, the R.B.I. has started publishing a new table (No. 13) on the lines of (1) suggested above. But it has also retained the table, which contains all the data that the new table (on reserve money) presents (an unnecessary duplication of data presentation) besides data on the sectoral composition of bank credit. Clearly, the R.B.I. must replace this table by a new one which gives the sectoral composition of only the credit of banks. Further, it should be designated as such. Besides eliminating the present duplication of the data presentation on reserve money, this would complete the presentation of all the data the table currently presents, and in a 'money supply theory neutral' form. It would also liberate the R.B.I. and others from the purely accounting frame of money-supply analysis. Any continued publication of the table, on the other hand, would offer proof enough for the charge that whatever the excuses offered, the R.B.I. is in fact committed to a purely accounting analysis of money-supply variations. Otherwise, why not give the data on the sectoral distribution of bank credit the correct name? Equally important, why retain a form of data presentation which is not only liable to misinterpretation, but has been and still is widely misinterpreted as something that 'explains' the behaviour of money supply in India.

Our preference is for a more detailed table on the credit operations of banks in place of the table. This could be constructed on the following lines:

TITLE: CREDIT OPERATIONS OF BANKS

A. *Sectoral distribution of bank credit*
1. *Government*
   (a) Central Government
   (b) State Governments

---

[8] We are using the term bank credit in the sense of credit from banks other than the R.B.I., whether extended to the government, the commercial sector, or the foreign sector.

2. *Commercial sector*
   (a) Loans and advances
   (b) Bills discounted
   (c) Investment in 'other approved securities'
   (d) Other investments

3. *Foreign sector*
   Net foreign exchange assets of banks

4. *Total bank credit*

B. *Financing of bank credit*

5. Net demand deposits of banks

6. Net time deposits of banks

7. Other net non-monetary liabilities of banks of which
   (a) Owned funds
   (b) Credit from the R.B.I.
   (c) Credit from the I.D.B.I.
   (d) Participation certificates
   (e) Bills discounting scheme
   (f) Other sources

8. Total demand and time liabilities

Less 9. Reserves
   (a) With the R.B.I.
   (b) Cash on hand

If possible, more detailed information under various heads and sub-heads may be incorporated.

2. The R.B.I.'s argument (2) in favour of the table, summed up above, confirms the charge that the R.B.I. is sticking fast to an accounting explanation of the sources of change in money supply. For it is only in an accounting sense, and not behaviourally, that the 'sectoral components of bank credit' can be called the 'sources of change in money supply.'

3. The claim that the table 'facilitates credit planning and forecasting' is unwarranted, because a mere 'disaggregation of total domestic credit into major user sectors' is not sufficient for either credit planning or forecasting. All that the table tells is 'how things have been', and not 'how things ought to be, or are planned to be, or are expected to be'. For credit planning, the R.B.I. must first specify social criteria for the rate of growth of total bank credit and its sectoral distribution, solve for such growth and distribution, and then use the various tools of credit control at its disposal to ensure that the actual conforms to the desired.

'Forecasting' is an equally ticklish affair. If bank credit is taken to be a fully R.B.I.-determined variable, which it is not, then all that the forecasting would entail would be periodic announcements of the R.B.I.'s policy decisions on the subject. But if the stock of bank credit is taken to be an endogenous variable, which it surely is and would necessarily be, so long as the fractional reserve system obtains or there are assets (such as currency) that compete with bank deposits in the asset portfolio of the public, the R.B.I. is in no position to specify on its own the stocks of bank credit at various points of time, though it can surely steer the course of such credit more or less around the charted time-path through the use of the control instruments at its disposal, provided the government also fully cooperates with the R.B.I. in the matter. In such a situation, the R.B.I. fully needs a theory of money supply or bank credit, which can reliably predict the money supply/credit consequences of particular policy actions and other changes taking place in the economy all the time. An accounting table can be no substitute for a properly articulated theory and an estimated empirical model based on it. The theory and an empirical model are absolutely necessary for successful credit planning.

3.6 The R.B.I. and the Money Multiplier

The R.B.I.'s attitude towards the money-multiplier theory of money supply is one of seeming ambivalence. It has offered the theory qualified recognition in a variety of ways. Time and again, it has spoken of the 'secondary expansion' of bank money/credit, which involves the money-multiplier process. Since 1972–3 it has regularly carried a brief discussion on the behaviour of the money-multiplier in India in its annual *Report on Currency and Finance*. Since the April–May 1978 issue of its monthly *Bulletin*, two new tables have been introduced: (1) 'Reserve Money And Its Components' and (2) 'Analysis of Sources of Change in Reserve Money.' Any separation of reserve money (or H) from ordinary money (M) presumes the existence of some kind of a money-multiplier relation between H and M, otherwise there is no point in looking at the components and sources of change in H. Lastly, the Second Working Group of the R.B.I. (1977) has disclosed that the money-multiplier approach 'has been adopted [by the R.B.I.] for *long-term projections* of credit/money supply for, say, the Fourth and Fifth Plan periods' (p. 88, my italics). However, it has added that 'the Bank's analytical frame [the table] provides a much better insight for the practical formulation of monetary policy, especially *in the short run*' (p. 88, italics mine.) Nevertheless, in view of our discussion in the previous section, any such credit claimed for the accounting analysis is totally un-warranted. And the difference between the two approaches—the money-multiplier and the accounting—does not lie in any difference between the length of the time period chosen, but in the empirical meaningfulness of the one and the total emptiness of the other.

The harsh truth is that the R.B.I.'s money-supply analysis is dominated by the accounting approach discussed in the previous two sections. The Second Working Group of the R.B.I. (1977) and some of its members individually (see Majumdar, 1976, and Shetty, Avadhani, and Menon, 1976) have rejected the money-multiplier approach on four main grounds:

1. The money-multiplier theory is 'a mechanistic approach to money supply determination', devoid of any 'serious operational significance'. This is not correct. Our brief discussion of the theory in Section 3.3 and in Appendix D should convince the reader that it is a behavioural theory. (Also see Gupta, 1976b.)

2. Banks alone cannot enlarge money supply/credit unless there are takers or there is demand for it. Theoretically, at least, this is true. But, in the money-multiplier analysis, the demand side for credit is neglected on the assumption that the supply of acceptable earning assets facing banks (i.e. the demand for bank credit from the commercial sector and the government) is highly elastic. With a relatively large and growing amount of public debt for about the last three decades, empirically, this is a highly realistic assumption to make (see Gupta, 1976b). Hence the possible difficulties arising from the demand for bank credit can be safely neglected most of the time. In addition the money-multiplier theory can still handle these difficulties via the reserve ratio of banks as one of the proximate determinants of the money multiplier.

3. 'The determination of money supply ... is the result of a complex process of interaction between *monetary* and *real* factors' (R.B.I., 1977, p. 87). Consequently, the money-multiplier theory cannot offer a satisfactory explanation of such a complex process, as it only looks at the monetary variables. The criticism betrays the lack of a full and proper understanding of the money-multiplier theory. The strength of this theory lies precisely in that this simple-looking theory provides a framework in which to capture systematically all the factors that may influence the supply of money and

also to explain and predict the effect on money supply of any autonomous changes in one or more of these factors.[9]

4. Following Goodhart (1975), it has been alleged that 'the [money-multiplier] approach fails to take into account the difficulties confronting the Monetary Authority in achieving any desired level of the monetary base (H) itself' (R.B.I., 1977, p. 88).[10] The charge is irrelevant to the theory *per se*, as it is not concerned with the 'control of H' problems. Its function is only to explain how changes in H and other factors bring about changes in M. For the purposes of monetary policy, though, difficulties in controlling H must be faced. In this context, the charge is unfounded. Firstly, it is only the money-multiplier approach which emphasizes the distinction between H and M and the importance of controlling H for controlling M. Then, the approach requires a consideration of the sources of changes in H, and examination of the nature of and the control problems connected with each of these sources, which we shall do in the following chapters. Thus, far from neglecting the 'control of H' problems, the money-multiplier approach to monetary planning lays greatest stress on them.

[9] See Cagan (1965) and Swamy (1975) as supporting illustrations of this claim. Also see Section 3.3 and Appendix D.

[10] The Second Working Group (R.B.I., 1977), however, had no right to bring forward the charge, because only in the preceding paragraph of its *Report* (p. 87) it had claimed that 'in the Indian system . . . both the monetary base and the money stock expansion have come to be regulated by the monetary authorities.'

CHAPTER 4
HIGH-POWERED MONEY

4.1 Introduction

The key to the controlled variations of money supply is the control of high-powered money (H). This is based on the first-approximation assumption that either m remains constant or it varies in a highly predictable manner. In order to know how to control H, we must know what the sources of variation in it are, their relative importance, their nature, and the *modus operandi* of each source. This knowledge is so important for monetary control that we devote this whole chapter to a study of the sources of changes in H. In most discussions of monetary control such a study is not attempted at all, for these discussions are not based on any explicit theory of money supply. This is a serious lacuna. Moreover, such discussions are inadequate in that they concentrate only on the monetary-control measures of the Central Bank. For success in monetary control, the government must also control appropriately its policy actions affecting H.

4.2 Sources of Change in High-Powered Money (H)[1]

In Chapter 3 high-powered money was defined empirically to comprise (1) currency held by the public, (2) cash reserves of banks, and 'other deposits' of the R.B.I.[2] Some (relatively small) part of currency is issued directly by the government, the rest is all Reserve Bank money (R.B.M.). The cash reserves of banks are held partly in the form of currency (government as well as Reserve Bank) as 'cash on hand' and partly as deposits with the R.B.I. Therefore, H can be redefined simply as the sum of government currency and R.B.M. held by the public and banks. In analysing the sources of change in H, this cross-classification of the components of H into government currency and the R.B.M. will be found very useful.

---

[1] Swamy (1975, Chapter 2) discusses these sources in detail.

[2] For an explanation, see Section 3.2. These deposits are held by the 'public'.

Government currency comprises one-rupee notes and coins and small coins. R.B.M. comprises (1) all currency notes other than one-rupee notes, (2) bank deposits with the R.B.I., and (3) 'other deposits' of the R.B.I. Thus, the R.B.M. has both a currency component and a deposit-money component. The latter is the sum of (2) and (3).

Of all the currency issued by the government, only a part is held by the public and banks; the rest is held by the R.B.I., mainly in its Issue Department as a backing against its own currency. The R.B.I. as the currency authority of the country is charged with the responsibility of maintaining at par the full convertibility of government currency into the rest of the country's currency and *vice versa*. As the agent of the Central Government, the R.B.I. is also entrusted with the task of putting into circulation all one-rupee notes and coins and most of the small coins. This the Bank does through its Banking Department. For the same reasons, the R.B.I. holds stocks of government currency on hand.

The government controls directly only the *total* issue of its currency, and this, too, within narrow limits, because it is wasteful to issue excessive amounts of this currency as a means of raising resources in place of borrowing from the R.B.I. How much of this currency is held by the public and how much by the R.B.I. is determined neither by the government nor the R.B.I. but by the public, because the latter is perfectly free to convert different kinds of currency into one another. Thus, if excessive amounts of government currency are issued to the public, it will exchange the undesired amounts of it for Reserve Bank currency at the currency chests of the Bank and the treasuries, and make the actual stock equal to the desired stock.

Structurally, government currency in the hands of the public and banks constitutes a small proportion of the total stock of H outstanding. In 1975–6 this proportion was only 7.3 per cent. Similarly, changes in government currency have also contributed only a small share to the observed total changes in H. For example, for the six years 1971–2 to 1976–7, changes in government currency have constituted, on average, only 6.1 per cent of the year-to-year changes in the average stocks of H. Therefore, for all practical purposes, changes in H amount to changes in the R.B.M. More important, changes in government currency are induced by changes in the R.B.M. The former are brought about to meet the public's demand for small coins (including one-rupee coins and notes) in relation to currency of higher denominations issued by the R.B.I. Therefore, changes in the R.B.M. are virtually responsible for all the observed changes in *H*. An analysis of the sources of change in the R.B.M. now follows, much the most interesting and complicated part of the analysis.

4.3 Sources of Change in Reserve Bank Money (R.B.M.)

Analysis of the sources of change in the R.B.M. begins with the balance-sheet identity for the R.B.I. in the following form:[3]

Monetary Liabilities + Non-Monetary Liabilities
= Financial Assets + Other Assets.

Or symbolically,

$$ML + NML = FA + OA,$$

$$\text{or} \quad ML = FA - (NML - OA),$$

$$\text{or} \quad RBM = ML = FA - NNML, \qquad (4.1)$$

where $NNML = NML - OA =$ Net Non-Monetary Liabilities.

What has been done above is very simple. First, both the liabilities and the assets have been classified under two heads each and, then, by a simple transposition of terms, equation (4.1) is arrived at. This defines the Reserve Bank money or the monetary liabilities of the R.B.I. as the excess of its financial assets over its net non-monetary liabilities. The latter are themselves defined as the excess of the non-monetary liabilities over the other assets of the R.B.I.

The purpose of arriving at equation (4.1) is to provide a simple framework in which to study the operations of multifarious factors which are responsible for the variations in the monetary liabilities of the R.B.I., i.e. the R.B.M. The important point to note is that the R.B.I. does not change *H* by a mere fiat or completely arbitrarily. Rather, there is an intricate but definite system whereby changes in the R.B.M. occur. An understanding of this system is of the utmost importance for the conduct of a successful policy of monetary control.

We may begin our analysis of the system of changes in the R.B.M. with the statement that all such changes occur as a result of the complex of transactions which the R.B.I. runs with the rest of the economy and the world in the discharge of its central-banking functions.

---

[3] This refers to the consolidated balance-sheet of the Issue Department and the Banking Department of the R.B.I.

All the R.B.I.'s transactors may be divided into four empirically meaningful sectors, viz. (1) the government (Central Government and state governments), (2) the banks (commercial banks and State co-operative banks), (3) the development banks, and (4) the foreign sector.

The R.B.I. does not deal with the foreign sector directly in all cases. Rather, most of the time, the transactions are between the constituents of the domestic sector and the foreign sector. The R.B.I. as the sole custodian of the country's foreign-exchange reserves bears the brunt of these transactions through variations in its foreign exchange assets, and thereby in H. Therefore, the admission of a separate foreign sector will raise a problem. If the transactions in foreign exchange are either on government account or on private account, the changes in H arising from dealings in foreign exchange become also *ultimately* attributable to these two domestic sectors— the government sector and the commercial sector. This point must be borne in mind while retaining a separate foreign sector, because this procedure will throw greater light on the working of economic forces which bring about changes in H.

Following the fourfold sector-classification of the R.B.I.'s transactors, all (net) financial assets of the R.B.I. are divided under the corresponding (four) sector-categories. Because of the lack of adequate information (to be discussed later), for the time being the net non-monetary liabilities of the R.B.I. are retained under one common head. Then, denoting Reserve Bank credit by R.B.C., equation (4.1) can be re-written in the following form:

R.B.M. = (1) net R.B.C. to government
+ (2) R.B.C. to banks
+ (3) R.B.C. to development banks[4]
+ (4) net foreign exchange assets of the R.B.I.
− (5) net non-monetary liabilities of the
R.B.I.   (4.2)

Correspondingly, any change in the R.B.M. will be the net sum of the changes in the balance-sheet components appearing on the right-hand side of equation (4.2) (with the same algebraic signs). Changes

----

[4] The R.B.I. designates this head as 'R.B.C. to the Commercial Sector' (see R.B.I., 1977, p. 105). For reasons for our redesignation of this head, see Section 10.1.

in the aforementioned five balance-sheet components will be called the sources of change in the R.B.M.

Before discussing each of these sources, the reader's attention is drawn to a serious conceptual problem involved in the R.B.I. classification of the sources of change in H. The R.B.I. classification is by the ultimate, and not the immediate, recipient of its credit. To illustrate, let us take the case of treasury bills. The R.B.I. buys them directly from the Central Government. It also purchases them from banks (and others). In the first case it lends directly to the government. In the second case, in the first instance, it provides accommodation to banks. If it is interpreted as providing credit to the government, it does so only indirectly through banks. The government, in the second case, borrows from banks. The banks hold treasury bills for some time. When in need of cash, they get these bills rediscounted from the R.B.I.

The conceptual problem that arises here is: through rediscounting does the R.B.I. extend credit to the government or to banks? One view can be that, since the treasury bills are the liability of the government, the credit is being extended to the government. This is supported by the consideration that, technically, rediscounting is a purchase/sale transaction. Therefore, the selling bank is, technically speaking, not borrowing. This is also the R.B.I. view.

But there is another view which goes against the R.B.I. practice of the consolidation of accounts. We have already seen in another context (Section 3.5) that in monetary analysis, such a consolidation of accounts can be treacherous. In general, in monetary analysis which deals with the layering of claims, it is not advisable to take short cuts. If we do, and speak only of the ultimate borrower and the ultimate lender, then all financial intermediaries, including banks, will evaporate into thin air. Then, given the R.B.I. policy, the resale of treasury bills by banks is a decision variable of banks, and not of the government. Once the bills have been sold to banks, the treasury loses all control over them. Thereafter, it is entirely up to the banks to decide whether and how long they hold the bills in their portfolios or when and in what amount they sell these bills to the R.B.I., subject, of course, to R.B.I. policy constraints. A recognition of this fact is important for the proper conduct of monetary policy. The argument that the rediscount of bills by the R.B.I. is not lending is purely technical, and not economic. Bill rediscounting is only one form of refinancing. It is commonly accepted that bills are a short-term *credit* instrument and that when the government is *selling* bills, it is *borrowing* funds for the short duration of ninety-one days. The same is true when these bills are resold. Now, the borrowing is done by the reseller—the banks in the present instance—for the remainder of the bills' lives.

For all these reasons, bills rediscounted by the R.B.I. for banks, whether they are treasury bills or commercial bills, should be considered as credit given to banks, who are the immediate recipients of it. This will not require any change in the presentation of the balance sheets of banks, but simply the re-classification of data by the R.B.I. The bills rediscounted by the R.B.I. for banks will be counted as a part of the R.B.C. to banks. For credit accounting, the treasury bills purchased from banks will be counted as a part of the ordinary *bank* credit to the government and commercial bills rediscounted for banks will be counted as a part of the ordinary *bank* (and not the R.B.I.) credit to the commercial sector.

4.4.1 Net Reserve Bank Credit to the Government

According to the R.B.I. (1977, p. 105), its net claims on the government comprise the following:

1. rupee securities held in the Issue Department,
2. treasury bills purchased and discounted,
3. investments in government securities (= total investment of the Banking Department − investments other than government securities including foreign securities held in Investment Account),
4. rupee coin in Issue and Banking Departments,
5. loans and advances to state governments,

less 6. government deposits with the R.B.I. (of the Central as well as state governments).

As pointed out earlier, the R.B.I. comes to acquire government currency as the central government's agent for the distribution (sale) of this currency to the public. It also holds stocks of government currency as the currency authority of the country to ensure full convertibility at par of the currency of different denominations. The government currency appears as an asset item on the R.B.I.'s balance sheet. It is a non-interest-bearing (monetary) debt of the government to the R.B.I. The variations in government currency held by the R.B.I. arise when its net purchases of this currency from the government differ from its net sales of this currency to the public and banks.

When government currency in the hands of the R.B.I. increases, other things being the same, H also goes up—not in the form of government currency but in the form of the R.B.M. This happens because the R.B.I. acquires additional government currency, whether from the government or the public or banks, only by paying for it in terms of its own money. Therefore, it is not only the issue of government currency to the public which raises H, the issue of government currency to the R.B.I. also raises it. We are, of course, assuming that the government does not add the sale proceeds of its currency to its cash balances, but spends them in the market.

The government's rupee securities include *ad hoc* and regular treasury bills and other securities of any maturity of the Government of India. They are *largely* the result of the Central Government's direct borrowing from the R.B.I. The R.B.I. as banker to the Central Government provides the latter with short-term finance through its purchase of *ad hoc* treasury bills. Besides, it also provides long-term finance to the Central Government as its banker and as the manager of the public debt, by taking a dealer's position in government securities. The important thing to note is that the Central Government is empowered to borrow any amount it likes from the R.B.I. The latter cannot impose any restrictions on such borrowings.

The R.B.I. as banker to the state governments also provides short-term loans and advances (called ways-and-means advances) to these governments to tide over imbalances in their ways-and-means position arising out of uneven flow of receipts in relation to disbursements. Besides, it gives them loans from the National Funds (Section 4.8) it operates. Unlike the Central Government, the state governments are not authorized to borrow any amount they like from the R.B.I.: the R.B.I. prescribes certain limits for the borrowings of individual states. The state governments, however, have been used to drawing beyond these agreed limits without any authorization by the R.B.I. This has given rise to the problem of 'unauthorized overdrafts'. At the end of June 1977 these overdrafts had aggregated to Rs. 319 crores. They aggravate the problem of monetary control, for, ultimately, they result in increased borrowing by the Central Government from the R.B.I. The *modus operandi* is simple. The unauthorized overdrafts are cleared by the Central Government against its *ad hoc* loans to the states or as advance payments to them in respect of their shares of taxes, grants-in-aid or as the Centre's assistance for state plans. The Central Government, in turn, raises funds by sales of *ad hoc* treasury bills to the R.B.I. Thus, the unauthorized overdrafts to the state governments end up as a loan to the Central Government over which the R.B.I. has no control.

We have combined the borrowing of the Central and state governments under one head as government borrowing from the R.B.I., because, whoever the borrower from the R.B.I., the effect on H of such borrowing is exactly the same. Similarly, for the generation of H, it does not matter whether the state overdrafts are authorized or unauthorized. These distinctions are, however, important for monetary control, because whereas the R.B.I. cannot impose any restrictions on its loans to the Central Government, it is empowered to do so in the case of the state governments. The problem of unauthorized overdrafts to the state governments has arisen because the R.B.I. is not willing to lend to these governments beyond a point.

Since the R.B.I. acts as banker to both the Central and state governments, they keep most of their cash balances (apart from small amounts of cash in their treasuries) on current account deposit with the R.B.I. These deposits with the R.B.I. are a non-monetary liability of the R.B.I., as, by definition, they are not included in H or M. In order to arrive at the net R.B.C. to the government, these deposits are subtracted from the gross R.B.C. to the government.

Holding other sources of change in H constant, a change in the net R.B.C. to the government would change H in the same direction and by an equal amount. But other sources of change in H may or may not remain constant when the net R.B.C. to the government changes. The last two of the other four sources, namely, net foreign exchange assets of the R.B.I. or net non-monetary liabilities of the R.B.I. may also change in either direction. Therefore, the conclusion frequently reached that the change in the net R.B.C. to the government measures the impact of government's transactions with the R.B.I. on H is, in general, not correct. Two adjustments must always be made in it—one arising from the government's net purchase/sale of foreign exchange from/to the R.B.I., the other arising from the change in the R.B.I.'s net non-monetary liabilities attributable to the R.B.I.'s lending to the government.

Suppose the net R.B.C. to the government has increased by Rs. 100 crores. If this is accompanied by a net government purchase of foreign exchange of the value of (say) Rs. 20 crores, this amount would flow back to the R.B.I. and H would increase by only Rs. 80 crores. In the event of the net government sale of foreign exchange of the same amount to the R.B.I. being the accompanying factor, the net change in H will rise to Rs. 120 crores. This point will be discussed more fully later in Section 4.7. We may, however, note that separate data for the net purchase or sale of foreign exchange on government account are not available. Yet the estimates for such transactions can be derived from the data on foreign exchange assets and transactions published by the R.B.I.[5]

The net credit which the R.B.I. extends to the government (or other sectors) is financed partly by the creation of monetary liabilities and partly by its net non-monetary liabilities. (A parallel example is provided by banks. Their loanable funds, too, are derived partly from their demand deposits—their monetary liabilities—and partly from their time deposits and other non-monetary liabilities.) Therefore, to the extent the increase in the net R.B.C. to the government is financed from the net non-monetary liabilities of the R.B.I., the increase in H due to the increase in the net R.B.C. to the government will fall short of the latter. However, data are not available whereby such a measurement or adjustment can be made. The problem involved will be discussed more fully under Section 4.8.

4.4.2 Net Reserve Bank Credit to the Government and Deficit Financing

The relation between the net R.B.C. to the government and that much-used but ill-defined term deficit financing of the government may now be briefly explained. There is no one commonly-accepted definition of deficit financing. In official documents a distinction is usually made between (1) budgetary deficit and (2) deficit financing. Even the Government of India uses the former in two different senses; one as given in its budget documents, the other as given in its annual *Economic Survey* (1976–7, p. 24 fn). Correctly speaking, the latter concept should be called deficit financing rather than budgetary deficit, as will become clear as we proceed with our discussion. The R.B.I. uses yet another definition of budgetary deficit. The Planning Commission mostly uses the term deficit financing without distinguishing it from budgetary deficit. Its meaning of deficit financing has, however, changed with each Plan up to the Third Plan. The Fifth and Sixth Plan documents have avoided defining the term.

[5] For details, see Swamy (1975), Appendix 1, Table 2.

All these (and other) uses of the term have created a great deal of confusion. In the budget identity, total receipts must equal total expenditure. Among all definitions of a budget deficit (or deficit financing), given a total expenditure, the difference arises only on the receipts side: regarding the receipts that are to be treated as constituting deficit financing. Once a decision in this regard has been made, the receipts that are defined to constitute deficit financing do not get included in total receipts, and, thus, also constitute budget deficit. Therefore, any distinction between the terms budgetary deficit and deficit financing is a contrived one. They are better left as one and the same. The *Economic Survey* (1976-7, p. 24 fn) tries to justify the distinction by saying that 'while budgetary deficit is derived from budgetary data, deficit financing has to be worked out from monetary data.' This is not sufficient ground for retaining the distinction.

We speak of the combined budget deficit of the Central government and state governments. The budget documents define budgetary deficit as the sum of net increase in the floating debt of the government and the net withdrawal of their cash balances. The floating debt comprises treasury bills of the Central Government and the R.B.I.'s ways and means advances and overdrafts to state governments.

The R.B.I.'s definition of the budgetary deficit is broader than that given above. Besides the above components, it also includes withdrawals from cash balance investment accounts and revenue reserve funds of states.

The *Economic Survey*'s definition is the narrowest. It measures budgetary deficit by the net increase in the R.B.I.'s holding of treasury bills and in the R.B.I.'s ways and means advances and overdrafts to states, plus net withdrawals from their cash balances by the Centre and the states. This definition differs from that in the budget documents only with regard to the coverage of treasury bills. The former includes only net increase in treasury bills held by the R.B.I., the latter net increase in all the treasury bills outstanding (whether held by the R.B.I., state governments, commercial banks, or others).

The Third and Fourth Plan documents define deficit financing as the increase in the net R.B.C. to the government. For the first time, the *Economic Survey* (1977-8, p. 25 fn) also gives explicitly this very definition. The differences with the several definitions of budgetary deficit given above can be easily worked out, as we already know the components of the net R.B.C. to the government from the previous sub-section.

What lies behind this way of defining deficit financing? Under the broadest definition used in the U.S.A., deficit financing is the net increase in the total indebtedness of the government (including net withdrawal from its cash balances). Why then is there a much narrower definition in this country? The objective seems to be to arrive at a definition which, more or less, measures the M-impact of the government's method of financing the budget. This is not attainable. For what deficit financing does directly, is increase H. The resulting increase in M is a certain multiple of the increase in H, depending upon the value of the marginal money multiplier.

Even if we want to define deficit financing as the exact measure of the H-impact of the government's method of financing its budget, the official definition will have to be appropriately modified in the light of the earlier discussion. First, deficit finance should be explicitly defined as the government finance raised through the creation of H. To give it a name, let us call it the H-definition of deficit finance. Thus defined, deficit financing will be given by

(i) increase in the net R.B.C. to the government,

$+$ (ii) increase in government currency with the public and banks,

$+$ (iii) net sale (or minus net purchase) of 'old' (previous years') issues of rupee securities by the R.B.I. to the public,

$-$ (iv) the part of (i) estimated to be financed by the increase in the net non-monetary liabilities of the R.B.I.

The following points about the H-measure of deficit financing may be noted:

1. Increase in the net R.B.C. to the government is not the same thing as deficit financing.

2. Since sale of government currency is also a monetary method of raising funds or since government currency also is a part of H, increase in such currency with the public and banks should also be included in the H-measure of deficit financing.

3. The rupee securities included in the net R.B.C. to the government cover both the 'old' issues and the current year's issues of dated securities. The latter are obviously the result of the current year's government borrowing from the R.B.I. But the stock of old dateds

with the R.B.I. does not stay unchanged. The R.B.I. buys and sells them under its open market operations. Any change in the net R.B.C. to the government is, therefore, the combined result of deficit financing and open-market operations. For analytical as well as policy purposes, the two must be separated. Hence the need for adjustment (*iii*).

4. The rationale for factor (*iv*) has already been offered in the previous sub-section.

5. Leaving out completely all government borrowing from the R.B.I. through the sale of dated government securities, as is done in all the definitions of 'budgetary deficit', is indefensible. The argument that the R.B.I. buys them as an intermediary or wholesaler with the intention of selling them again to the public and banks, so that their 'temporary' purchase by the R.B.I. can be ignored, is misplaced. For during the time the R.B.I. holds any such securities, it does extend credit to the government and thereby does create H.

6. In the H-measure of deficit financing no adjustment has been made for the net purchase of foreign exchange by the government. This is because purchase of foreign exchange is not treated as a budgetary operation. Whatever use is made of funds raised through new H by the government—whether they are spent domestically or abroad—has nothing to do with the method of financing government expenditure. And deficit financing is purely a question of the method of financing. This neither requires nor suggests that while looking at the H-impact of the total government operations the reduction in H consequent on the government purchase of foreign exchange should be neglected. On the contrary, such H-impact must be considered.

Interestingly, it is fully consistent with the H-approach to deficit financing to allow for any budgetary support from net foreign aid even though the latter yields rupee funds to the government through sale of foreign exchange. For, from the budgetary point of view, any matching government expenditure does not leave any uncovered gap or deficit. The resulting expansion of H is a consequence of the sale of foreign exchange, whatever the state of the budget.

7. If deficit finance were to be defined differently as the net current borrowing from the R.B.I., factors (*ii*) and (*iv*) given above, would not enter its empirical measurement.

8. Under the current (1978) state of data availability the H-measure of deficit finance is not exactly computable, unless we know

the composition of the R.B.I.'s open market operations in terms of current issues and old issues of government securities.

4.5 Reserve Bank Credit to Banks

The R.B.I. provides credit to banks through loans and advances against government securities, usance bills or promissory notes as collateral, and through the purchase or rediscounting of internal bills as well as treasury bills. The R.B.I., however, does not measure its credit to banks in this manner. It classifies the commercial bills purchased and discounted by it as a part of its credit to the commercial sector, and not to banks (see R.B.I., 1977, p. 105). Similarly, it classifies treasury bills discounted by it for banks as its credit to the government, and not to banks.

For reasons already discussed in Section 4.3 this is not a correct practice. In our view the bills (commercial or treasury) rediscounted for banks by the R.B.I. should be counted as a part of the R.B.C. to banks, and not to the commercial sector or the government. In turn, for credit accounting of the sectoral allocation of *bank* credit, the commercial bills rediscounted with the R.B.I. should be counted as a part of ordinary bank (and not R.B.I.) credit to the commercial sector, along with the bills purchased and discounted by banks and still in their hands. Similarly, the treasury bills discounted by the R.B.I. for banks should be counted as a part of ordinary bank (and not R.B.I.) credit to the government, along with other treasury bills purchased by banks and still in their hands.

Such a view suggests a neater classification, too. Once the internal bills rediscounted for banks are treated as a part of the R.B.C. to banks (and not to the commercial sector, as at present), the rest of the R.B.C. to the commercial sector can (and should) be redesignated as 'Reserve Bank Credit to Development Banks', because this is what it is. Like banks, these institutions are also financial intermediaries, and operate as such. For purposes of monetary control, too, it is best to recognize them directly. The borrowing of banks will be discussed in detail in Chapter 8.

4.6 Reserve Bank Credit to Development Banks

A large part of what the R.B.I. calls 'R.B.C. to the Commercial Sector' has been redesignated 'R.B.C. to Development Banks'. For the R.B.I. does not provide credit to the commercial sector directly, but only indirectly through banks and development banks. According to the R.B.I.'s own classification, what it calls 'R.B.C. to the Commercial Sector' comprises the following (see R.B.I., 1977, p. 105):

1. investments in bonds/shares of U.T.I., I.F.C.I., S.F.C.s, etc. and co-operative bank debentures,
2. loans to I.D.B.I., A.R.D.C., and 'others', and
3. internal bills purchased and discounted (under the Bills Rediscounting Scheme).

We have already argued above (Sections 4.3 and 4.5) that the last item mentioned above should be, correctly speaking, interpreted as a part of the 'R.B.C. to banks'. On similar grounds, the first two items put together should be designated the 'R.B.C. to Development Banks'. This as well as the nature and composition of this component of the R.B.C. is discussed fully in Chapter 10.

4.7 Net Foreign Exchange Assets of the R.B.I.

The gross foreign exchange assets of the R.B.I. comprise (1) gold coin and bullion, (2) foreign securities including those held in the Investment Account, and (3) balances held abroad. From this, foreign exchange liabilities represented by the I.M.F. A/C No. 1 less 'the portion of India's I.M.F. quota subscription and some other payments in rupees', are subtracted to arrive at the *net* foreign exchange assets of the R.B.I. Under the old classification, the entire I.M.F. A/C No. 1 was treated as a foreign exchange liability of the R.B.I. Under the new classification, a part of the I.M.F. A/C No. 1, viz. 'the portion of India's I.M.F. quota subscription and some other payments in rupees', is classified as a non-monetary liability of the R.B.I. Only the rest is treated as its foreign exchange liability.

The I.M.F. holds two kinds of accounts with the R.B.I., A/C No. 1 and A/C No. 2. The former is the major account in which 'the portion of India's I.M.F. quota subscription and some other payments in rupees' are credited and through which all the major transactions with the I.M.F. involving 'purchase' of foreign currencies ('sale' of rupees) and 'repurchase' of rupees are routed. Technically, this is a frozen account. For day-to-day use, the I.M.F. maintains another account with the R.B.I., called A/C No. 2. This is a very small current account. Deposits in it are included in the 'other deposits' of the R.B.I., which are a part of H as well as M.

The foreign exchange assets of the R.B.I. *less* its gold holding represent the Reserve Bank credit to the foreign sector. For, whatever the form in which these assets are held, whether cash, fixed deposits or foreign securities, they all are the financial liabilities of the foreign sector. Therefore, the accumulation of foreign exchange reserves (excluding gold) represents the outflow of domestic savings abroad via the R.B.C. to the foreign sector.

The R.B.I. is the custodian of the country's foreign exchange reserves. It also acts as the controller of all foreign-exchange transactions. As such it regularly buys and sells foreign exchange against Indian rupees. All such transactions have a direct impact on H. When the R.B.I. buys foreign exchange, it pays for it in terms of its own money and the supply of H in the economy increases. Conversely, when the R.B.I. sells foreign exchange, it receives payment from the buyer of foreign exchange or its bank in the form of H and the supply of H goes down. Since the buying and selling of foreign exchange by the R.B.I. goes on all the time, what matters for changes in H is the difference between the two. Thus, a deficit in the balance of payments decreases the supply of H, whereas a surplus in it increases the supply of H, other things being the same.

There are, however, institutional arrangements whereby the above relation between foreign exchange accrual/disposal and changes in H are modified. Two such cases will be explained briefly.

In the case of drawals from the I.M.F., foreign currencies are purchased against rupees from the I.M.F. When such drawals are made, the (gross) foreign assets of the R.B.I. increase. But the amount of H in the economy does not change, because the R.B.I. credits the rupee payment to the I.M.F. A/C No. 1—a frozen account. Similarly, when repayments are made to the I.M.F. (i.e. rupees are 'repurchased' from the I.M.F.), the foreign assets of the R.B.I. and the balance in I.M.F. A/C No. 1 go down by an equivalent amount without any change in H.

These, however, are immediate effects. There will be further effects which may change H. For example, in the case of the drawals from the I.M.F., the R.B.I. gains foreign exchange. When it sells this foreign exchange to the public, H will go down. This, however, is a separate transaction—separate from the I.M.F. drawals *per se*. Similarly, if foreign exchange is sold to the government, the effect on H will vary with the method of financing the purchase of foreign exchange by the government. This is discussed below.

If the government pays for its purchase of foreign exchange by borrowing an equal amount of it from the R.B.I. or by drawing down its deposits with the R.B.I., *H* with the public will remain unchanged. The *H*-contractionary effect of the sale of foreign exchange by the R.B.I. is offset exactly by the *H*-expansionary effect of the equal amount of *net* government borrowing from the R.B.I. If, instead, the government finances the purchase of foreign exchange from revenue surpluses or from domestic borrowings, *H* will go down. Even if, initially, the government pays for the foreign exchange from its borrowings from the R.B.I., after a time *H* may go down, when the government repays its borrowings from the sale proceeds of the imports. (In such a case, the government is acting only as an intermediary between the R.B.I. and the public.) Majumdar and Patil (1975) have provided an example of such a case. In 1974–5 the Central Government utilized foreign exchange accruing from the I.M.F. drawals for financing the imports of food, fuel and fertilizers —all three of which were sold eventually to the public. Thus, in the final analysis, the I.M.F. drawals led to a reduction in *H*.

A few implications of this discussion will be noted.

1. It is not the total budget deficit of the government (or the total net government borrowing from the R.B.I.) that impinges on *H*, but this deficit *minus* the government purchase of foreign exchange from the R.B.I., if the further effects of the use of foreign exchange are ignored. Government borrowings from the R.B.I. for financing its foreign exchange purchases do not increase *H*.

2. External assistance to the government provides budgetary support to it. For the foreign exchange gained, when sold to the R.B.I., is converted into rupee resources. The I.M.F. drawals *per se* do not provide any budgetary support in this sense. However, when mediated through the borrowings from the R.B.I. and when these borrowings are adjusted for the foreign exchange purchased (see point 1), the I.M.F. drawals also can be treated as additions to budgetary resources.

3. Drawing down the accumulated foreign exchange resources to meet the balance-of-trade deficit has two mutually-reinforcing anti-inflationary effects, provided the purchase of foreign exchange is not financed by net borrowings from the R.B.I. This is clear enough for the trade deficit on private account. On the one hand, such a deficit reduces the supply of money (by reducing *H*) and thus reduces the excess demand pressures in the market for goods and services; on the other hand, the import surplus increases the supply of goods in the market. When the government is involved, it may finance its

entire purchase of foreign exchange by additional borrowings from the R.B.I. Then the *H*-effect will be absent. Only the supply-of-goods effect will operate in the market. Only when the sale proceeds of goods are used to reduce the borrowings from the R.B.I. will the *H*-effect come into operation.

Since about the middle of 1975 foreign exchange reserves (excluding gold and S.D.R.s) have grown at a rapid rate. At the end of March 1975, they amounted to Rs 611 crores. By March 1976 they had grown to Rs 1,492 crores—a net addition of Rs 881 crores. After one more year, at the end of March 1977, they stood at Rs 2,863 crores, giving an average monthly accretion of Rs 114 crores over the year. Over the year 1977–8, they increased further to Rs 4,500 crores at the end of March 1978.

Such a rapid accumulation of resources has been due to several factors, the most important of them being large inflows of private remittances from abroad, larger net inflows of external assistance, and improvement in the balance of trade. Private remittances have been flowing in at an average monthly rate of about Rs 100 crores. Net external aid for 1975–6 and 1976–7 was Rs 949 crores and Rs 667 crores, respectively, when it was only Rs 419 crores for 1974–5. The balance of trade was estimated to show a surplus of Rs 72 crores for 1976–7, when it showed a deficit of Rs 1,190 crores for 1974–5 and of Rs 1,216 crores for 1975–6.

This reserve accumulation has been an important source of increase in *H*, especially over 1976–7 and 1977–8.

4.8 Net Non-Monetary Liabilities of the R.B.I.

The net non-monetary liabilities of the R.B.I. are a sizeable item. They have grown very fast in recent years. On the last Friday of March 1977 they were provisionally valued at Rs 2,833 crores. A large part of them are the owned funds of the R.B.I. held in various forms as reserves and contributions to the National Funds (see below). Compulsory deposits of the public are another big component.

More specifically, the net non-monetary liabilities are the excess of the non-monetary liabilities over 'other assets'. Till about the middle of 1973 the latter used to comprise mainly premises, furniture, fittings, etc. Since then a rapidly growing and big item in the form of 'advances to certain scheduled commercial banks under special arrangements in respect of their investments abroad' has started appearing among 'other assets'. Further information about the nature of these advances and their special treatment is not available. Non-monetary liabilities of the R.B.I. comprise the following:

1. paid-up capital (Rs 5 crores) and reserves (Rs 150 crores),
2. contributions to the three national funds, namely, National Agricultural Credit (Long-Term Operations) Fund, National Agricultural Credit (Stabilization) Fund, and National Industrial Credit (Long-Term Operations) Fund—these contributions had accumulated to a total of Rs 1,375 crores by the end of March 1977; they are made out of the annual income of the R.B.I. (see Chapter 10),
3. Reserve Bank Employees' Pension Fund, Provident Fund, and Co-operative Guarantee Fund,
4. an offset of Rs 43 crores to assets held against Indian currency returned by Pakistan awaiting adjustment,
5. balances under the Compulsory Deposit Scheme,
6. portion of India's I.M.F. quota subscription and some other payments in rupees included in I.M.F. A/C No. 1,
7. bills payable, and
8. other liabilities.

For the reason given below, the R.B.I. calls such liabilities 'non-identifiable'. Apart from them, there are two more components of non-monetary liabilities, namely, government deposits with the R.B.I. and a portion of the I.M.F. Account No. 1. They are not included in this list, as they are 'identifiable'; the former are R.B.I.'s non-monetary liabilities to the government sector and the latter to the foreign sector. Therefore they are treated differently. Each is transferred to the account of the sector of which it is identified as an asset. This helps in arriving at the *net* R.B.C. to these sectors. Thus government deposits are subtracted from the R.B.C. to the government to arrive at its *net* credit (to the government), and the I.M.F. Account No. 1 less 'the portion of India's I.M.F. quota subscription and some other payments in rupees' is subtracted from the foreign exchange assets of the R.B.I. to arrive at its *net* foreign exchange assets.[6]

---

[6] Similarly, item 3 of the non-monetary liabilities listed above, namely, the sum of Reserve Bank Employees' Pension Fund, Provident Fund and Co-operative Guarantee Fund, is R.B.I.'s identifiable non-monetary liability to the commercial sector. Therefore, it should have been netted from the R.B.C. to the commercial sector in the R.B.I.'s accounting analysis. The same is true of item 5—compulsory

The role of the net non-monetary liabilities of the R.B.I. as a source of change in H is among the least understood. We shall therefore now attempt to make it better understood.

We have seen above how the R.B.I.'s transactions with the various sectors result in its acquisition of (net) financial assets as well as the creation of H. But the important point to note is that not all the acquisition of (net) financial assets is by the creation of H, but that a part of this acquisition is also supported by its net non-monetary liabilities, like its owned funds, compulsory deposits of the public, etc. The larger these non-monetary sources of credit for the R.B.I., the less it has to depend upon the creation of new H to finance its credit. Accordingly, an increase in net non-monetary liabilities of the R.B.I. reduces H, whereas an increase in any other source of change in H increases H by a like amount.

It would, therefore, be incorrect to say that changes in the R.B.M. occur only with changes in the net R.B.C. and changes in the net foreign exchange assets of the R.B.I. The changes in its net non-monetary liabilities must also be brought into the picture. At the aggregrate level, this can be very easily understood with the help of equation (4.1).

A practical problem arises when it comes to measuring the net R.B.M. effects of the transactions of the various sectors with the R.B.I. We have seen above that, with minor exceptions, we can measure the changes in the R.B.I.'s net financial assets arising from its transactions with each individual sector. But a similar sector-wise breakdown of the net non-monetary liabilities or of the matching assets is not feasible. This is what creates the problem of non-identifiability of the net non-monetary liabilities.[7]

But without a sector-wise breakdown of variations in the net non-monetary liabilities, we cannot measure exactly the net H-effect of an individual sector's transactions with the R.B.I. only on the basis of the variation in that sector's (net) indebtedness to the R.B.I. For

deposits of the public. It is not clear why the R.B.I. has not taken such a step. For us, it does not matter, because we do not have a separate category of 'the R.B.C. to the commercial sector'.

[7] Basically, the problem arises because a large part of the net non-monetary liabilities constitutes the net worth of the R.B.I. And net worth is what the R.B.I. owes to itself, not to others. On the asset side, too, we cannot say what particular assets have been purchased with owned funds and what with 'created' funds. For funds from all sources make one common pool.

even in the case of an individual sector, equation (4.1) holds, and its contribution to a change in the R.B.M. is equal to the change in this sector's net indebtedness to the R.B.I. *minus* the change in the net non-monetary liability (or the matching asset) of the R.B.I. attributable to this sector.

One simple way out of the difficulty would be to assume that the R.B.I.'s assets matching in value its net non-monetary liabilities are distributed sector-wise in the same proportion in which the net financial assets of the R.B.I. are distributed. This will mean *assuming* that the R.B.M.-effects of the transactions of the various sectors are distributed in the same proportion in which the net R.B.C. to these sectors is distributed. This assumption is much better than the current R.B.I. practice of characterizing the net non-monetary liabilities as 'unidentifiable' and leaving them undistributed sector-wise. On our assumption, the absolute contribution of each sectoral source to the observed changes in the R.B.M. can be measured reasonably well. This has been done in the next section for the period 1970-1 to 1976-7.

One caveat may be entered here. As an alternative to the rough rule of thumb for allocating the N.N.M.L. sector-wise proposed above, it may be suggested that at least for the sums accumulated in the three National Funds—and these sums constitute a large part of the total N.N.M.L.—the actual sectoral disbursement of funds made from these Funds may themselves be used for the sector-wise allocation of this component of the N.N.M.L. for the R.B.M. analysis. That is, we know that these Funds are used to make loans and advances to development banks (see Chapter 10), state co-operative banks, and state governments. Then the actual disbursements made from these Funds can be netted out both from the R.B.C. to these sectors (and the R.B.I.'s N.N.M.L.) to arrive at each sector's contribution to the R.B.M. This will further reduce the non-identifiable part of the N.N.M.L. Under this dispensation, the 'R.B.C. to Development Banks' will not contribute anything to the R.B.M., as all such R.B.C. is made from the National Funds (see Chapter 10).

The above alternative must be rejected. For it assumes an unwarranted equation between the accounting source of credit and the true source of credit in the economic sense. In the ultimate analysis, *all* R.B.C. is financed partly from the monetary and partly from the net non-monetary liabilities of the R.B.I. And all the sectors compete among themselves for the R.B.C., that is, for the R.B.I.'s monetary

and net non-monetary liabilities. Therefore, simply because, under the prevailing institutional arrangements, the 'R.B.C. to Development Banks' comes from the National Funds in the accounting sense, it does not follow that the Development Banks have a unique right to it in the same sense in which (say) the government has a right to its deposits with the R.B.I. Alternatively speaking, if no loans were made to the Development Banks, the funds so released, other things being the same, would become available to other borrowers of the R.B.I. Hence our rejection of the alternative suggestion. The N.N.M.L. of the R.B.I. must be apportioned among all its 'debtors' in some economically rational way, e.g. the one we have suggested above.

4.9 Relative Importance of Different Sources of Change in H

The contribution of each source to the generation of H outstanding and to the observed annual changes in H has varied from year to year. The relevant data for the years 1970–1 to 1976–7 are given in Table 4.1. They relate to the unadjusted sources of H-generation. From them, source-wise annual changes in H can be easily derived. The data are annual averages of 'last Friday of the month' figures. Our classification of the sources differs from that of the R.B.I. in two respects: (1) the redesignation of a part of what the R.B.I. calls 'R.B.C. to the commercial sector' as 'R.B.C. to Development Banks', and (2) the inclusion of 'commercial bills discounted with the R.B.I.' in 'the R.B.C. to banks'.

As argued earlier, the N.N.M.L. of the R.B.I. (Column 6, Table 4.1) deserve to be allocated among the first four sources of H-generation along the lines suggested already. We have attempted such an allocation. For any year, the relative share of R.B.C. to a particular sector in the total R.B.C. was calculated. Multiplying the N.N.M.L. of that year by the proportion so calculated yielded that sector's absolute share of the N.N.M.L. of the R.B.I. for the year. The excess of R.B.C. to that sector over the latter, then, tells us how much of R.B.M. creation can be attributed to the R.B.C. to that sector for that year. The resultant picture for the years 1970–1 to 1976–7 is presented in Table 4.2.

A summary of the figures in Table 4.2, in ratio form, is presented in Table 4.3.

The following points revealed by Table 4.3 are worth noting:
1. the relative dominance of the 'R.B.M. due to Government' as

TABLE 4.1

UNADJUSTED SOURCES OF *H*-GENERATION

(*Rs. crores*)

Year	R.B.C. to government	R.B.C. to banks	R.B.C. to development banks	R.B.C. to foreign sector	Government currency	N.N.M.L. (R.B.I.)	H $[(1)+(2)+(3) +(4)+(5)-(6)]$
	(1)	(2)	(3)	(4)	(5)	(6)	(7)
1970-1	3,569	541	100	619	372	624	4,577
1971-2	4,333	441	157	586	398	863	5,052
1972-3	5,077	318	206	561	428	1,057	5,532
1973-4	6,160	511	269	588	485	1,237	6,777
1974-5	6,612	748	400	504	520	1,540	7,244
1975-6	7,228	897	526	481	549	2,194	7,487
1976-7	6,848	1,387	653	1,708	557	2,563	8,589

Source: R.B.I., *Bulletin,* January 1977, pp. 128-34 (for 1970-1 to 1975-6); R.B.I., *Report on Currency and Finance,* 1976-7, Vol. II, Statement 27 (for 1976-7).

Note: The figures are rounded off. Therefore they are subject to slight approximation errors.

TABLE 4.2

ADJUSTED SOURCES OF *H*-GENERATION

(Rs. crores)

Year	R.B.M. due to government	R.B.M. due to banks	R.B.M. due to development banks	R.B.M. due to foreign sector	Total R.B.M. [(1) + (2) + (3) + (4)]	Government currency	H [(5) + (6)]
	(1)	(2)	(3)	(4)	(5)	(6)	(7)
1970–1	3,108	471	87	539	4,205	372	4,577
1971–2	3,655	372	132	495	4,653	398	5,052
1972–3	4,205	263	171	464	5,104	428	5,532
1973–4	5,149	427	224	492	6,291	485	6,776
1974–5	5,380	608	326	410	6,724	520	7,244
1975–6	5,493	682	399	365	6,938	549	7,487
1976–7	5,192	1,051	494	1,295	8,032	557	8,589

Note: The figures are subject to slight approximation errors due to being rounded off.

a source of H-generation and as a source of change in H;

2. a big change in the structural composition of the sources of change in H as well as in their relative contributions to the observed change in H for 1976–7 from the average pattern for the previous five years.

These points have been taken note of earlier, too, in our discussion in the present chapter.

TABLE 4.3

STRUCTURAL COMPOSITION OF THE ADJUSTED SOURCES OF
H-GENERATION (PERCENTAGE)

Adjusted Sources of H-Generation	5-year (1971–2 to 1975–6) average		1976–7	
	Average share in H outstanding	Average share in ΔH	Share in H outstanding	Share in ΔH
(1)	(2)	(3)	(4)	(5)
1. R.B.M. due to government	74.40	80.33	60.45	− 27.30
2. R.B.M. due to banks	7.18	7.75	12.24	33.54
3. R.B.M. due to development banks	3.76	14.70	5.75	8.63
4. R.B.M. due to foreign sector (foreign exchange reserves)	7.20	− 9.93	15.08	84.40
5. Government currency	7.46	7.15	6.48	0.72
Total	100.00	100.00	100.00	100.00

Source: Table 4.2.

4.10 Is H an Autonomous Variable?

The money-supply analysis of the previous chapter had assumed that H is an autonomous, policy-determined, variable. That is, that the authorities (the government and the R.B.I.) determine what the

amount of H outstanding at any time would be.[8] We want to examine in this section how far and in what sense this is a reasonable assumption to make. The discussion will throw additional light on the nature of the sources of change in H.

Briefly, we may say that in the strict form stated above, the assumption is not correct. For it is not only the decisions of the authorities which lead to the generation or destruction of H, it is also the decisions of the public and banks which contribute to it. For example, if the banks so desire, they can change H within narrow limits by varying their borrowings from the R.B.I. Similarly, the development banks themselves can affect H by varying their borrowings from the R.B.I. Yet, despite this and for reasons given below, it would be correct to say that the *net* variations in the stock of H are definitely within the close control of the authorities. This is all the more so for 'adjusted H' (H^*)—the variable in place of unadjusted total H that matters for M. H^* can be controlled further than H by impounding or releasing reserves of banks through appropriate variations in the statutory reserve ratio of banks (see Appendix E). If the authorities so desire, and barring exceptional circumstances, they can make the *average* value of H^* outstanding over any period that they like within a sufficiently narrow margin, so that, for all practical purposes, it would be true to say that H^* is very much a 'policy-controlled' variable, though not a direct policy or control instrument. It is only in this qualified sense that the usual assumption of the money-supply analysis that H^* may be treated as autonomously given to the system may be justified. How the target H^* can be attained is the key problem of monetary control and a major concern throughout the rest of the book.

From policy (control) point of view, all *changes in H* (not H^*) can be classified under two broad heads: (1) autonomous or discretionary changes, and (2) endogenous or non-discretionary changes. Symbolically, we represent the former by ΔH_1 and the latter by ΔH_2,[9] so that

$$\Delta H_1 + \Delta H_2 \equiv \Delta H. \tag{4.3}$$

[8] All authorities, by definition, are assumed to be outside the public. Hence, all variables determined by the authorities, whether it is government expenditure, tax rates, or H, become autonomous, or a given datum to the public. That is why we have clubbed together the government and the R.B.I. (Also see Section 5.1.)

[9] Correspondingly, we define H_1 and H_2 as the autonomous and endogenous components of H, respectively.

Autonomous changes in H are determined directly by the policy-making authorities—the government and the R.B.I. They are fully the autonomous decision-variable of the authorities. On the other hand, the endogenous changes in H are decided by the public, banks, and development banks, given the terms and conditions under which the R.B.I. is willing to produce such changes. That is, the R.B.I. determines only the terms and conditions on which it is willing to produce ΔH_2, and not the actual amount of it. The public and banks determine the latter.

Endogenous changes in H arise as a result of the performance of certain central-banking functions by the R.B.I. towards the public and banks; for example, its function as the controller of the country's foreign exchange for the public, or its function as the banker to banks, including development banks. Looked at from the other side, endogenous changes in H arise through the borrowing by banks and development banks from the R.B.I. and the foreign exchange activities of the public. To sum up, in the case of autonomous changes in H, the initiative lies with the government and the R.B.I.; in the case of endogenous changes, the initiative lies with the non-policy-making transactors—the public and the banks—subject, of course, to certain restrictions. Therefore, it is only the autonomous change in H (i.e. ΔH_1), and not the whole of ΔH, that can be called a policy variable.

For monetary-policy discussion a given ΔH (not to speak of ΔH^*) should never be made its starting point. The presence of ΔH_2 must be explicitly recognized and its behaviour analysed. The authorities can more or less control it, but not fix its value. Also ΔH_1 is not one homogeneous whole. The values of some of its components may be decided largely by extra-monetary considerations. This may require offsetting operations by the R.B.I. Then, a large part of the use of monetary-control measures is concerned with making ΔH^* conform to the desired ΔH^* of the authorities. If *all* ΔH is determined directly by the authorities, there will be very little left for the monetary-control measures to control. Then ΔH would become purely a matter of autonomous policy specification, which is not true.

Earlier in this chapter, the different sources of change in H were identified. The changes from all these sources will now be classified under two heads: autonomous and endogenous. This will require bisecting changes in H from various sources along autonomous/

endogenous lines. For this purpose, we need look at only the R.B.M. along with the government currency.

The autonomous changes in H, according to our definition,[10] will comprise

1. changes in the R.B.M. due to government, gross of (3) below and including changes arising from the open-market operations of the R.B.I.,
2. changes in the discretionary component of the R.B.M. due to banks and development banks, and
3. net purchases or sales of foreign exchange by the government.

The endogenous changes are the remaining changes in H, namely,

1. changes in government currency held by the public (see Section 4.2),
2. changes in the non-discretionary component of the R.B.M. due to banks and development banks, and
3. net purchases or sales of foreign exchange by the public.

Whereas data are available for component 1 under both kinds of change, and they can be estimated with some effort for component 3,[11] they can be only arbitrarily arrived at for component 2. Therefore, the reader's attention will be drawn only to Table 4.3, and a further quantification will not be attempted. It is apparent from these figures that over the period 1971–2 to 1975–6, on average, ΔH_1 heavily dominated ΔH_2. Broadly speaking, this was also the situation for the earlier period since the early fifties (see Swamy, 1975, Chapter 2). The year 1976–7 has been markedly different from others in that during this year ΔH_2 (mainly due to net foreign exchange purchases by the R.B.I. and also due to the R.B.M. created for banks—discretionary and non-discretionary combined) has dominated the scene. But, for the period up to 1975–6, it can be said that ΔH was largely a policy-controlled variable.

4.11 The Problem of H-Management during 1976–7

Since about the end of March 1976 the problem of managing ΔH_2 has (apparently) become more difficult than before. The chief

---

[10] For a narrow definition of an autonomous change in H, see Swamy (1975, Chapter 2). She defines it as only the change determined by the R.B.I. This would leave out the government-determined change in H.

[11] For a detailed discussion for the period 1952–3 to 1970–1, see Swamy (1975, Chapter 2).

reason is said to be a large inflow of foreign exchange into the country, which the R.B.I. has necessarily to buy and pay for by creating new H. The R.B.I. has no control over the factors governing this inflow of foreign exchange. Nor does anyone want to stop the inflow. The government, of course, must take adequate measures for the effective utilization of foreign exchange reserves and not accept their excessive accumulation. But, while the net addition to these reserves continues to be substantial, what can the R.B.I. do to control the monetary consequences of this accumulation? More specifically, what could the R.B.I. have done and what did it actually do during the year 1976–7 in this respect? Was the R.B.I. as helpless to control the resulting monetary situation as it is sometimes made out to be? Did the monetary policy followed by the R.B.I. over the year worsen or improve the money-supply position?

The relevant facts are summed up in Table 4.4. They give a source-wise break-down of the actual change in average H for 1976–7 over that for 1975–6.

The figures in Table 4.4 reveal a very interesting story. The increase in average R.B.C. to the foreign sector (through the accumulation of foreign exchange assets with the R.B.I.) was, undoubtedly, very large. But there were attenuating developments, too. The average R.B.C. to the government and state co-operative banks fell by a total of Rs 450 crores. Add to this the substantial increase of Rs 370 crores in the average N.N.M.L. of the R.B.I. Put together, these sources provided the R.B.I. with Rs 820 crores of disposable credit, not requiring fresh creation of H. Thus, the situation was manageable. It worsened, in large measure, due to the excessive R.B.C. to banks—very much within the direct control of the R.B.I. In the context of excess expansion of H (and of bank reserves) from other sources, the situation required curtailment of the R.B.C. to commercial banks, and not substantial increases of it, as the R.B.I. actually did.

The R.B.I. has tried to justify its overly liberal credit to banks on the ground that such support was necessary to enable banks to finance public food procurement. The R.B.I. followed a rule according to which the whole or a part of the total bank credit for public food procurement above a certain level could be refinanced by the R.B.I. The minimum level of such credit not eligible for refinance was revised upward from time to time as well as the portion of excess eligible for refinance (see Section 8.8).

TABLE 4.4

SOURCE-WISE CHANGE IN AVERAGE *H*
(1976–7 over 1975–6)

(Rs crores)

Sources of Change in *H*	Amount of Change
(1)	(2)
1. R.B.C. to government	− 380
2. R.B.C. to banks	490
(a) Scheduled commercial banks	560
(b) State co-operative banks	− 70
3. R.B.C. to development banks	127
4. R.B.C. to foreign sector	1,227
5. Government currency	8
6. N.N.M.L. of the R.B.I.	370
Addenda	
7. Total change in *H*	1,102
[(1) + (2) + (3) + (4) + (5) − (6)]	
8. Neutral change in *H*	295
(at 4 per cent of average *H** of Rs 7,369	
crores for 1975–6)	
9. Excess change in *H* [(7) − (8)]	807

Source: Table 4.1. The figure for R.B.C. to state co-operative banks has been
computed from the monthly data given in the R.B.I. *Report on Currency and
Finance, 1975–6* (Statement 38) and *1976–7* (Statement 41).

Was this justifiable in the overall context of monetary stability?
The banks had sufficient extra lendable resources. If the public food
procurement was a priority activity for the authorities, it should have
been so for the nationalized banking system too. The priority system
should imply only a reallocation of the total bank credit, not the
increase in its nominal size beyond its safe limit. If the limit is not
honoured in nominal terms, but exceeded, the resulting inflation
merely reallocates real credit among various bank borrowers, including the government, without succeeding in expanding real credit.
Therefore, unless the R.B.I. was interested in the resultant reallocation of real credit through inflation, nothing is gained and much is
lost through credit inflation (see Gupta, 1978a). A responsible monetary authority should eschew the path of credit inflation.

The R.B.I. did try half-heartedly to bring the situation somewhat

under control. It tried to impound some reserves of banks through variations in the average/marginal statutory reserve ratio of banks. This ratio was raised from 4 to 5 per cent with effect from 4 September 1976, and then to 6 per cent with effect from 13 November 1976. In addition, banks were asked to deposit with the R.B.I. 10 per cent of their incremental demand and time liabilities accruing since 14 January 1977. The banks did not observe fully the enhanced reserve requirements and got away with paltry penalties. The measures were successful in the actual average impounding of only Rs 97 crores of bank reserves for the year, over the required reserves given by the 4 per cent statutory reserve ratio that prevailed during 1975–6. Thus, the additional amount of R.B.C. to commercial banks of Rs 560 crores was about six times the additional amount of reserves impounded.

If the R.B.I. was truly serious about monetary stability and conscious of its inability to expand real credit by sheer manipulation of nominal credit, it should have enforced strictly the statutory reserve requirements on defaulting banks, resorted to larger impounding of reserves, preferably by hiking up further the incremental reserve ratio, exercised tighter control over its credit to banks, and made it truly scarce. All these measures are and were within the ambit of the R.B.I.'s authority.

CHAPTER 5

PLANNING CONTROL OF MONEY SUPPLY

5.1 Introduction

How can variations in money supply be controlled? What control strategy should the authorities adopt? What determinants of money supply should they try to manipulate and why? The answers must rest on an empirically meaningful and reliable theory of money supply. The effort in the previous two chapters has been to provide such a theory and detailed analysis of H—the key determinant of money supply. Once it is realized that the money multiplier (m) connecting H^* (i.e. adjusted H) with M is largely an endogenous and not a policy variable and that the proximate determinants of m are not easily and quickly manipulable by policy measures (see Appendix C), the most practicable course for monetary control left with the authorities is to control H^*.

This provides the chief basis for the approach to monetary control measures discussed in this book. The strategy, very simply stated, is: 'control H to control M'. It was with this end in view that the whole of the previous chapter was devoted to the understanding of the sources, the mechanism, and the nature of changes in H. This sets the stage for the design and execution of various monetary-control measures.

Next, we define monetary-control measures as all those measures which the authorities can take to bring about changes in M and the term 'authorities' broadly to include both the R.B.I. and the government. The usual practice is to call the former the monetary authority and the latter the fiscal authority and to treat, for purposes of monetary control, the activities of the government on the same footing as those of banks and the public, the monetary consequences of all of which the Central Bank as the sole monetary authority is supposed to bring under control. But on account of the special institutional relations between the R.B.I. and the Central Government under

which the latter can borrow any amount from the R.B.I., the monetary authority of the R.B.I. is severely limited, and the government comes to exercise enormous monetary powers. On other counts, too, for all practical purposes, the R.B.I. is like a department of the government. Therefore, it is of the utmost importance for sensible monetary analysis as well as planning to recognize this fact explicitly and to make the government jointly responsible with the R.B.I. in the task of monetary planning and control with government as the senior partner. This marks an important departure from the traditional approach to monetary planning. We are strongly of the view that without the government's full and active co-operation no plan of monetary control for monetary stability can ever be successful. By itself the R.B.I., with the control powers at its disposal, can hope to control the course of M only within relatively narrow limits, given the volume of deficit financing by the government year after year. Therefore, a chief prerequisite for successful monetary control is the control of deficit financing by the government. The precise implications of neutral-money policy for the government's deficit financing will be worked out later in the chapter.

5.2 Neutral Trend-Variations in H

In Chapter 2 we had argued that monetary policy in India should be so conducted as to generate neutral trend-variations in money supply. But variations in M are *largely* a function of the variations in H (see Chapter 3 and Appendix E). Therefore, it follows that the variations in H should be so controlled as to produce neutral trend-variations in M. We call such variations in H neutral trend-variations. How to determine the quantum of neutral trend-variations in H per year? This is the problem of ΔH-*budgeting*.

To solve this problem, we make use of the money-supply equation (3.5) to give us

$$\Delta M = b \cdot \Delta H \qquad (5.1)$$

where b is the marginal money-multiplier.[1] We have chosen to operate with equation (3.5), because the empirical evidence on money supply in India analysed in Appendix F.1 favours it over equation (3.4). As a first approximation dictated by the need for simplification,

---

[1] For qualitative analysis, we shall revert to the use of the average money multiplier m.

we have ignored the impact of rates of interest on money supply. In a fuller model this impact should be duly incorporated.

Using equation (5.1), we can solve for ΔH for a particular year in terms of the target value of ΔM for that year given by the application of the flexible trend rule of Section 2.7. This gives

$$(\Delta \hat{H})_t = \frac{1}{b} \cdot (\Delta \hat{M})_t \tag{5.2}$$

where the hat ($\wedge$) over H and M indicates that they are target values of these variables. It is this value of ΔH which the authorities should try to ensure for the tth year. Since the supply of H is affected by numerous factors, a lot of H-management through offsetting actions from day to day will be required by the R.B.I. to keep the course of H along its charted trend path.

The trend rule policy for H-management, however, would have to be followed with a degree of flexibility. This flexibility will be required on the two counts discussed below.

Busy Season / Slack Season

The Indian money market is said to be marked by two well-defined seasons, called the busy season (November–April) and the slack season (May–October), as the demand for short-term funds goes up or down, respectively. The seasons themselves are associated with the movement of crops, the busy season coinciding with the marketing of kharif (winter) crops and the slack season with that of rabi (summer) crops. Therefore, the R.B.I. has been following a pro-seasonal monetary policy, making more funds available to banks during the busy season and withdrawing surplus funds during the slack season. The rationale for such a pro-seasonal policy rests on the structural features of the Indian economy, viz. the dominance of agriculture in the economy, its seasonal character, governed largely by natural factors, and the growth of agro-based seasonal industries. If the R.B.I. adopts a season-neutral monetary policy, much avoidable harm will be done to the Indian economy. However, the R.B.I. must study carefully the changing seasonal character of the Indian economy as well as the money market and make suitable adaptations in its seasonal policy. For example, it must take full cognizance of the fact that with the growing increase in double-cropped area and increased cultivation of rice (the major kharif crop) as a rabi crop, especially in the Punjab and Haryana, growing industrialization,

7

and a marked shift in the distribution of bank credit from trade to industry, the traditional money market seasonality has become much less pronounced. The Bank must also make sure that there is not an excessive expansion of bank credit during the busy season. Also, it must ensure that its pro-seasonal credit policy does not encourage artificially purely-seasonal activities. It has been observed in recent years that the traditional slack-season contraction of credit is fast disappearing. Does it indicate a change in the seasonal character of the Indian economy or the working of excess-demand pressures encouraged by an inflationary psychology? The question deserves careful study. If the slack-season contraction of credit does not counterbalance the busy-season extra expansion of credit, this will result in excessive expansion of money supply over the year and generate inflationary pressures in the economy. This must be avoided. Over the year the trend rule must be adhered to.

In September 1976, the R.B.I. had announced that it was giving up its traditional basis of credit policy linked with busy-season slack-season distinction in favour of annual perspective credit planning with quarterly reviews. Its annual *Report on Currency and Finance* (1976–7) published a year after had, however, carried the traditional slack-season busy-season format of credit policy review. And nothing further has been heard about the perspective credit planning.

Seasonal and Other Changes in m

The immediate target variable of monetary policy is M. We use changes in H^* as an instrumental variable to produce desired changes in M. This is done on the basis of a presumed or expected behaviour of m. But m may not behave in the expected manner. It may fluctuate around its expected trend value over (say) the year. What should be done? If the changes in m are very small, irregular, and brief, they can be ignored. If they are not, they would call for compensatory adjustments in the trend variations in H.

We have already recognized the need for pro-seasonal bias in changes in M and so in H^*. This bias for changes in H^* gets heightened when we note the seasonal behaviour of m. Swamy (1975, Chapter 6) has found that m behaves contra-seasonally, contracting during the busy season and increasing during the slack. The major explanation for this kind of behaviour, according to her, is the pro-seasonal behaviour of the currency–deposit ratio (c). c goes up during the busy season as the public moves out of bank deposits into cur-

rency, and it moves down during the slack season when the reverse flow of currency takes place into banks. Other things being the same, a rise in c leads to a fall in m, and if H^* is allowed to grow along its trend path, this will mean a fall in the rate of growth of M below its trend rate. This will cause seasonal monetary stringency and hamper the flow of economic activity, both clearly unintended as well as undesired. Therefore, the R.B.I. would be right in making pro-seasonal changes in H^*, not only to compensate for contra-seasonal changes in m, but also to provide for the desired pro-seasonal change in M.

Non-seasonal changes in m can also arise from time to time and from varied sources. One advantage of the 'm-theory' is the assurance that all these influences on m will operate through its proximate determinants (see Appendix D). The behaviour of these determinants can be observed easily and quickly. The factors causing changes in them need to be identified, the nature of these factors understood, and the necessary corrective changes made in the course of H^* in the light of the m-theory.

5.3 Deficit Financing and Neutral Increases in H

What is the implication of the previous section for the deficit financing of the government? In Section 4.4.2, we have already studied the relation between deficit financing and increases in the net R.B.C. to the government. Several adjustments are required to move from one to the other. To recall, the H-measure of deficit finance is given by

      1. increase in the R.B.M. due to the government,

plus 2. increase in government currency with the public and banks,

plus 3. net sale (or minus net purchase) of 'old' (i.e. previous years') issues of rupee securities by the R.B.I. to the public, so as to allow for the open market operations of the R.B.I. in such securities.

Since no information is available on component 3, we are constrained to leave it out of our measure of deficit finance. Let us call the sum of components 1 and 2 a 'crude' measure of deficit finance. This crude measure will be an underestimate (overestimate) of the true measure of deficit finance by the amount of the net open market sale (purchase) of 'old' government securities by the R.B.I.

Most of the time, deficit finance crudely measured has been a major source of change in H (see Table 4.3) and so it must also share a major part of the responsibility for excess increases in H. Deficit financing is a decision variable of the government and the R.B.I. has 'practically' no control over it.[2] Therefore, the government alone is capable of keeping it under check by exercising the necessary self-discipline. What our analysis of neutral increase in H does, is tell what should be the desirable increase in H from all the sources of change in H during any particular year. From this we must now derive the 'neutral' amount of deficit financing.

Such a derivation in the form of a rigid formula is neither feasible nor desirable, though a rough rule-of-thumb can always be devised. Therefore, we only spell out here the considerations which should be involved in the determination of deficit financing *from the side of H-generation*. For this, our discussion of the sources of change in H in the previous chapter provides all the necessary basic information. The simple point is that deficit financing is only one of the sources of change in H. Therefore, for the changes in H from all sources to add to a stipulated ΔH for a particular year, one of the sources, be it deficit financing or some other source, must act as the balancing or as the residual item.

Suppose we choose deficit financing as the balancing item. Then, how will the neutral amount of deficit financing be arrived at?

Let us start with the following identity:

$$\Delta H \equiv D + \Delta B + \Delta DB + \Delta F \qquad (5.5)$$

where
$$D = \text{Deficit finance (crudely measured),}$$
$$B = \text{R.B.M. due to banks,}$$
$$DB = \text{R.B.M. due to development banks, and}$$
$$F = \text{R.B.M. due to foreign sector (or due to foreign exchange assets of the R.B.I.).}$$

Any of the terms in identity (5.5) may be positive or negative. Positive ΔF will mean net purchase of foreign exchange by the R.B.I. Negative ΔF will mean net sale of foreign exchange by the R.B.I. and correspondingly net purchase of foreign exchange by the government and/or the public. Let us use the symbol $\wedge$ over a

---

[2] We use the word 'practically' to allow for some formal check the R.B.I. has on deficit financing of state governments.

variable to denote its desired or target value. Then, identity (5.5) can be rewritten as:

$$\hat{D} \equiv \Delta\hat{H} + (-\Delta F) - (\Delta B + \Delta DB). \qquad (5.6)$$

What this identity tells is elementary, but important: that, given $\Delta\hat{H}$,

1. the greater the net sale of foreign exchange by the R.B.I. from its foreign exchange reserves, whether to the government or the public, the larger the value $\hat{D}$ can take; and
2. the larger the R.B.M. due to banks or development banks, the smaller the value of $\hat{D}$. Thus, the former is seen to compete with the latter.

This suggests that in planning neutral deficit financing, having determined $\Delta\hat{H}$, the authorities must further determine:

(a) the portion of $\Delta\hat{H}$ they would like to lend to banks ($\Delta\hat{B}$) and development banks ($\Delta\hat{DB}$),
(b) the extent of drawal of the net foreign exchange reserves of the R.B.I. ($-\Delta\hat{F}$),

such that

$$\hat{D} + \Delta\hat{B} + \Delta\hat{DB} + (-\Delta\hat{F}) \equiv \Delta\hat{H}. \qquad (5.7)$$

At this stage of planning neutral deficit financing and neutral change in H, we are free to fix the open market operations of the R.B.I. at zero level, so that they can be utilized to correct any deviation of actual ΔH from $\Delta\hat{H}$, which are sure to arise in actual life.

Identity (5.7) may be called 'neutral ΔH-budget identity'.

Planning for neutral money would require that the 'ΔH budget' be prepared by the authorities well before the commencement of a new financial year. The job should be entrusted to the R.B.I. which should submit its proposals to the Central Government for final approval and acceptance. Once the estimate for $\hat{D}$ has been accepted, the Central Government and the state governments should decide among themselves how the total allowable cake of deficit financing is to be divided among the various claimants. It is no use carrying on with the fiction that the Central Government alone has the right to benefit from it, because the state governments do draw upon it in various ways, which both involves horizontal inequity as among

states and goes against the tenets of any rational policy-making or planning. Further, there is no weighty reason for denying the state governments a share in the real resources the authorities capture from the public by issuing paper money. Like income tax or shared excises, deficit financing can also be treated as a common source of 'revenue' to the governments and should be shared among them in a rational manner. This would also help contain total deficit financing by the government. The government must realize that, like other methods of raising funds, the method of deficit financing also has well-defined limits.

CHAPTER 6

OPEN MARKET OPERATIONS

6.1 Introduction

In the previous chapter we had emphasized (1) that the key to the control of M is the control of H and (2) that, in the Indian set-up, barring exceptional developments, such as large and continued accumulation of foreign exchange assets with the R.B.I., the key to the successful control of H is the control of deficit financing by the government. The recognition of this fact by all concerned is essential for appreciation of the limits within which the R.B.I. can operate to manipulate monetary levers and the prerequisite for maintaining the growth of money supply along its neutral-growth path. This should not, however, be misinterpreted to mean that the R.B.I., in the face of an excess budget deficit, is altogether helpless. This is not true. For within limits, the R.B.I. can fight it out, if it so desires, with the help of the tools at its disposal. These limits, however, can soon be reached if the supply of money is subjected to persistent, one-way, heavy pressures in the upward direction by continued excess deficit financing of the government and/or persistent heavy accumulation of foreign-exchange assets with the R.B.I. We shall study the traditional methods of monetary control, bearing this factor in mind.

6.2 R.B.I.'s Instruments of Monetary Control

The traditional instruments of monetary control open to the R.B.I. are the following:
1. open market operations,
2. changes in statutory reserve requirements for banks,
3. changes in the bank rate and in the conditions governing access of banks to the Reserve Bank credit,
4. changes in secondary reserves or the statutory liquidity ratio of banks,
5. changes in the Reserve Bank credit to development banks, and

6. moral suasion.

In the present chapter, after a brief study of moral suasion, we discuss open market operations of the R.B.I. Other instruments of monetary control will be discussed individually in the following chapters. (For other discussions on the subject, see Friedman, 1959; Aschheim, 1961; Sen, 1967; and Ghosh, 1971.)

6.3 Moral Suasion

Moral suasion is a combination of persuasion and pressures which a Central Bank is always in a position to use on banks in general, and errant banks in particular. This is exercised through discussions, letters, speeches, and hints thrown to banks. For example, the R.B.I. periodically issues letters to banks making clear its policy positions and urging banks to fall in line. Moral suasion can be used both for quantitative control of credit and money supply, and for qualitative control of credit, i.e. control over the distribution of bank credit. In this book we are concerned only with the former. In this respect moral suasion can be used by the R.B.I. to urge banks to keep a larger proportion of their assets in the form of government securities, lend their help in developing a broad and active market in treasury bills and other government securities, and not borrow excessively from the Bank when it is engaged in fighting the forces of inflation. It is also a standing practice of the R.B.I. to advise banks at the beginning of the slack reason (May–October) each year to reduce their indebtedness to the Bank over the slack-season period. All these actions are different ways of controlling the expansion of H, and so of M. But it is very difficult to say how far such advice is heeded by banks. Nor can we measure its contribution to the monetary-control mechanism. Nonetheless, it cannot be denied that moral suasion measures do offer some scope for the R.B.I. to exercise control over money supply.

6.4 Open Market Operations

As yet we do not have one commonly accepted *empirical* definition of the open market operations of the R.B.I. Loosely speaking, they are understood to refer to the purchase and sale of all government securities of any maturity by the R.B.I. on its own account.[1]

---

[1] The R.B.I. (Banking Department) purchases government securities not only on its 'own account' but also 'on account of others'—the Central Government, state governments and other approved bodies for whom it acts as banker. The

However, this is not correct, because the R.B.I., as the government's banker, purchases even *ad hoc* treasury bills and other non-marketable securities (including funded treasury bills) of the Central Government (which it holds in its Issue Department as backing against its note issue), and these cannot be sold to the public. Therefore, a second definition would leave out such purchases and define open market operations only to comprise the purchase and sale of *marketable* government securities by the R.B.I. on its own account. Such securities would include treasury bills as well as dated securities of the government.[2]

The R.B.I. has adopted a still narrower definition according to which its purchase of securities directly from the government are excluded and only its purchases and sales of government securities from/to the public and banks (on its own account) are said to comprise its open market operations (see Swamy, 1975, p. 50). The reason advanced is that the R.B.I. buys these securities almost entirely as an intermediary in the sale of government securities. Since the R.B.I. is charged with the responsibility of managing the public debt a practice has developed under which the R.B.I. buys all the unsold stock of new government loans at the end of the subscription period and thereafter keeps them on sale in the market on its own account. Therefore, such purchases of government securities by the R.B.I. are not genuine market purchases. They constitute only an internal arrangement between the government and the R.B.I. whereby the new government loans are sold on 'tap', not directly by the government, but through the R.B.I.

The R.B.I.'s position is logically sound. The open market opera-

transactions on the government's Cash Balance Investments Account are, clearly, not open market transactions of the R.B.I., as the R.B.I. carries them out on behalf of others. The transactions on the government account, no doubt, affect the quantity of H. But this is taken care of by concentrating attention on the cash balances of the government. Any net withdrawal from these balances has already been defined as a component of deficit financing (see Section 4.2). Transactions in government securities on account of other approved bodies do not involve any change in H.

[2] In practice, almost the entire open market operations of the R.B.I. are conducted in dated securities, as the treasury bill market in India is very narrow and undeveloped. The R.B.I. does purchase small amounts of treasury bills from banks, state governments and others, but not at its own initiative. Therefore, all such purchases are clubbed together with treasury bills purchased and discounted (see R.B.I., 1977, Table 2, Col. 26). All treasury bills sold by the R.B.I. are in its capacity as the government's agent.

tions should only refer to the Bank's operations with the public and banks. But the implications of this correct definition of open market operations for the government's definition of its deficit financing must also be understood. We have already discussed these implications in Section 4.2. Together they explain how a part of the Reserve Bank credit to the government escapes inclusion in deficit financing, whereas it is, truly speaking, a component of such financing. This deficiency in the official measure of deficit financing must be corrected by the Ministry of Finance and the R.B.I.

The theory of open market operations is simple and straight-forward. Every open market purchase by the R.B.I. increases H by an equal amount; every sale decreases it. Thereafter, the money-multiplier process takes over and affects the supply of M in the standard way. It matters little whether the R.B.I. buys or sells securities from/to banks or the non-bank public except that in the former case the reserves of banks are affected directly, in the latter case indirectly. We are, of course, assuming that the banks remain fully loaned up all the time; i.e. that their actual excess reserves are always equal to their desired excess reserves. There are side effects, too, via changes in the government bond rates of interest. But, as we shall explain below, in the context of a largely captive government bond market in India, the interest-rate effects of the R.B.I.'s open market operations on the supply of money whether through changes in the proximate determinants of m or through induced changes in H through other sources, such as the borrowings of banks from the R.B.I., are of the second order of smalls and of uncertain direction. Therefore, they are best left out of our present discussion.

Open market operations are generally regarded as technically the most efficient instrument of monetary policy, provided (1) the market for government securities is well-organized and developed, reasonably broad, deep and resilient; (2) the Central Bank has enough capacity to buy and sell securities, and (3) it is also unencumbered by other considerations to do so for monetary-policy purposes. These operations in themselves are a highly flexible tool. They can be used continuously in widely-varying amounts, one way or the other as required, and at the option of the Central Bank. They are easily reversible in time. They involve no public announcement as changes in the bank rate or changes in the statutory reserve ratio or in the statutory liquidity ratio of banks do. Thus, they do not carry 'an-

nouncement effects' with them and do not attract public attention. Their *direct* effect on H is immediate and the amount of H *directly* created or destroyed by them is determined precisely. From this it does not, of course, follow that their net effect also is determined precisely, when the induced effects via the induced interest-rate changes and the induced offsetting borrowing/repaying actions of banks from the Central Bank and any other indirect effects are also taken into account. Any wide-awake Central Bank must always keep a close watch on these indirect effects, try to anticipate them as best as it can, and tailor its open market operations accordingly.

In India, however, the open market operations of the R.B.I. have not been a powerful instrument of monetary control. This is because, of the three conditions for the realization of the full potential of such operations, only the second is fully satisfied, and the other two only partly. The R.B.I. has more than adequate capacity to buy and sell securities. After the Reserve Bank of India (Amendment) Act, 1951 the Bank is authorized to buy and sell securities of any maturity and in any quantity of the Central Government, a state government, or of a local authority specified by the Central Government. Securities fully guaranteed as to principal and interest by any such government or authority are, for this purpose, deemed to be securities of such government or authority. Usually, however, the Bank restricts its open market operations to Central Government securities. Even then the limits within which the R.B.I. can affect the amount of H, and thereby M, through its open market operations alone are very wide. At the end of March 1976, if the R.B.I. were to buy all outstanding marketable Central Government securities including treasury bills with the banks and the public, it could increase the stock of H by about 74 per cent. On the other hand, if it were to make an open market sale of its entire holding of Central Government securities including treasury bills, it could buy up about 89 per cent of outstanding H.

The present state of development of the gilt-edged market, however, is a big handicap. Usually, it is taken as a reflection of the overall financial development of the economy. But it must be emphasized that the development of the gilt-edged market, instead of being purely dependent on the development of money and capital markets in the country, can itself be used as an instrument for fostering the growth of broad, deep, and resilient money and capital markets. And for this, the R.B.I. can and should play a greater promotional role

than it has so far. The present state of the gilt-edged market along with suggestions for developing it further is discussed in the next section.

Another big handicap from which the R.B.I.'s open market operations as an instrument of monetary policy suffer is that these operations are dominated by considerations of public-debt management and are effectively a part of such management. As banker to the government, the R.B.I. manages entirely the public-debt operations of the Central Government as well as state governments. This has the advantage that the official operations in public debt are not subject to dual control—that of the R.B.I. and the treasuries—and, therefore, do not raise any problem of co-ordination of the debt operations of various official agencies. But, at the same time, it has also meant subservience of monetary-policy objectives to debt-management objectives.

The officially stated main objective of the open market operations of the R.B.I. has been to assist the government in its borrowing operations and maintain orderly conditions in the gilt-edged market. To that end, open market operations have been used to 'groom' the market by purchasing securities nearing maturity to facilitate redemption. On the one hand, this puts cash in the hands of investors which the latter can use to subscribe to new loan floatations; on the other hand, this helps lengthen the average maturity of the government debt outstanding. The same objective is, of course, also pursued by making cash-cum-conversion issues of new loans under which a part or whole of the payment for a new subscription can be made in the form of outstanding amounts of a designated loan or loans. Thus, fresh borrowing and refunding operations are combined. Simultaneous issues of new loans of different maturities are also made.

The Bank makes available on tap all the time a large variety of old issues to cater to the diverse demands of investors and to broaden the gilt-edged market by bringing in more and more investors. For this purpose, it operates through recognized brokers who are regularly briefed on the various securities the Bank is willing to buy and sell and the rates at which it is prepared to do so. The Bank keeps on varying the list of securities for sale according to circumstances, such as the stock position of a loan with it, the approach of the interest payment date, and the demand conditions in the market. 'Switch' operations involving purchase of one security against sale of another are quite frequent and have been developed as a special instrument

of debt management. Though generally the switches are from shorter-dated to longer-dated loans, the stated intention of the R.B.I. is to help cater to the shifting asset preferences of investors with respect to maturity distribution and also to establish and maintain a harmonious pattern of yield as seen fit by the Bank. Switches affect only the maturity composition of debt, not its size.

Being in a near-monopolist's position or the main reservoir of government securities, it is pretty much in a position to fix effectively the prices of government securities (at least in the short run). It does, however, revise, up or down, in gradual steps, the prices of these securities according to the state of demand in the market and its expectations of the future. But as we shall see in the next section, since a large part of the government securities market is statutorily captive, the authorities have a substantial control over the demand side of the market as well.

Open market operations have also been used to provide seasonal finance to banks, but they ceased to be the primary channel of such finance from mid-November 1951. After this date the R.B.I. stopped buying passively whatever securities banks would offer to it, instead encouraging them to borrow from it against government securities as collateral. This brought the bank rate as an instrument of monetary control into (limited) operation. It also allowed the Bank to use open market operations in a more selective, discretionary, and discriminatory manner. Nevertheless, by the Bank's own admission, these operations have not been made much use of for influencing the availability and cost of credit or for controlling changes in the stock of money. Any changes in the stock of money that do come about owing to its open market operations are incidental to the debt management operations. From this to say that 'open market operations have nevertheless been in line with the Bank's monetary policy' (R.B.I., 1970, p. 56) is a gross overstatement, unsupported by facts. For if the Bank's claim were true, excess increases in the stock of money would have been more or less non-existent, unless, of course, the Bank were to assert that the actual increases have by no means been excessive.

The truth of the matter is that at no stage has the R.B.I. evaluated quantitatively the contribution of its open market operations to monetary management. The R.B.I. study by Chandavarkar (1964) gives only a good description of open market operations with primary monthly data, but no assessment of their adequacy or other-

wise. For later years, even similar monthly data have not been published by the R.B.I. The *Report on Currency and Finance* of any year gives only the aggregate figures of open market purchase, sale, and net sale/purchase for a whole year. The *Report* for 1976-7 has omitted even this information. For the years 1967-8 and 1968-9, too, even annual figures have not been published. This is indicative of the casualness with which the R.B.I. treats the provision of information on its open market operations for any independent evaluation.

The degree of adequacy of the R.B.I.'s open market operations for monetary management for any year can be judged only against a quantitatively specified target ΔH—the variable that open market operations affect directly—after due allowance has been made for reserve impounding or release through variations in statutory reserve requirements for banks (see Chapter 7 and Appendix E). The R.B.I. has never clearly stated the desired or target variation in H. The trend rule (see Chapters 2 and 5) gives us one way of working out desired (neutral) variations in H. But knowing them is not enough for evaluating the quantitative contribution of open market operations to the over-all control of H by the R.B.I. We also need monthly data on the R.B.I.'s open market operations. For the annual average change in H achieved through open market operations will be given by the average of the cumulative monthly totals of net open market operations over a year. Only in the R.B.I. study by Chandavarkar (1964) are monthly data for the period 1948-9 to 1963-4 given. From these monthly data cumulative monthly totals and their averages can, of course, be calculated. But similar data for later years have not been published by the R.B.I. In the absence of such data, a meaningful quantitative evaluation of open market operations as a tool of monetary control cannot be attempted. The R.B.I. should fill this data gap.

Coming to other aspects of open market operations, we note that they have undoubtedly helped the government and the market for its securities. The market has been reasonably stable—not subject to violent fluctuations. It has also grown in size. The interest cost of debt to the government has also been kept quite low. All this has been made possible largely through the extension and growth of the captive sector of the gilt-edged market. Under Indian conditions this is perhaps unavoidable, but for a faster development of this market and for making it broader (so as to attract funds in greater volume and from all sorts of investor groups) as well as deeper (so that

sufficient orders for buying and selling exist both below and above the market), the interest-rate mechanism should also be allowed to play a greater role. One way worth examining is the dual-interest-rate policy with respect to the statutorily required and the free components of the holdings of government securities. This is analogous to the dual-price policy for, say, sugar, under which till 15 August 1978 there used to be one price for levy sugar fixed by the government and another price for free sale sugar which was determined in the free market. Another important suggestion—that concerning the development of the market for treasury bills—will be discussed in the next section.

6.5 Main Features of the Indian Gilt-Edged Market

The main features of the Indian gilt-edged market are:

1. *Dominance of Financial Institutions*. The gilt-edged market is dominated by financial institutions, and among them by commercial banks. At the end of March 1975, the total amount of marketable Central and state government securities outstanding (excluding treasury bills and some small special issues) was Rs 8,340 crores. Its ownership distribution is given in Table 6.1.

TABLE 6.1

OWNERSHIP DISTRIBUTION OF CENTRAL AND
STATE GOVERNMENT SECURITIES
(End of March 1975)

Category of holders	Percentage to total
(1)	(2)
1. State governments	2.8
2. R.B.I. (own account)	28.2
3. Commercial banks	32.9
4. L.I.C. of India	14.1
5. Provident Funds	18.9
6. Others	3.1
Total	100.0

Source: Reserve Bank of India, *Report on Currency and Finance, 1976-7*, Vol. II, Statement 83.

Table 6.1 gives a broad idea of the present structure of ownership of the marketable public debt. The last category includes such holders as co-operative banks, general insurance companies, local authorities, trusts, individuals, joint stock companies, Industrial Finance Corporation of India and State Industrial Finance Corporations, non-residents (foreign central banks and governments), etc. Table 6.1 makes clear the dominance of financial institutions, and among them of commercial banks, in the ownership of marketable government debt held by the non-government sector. As we shall see below, this has helped the R.B.I. to exercise substantial control over the demand side of the market for government securities.

2. *Captive Market.* A second important feature of the gilt-edged market in India is that a large part of it is captive. The captivity is ensured through statutory investment requirements imposed on designated financial institutions. The R.B.I. itself is the most captive holder of government debt. Moreover, we are interested in analysing the characteristics of the market for gilt-edged securities the R.B.I. faces for its open market operations. For this, we must concentrate our attention on the non-government holders of public debt, excluding the R.B.I. Commercial banks, the single most important holders of government securities, holding as much as one-third of the total marketable government debt outstanding, are subject to a 'statutory liquidity' requirement. Under this, they are required to hold a certain minimum percentage of their demand and time liabilities in the form of 'liquid assets', defined statutorily to comprise excess reserves, balances with other banks on current account, and investments in unencumbered government and 'other approved' securities (see Chapter 9). Similarly, the L.I.C. of India, the General Insurance Corporation of India and its subsidiaries, provident and trust funds, are required statutorily to invest specific minimum proportions of their total investible funds (or fresh annual accrual of investible funds in certain cases) in Central and state government securities and government guaranteed bonds. The minimum proportions vary between 25 and 50 per cent of investible funds. With the growth in demand and time liabilities of banks and investible funds of other institutions, the captive market for government securities automatically grows. In addition, the statutory investment requirements can themselves be manipulated.

Full information is not easily available about the statutory component of actual investment of financial institutions in government

securities. Moreover, from the way such requirements are stipulated, it is hard to compute them exactly. Nevertheless, it would be broadly true to say that the proportion of the discretionary component of investment in government securities by financial institutions is very small. Consequently, apart from some seasonal operations by commercial banks, transactions in old governments are relatively small. Most transactions are of the nature of switch operations either with the R.B.I. or among other financial institutions themselves through brokers. This keeps the government securities market narrow as well as shallow.

3. *R.B.I. Monopoly*. The R.B.I. occupies a virtual monopolist's position in the market for gilt-edgeds. This is so not only in the case of treasury bills, but also for dated governments. At any time, the R.B.I.'s stock of marketable government securities (old and new issues) is several times the free or discretionary (or disposable) stock of such securities with any single financial institution as a potential seller of these securities in the market. Moreover, as the manager of the public debt, the Bank can expand the stock-supply of such debt virtually to any extent it deems desirable. In addition, it is the only institution which is continuously in the market, making 'tap' sales of government securities, new and old, and of various maturities, entering into switch operations, and also standing ready to buy all governments at prices close to its selling prices of comparable maturities, with of course some spread. Thus, it is the only institution which can be called *the* dealer in government securities. Commercial banks and other financial institutions also buy and sell government securities on their own account. But they do so as investors, not as dealers. They are not specialists in buying and selling government securities and are not out to make money purely, or even mainly, from such activities. Therefore, they do not 'make' market in government securities in the sense a true 'dealer' in them does. They are not continuously in the market, but only when investment, liquidity, or portfolio-balance considerations send them to the market.

The R.B.I. has made good use of its monopolist-dealer position in the gilt-edged market for purposes of debt management. It has been successful in keeping it steady and orderly, avoiding any sharp fluctuations, meeting the portfolio needs of various investors for differing maturities, and keeping the interest cost of public debt to the exchequer sufficiently low. Of course, in all this, it has been helped a good deal by the statutory investment requirements. On the

debit side, it has not been able to develop much of a market for treasury bills. The market for dated governments has also not grown as fast as it could with better over-all monetary management.

4. *Brokers' Market.* As an extension of this feature we may specifically say that (except the R.B.I.) there are no dealers in government securities who make continuous market in government securities and who are always ready to buy and sell such securities on their own account in whatever amount offered or desired at market-clearing prices. Instead, all that we have are firms of brokers who mediate between prospective buyers and sellers of government securities, including the R.B.I., so far as transactions among old issues of such securities are concerned. (The R.B.I. accepts directly only subscriptions to new issues.) This feature of the Indian gilt-edged market is both a cause and effect of the relative narrowness as well as shallowness of the market. We have already discussed the other factors contributing to this state of the market, and now discuss one more contributory factor in some detail.

5. *Undeveloped Treasury Bill Market.* Treasury bills with 91-day maturity are only issued by the Central Government. The market for such bills is highly undeveloped and narrow—the 'public' buyers are almost entirely the commercial banks. We are of course excluding the R.B.I. and the state governments, who are not treated as a part of the public. At the end of March 1977, the total amount of treasury bills outstanding was of the value of Rs 5,372 crores. Of this, about 67 per cent were held by the R.B.I., 19 per cent by banks, 12 per cent by state governments, and only 2 per cent by others.

In countries like the U.S.A. and the U.K., treasury bills constitute the most important short-term paper and the stock-in-trade of the money market. The market in such bills in these countries is very broad and active as against the undeveloped treasury bill market in India. This is a little surprising when we look at the level of development of other financial markets and note that treasury bills are the most liquid and credit-risk-free short-term asset which offer a reasonably good return. Is there something wrong with the structure of the money-market organization? Is there a gap in it which needs to be filled up?

Under the present arrangement (since 12 July 1965) the R.B.I. sells treasury bills (on behalf of the Central Government) on tap throughout the week at a rate determined by it. The rate is varied from time to time according to changes in market conditions. Since

1965 it has varied from the low of 3 per cent attained during 1969–70 to the high of 4.6 per cent prevailing since 23 July 1974. The R.B.I. also rediscounts these bills not only for banks, but also for state governments as well as approved bodies. All this, however, has not been sufficient to attract short-term funds in treasury bills in a reasonably big way.

The major reason for this state of affairs seems to be the continuance of a gap in the organizational structure of the Indian money market, namely, the absence of any dealers in treasury bills. The working of market forces has not encouraged private enterprise to assume this role. In such a situation it is for the government to take special steps to fill this gap by, say, setting up a subsidiary of the R.B.I. to deal in treasury bills (and maybe all other government securities as well). The major task of this subsidiary should be to develop an active market in treasury bills. For this, it would have to seek out actively throughout the country pools of short-term surplus funds with new potential customers, such as non-bank financial institutions, joint stock companies, and other large firms and institutions, educate their holders about the possibilities of profitable investment of even very short-term funds in treasury bills—which offer a very high degree of liquidity, no credit risk, and very little risk of capital loss—even borrow from them on a virtual call-loan basis, and establish a network of active, live, and continuous contact with them, both for drawing in their temporarily surplus funds and for buying bills from them.

In developing this sort of business, an efficient system of communications and an equally efficient arrangement for the quick remittance of funds will be crucial. The R.B.I. must ensure the satisfaction of the latter condition. It will, of course, have to surrender all its government agency business in treasury bills to its proposed subsidiary, including direct rediscounting (of treasury bills) for banks and other approved bodies. Such a rediscounting facility should be extended only to its proposed subsidiary. This would be necessary to enable it to meet its unforeseen demands for cash which it cannot raise immediately in the market without disturbing the treasury bill market greatly. All other holders of treasury bills, including banks and state governments, would transact business in these bills with the proposed subsidiary—R.B.I.'s special dealer in treasury bills—or at times, among themselves. The subsidiary would always be willing to buy and sell treasury bills at prices which it would make

and revise (within a narrow range) according to changes in market conditions and expectations about them. The R.B.I., of course, should remain free to buy and sell treasury bills on its own account in the open market, including its own subsidiary. The proposed subsidiary, after a time, should be able to meet its expenses, and also earn a handsome profit from the spread between its purchase price and selling price and large turnover amount.

If an active treasury bill market is cultivated, there will be substantial advantages. The excessive dependence of the government on the R.B.I. to meet its needs for short-term funds will be reduced. This will cut down the quantum of excessive deficit financing and thereby the most important source of excessive H-expansion. The short-term funds invested in treasury bills through the R.B.I. subsidiary (special dealer in treasury bills) will come largely from the public (leaving out the state governments), and not from the fresh creation of H as happens at present, whenever the R.B.I. purchases the bills.

From where will the short-term funds come to be invested in treasury bills? Again, we leave out the state governments, and also leave out commercial banks, which are already in the market for treasury bills. The potential new investors in treasury bills will be non-bank financial and non-financial corporations and other large firms and institutions. At present they keep their very short-term funds on current account with banks. Let us define very short-term funds as funds which are available for investment for any period from 7 to 91 days, provided such an investment is highly liquid so that it can be cashed immediately with only a small degree of risk of capital loss. Current-account funds with banks do not earn their holders any interest. Yet surplus cash is kept for earning the goodwill of banks or to meet the 'minimum balance' requirement banks impose on their borrowers. Over and above this, there must be some more very short-term funds, too, which firms are compelled to hold in the form of cash because no credit-risk-free short-term investment paper is available to them which is highly liquid. Treasury bills can fill precisely the need for such a paper, if a market in them is developed. Moreover, at least a part of the so-called 'goodwill' funds and very short-term (under three months) time deposits with banks will also be diverted into treasury bills.

Thus the development of the treasury bill market will largely mean a diversion of funds from bank deposits to treasury bills. This will

also mean a reduction in the direct demand for these bills from banks, unless the R.B.I. reduces its liberal credit to banks and thereby induces them to hold a higher proportion of their assets in the form of high-liquidity assets such as treasury bills. But why is such a planned diversion of funds or the substitution of one kind of financial asset (treasury bills) for another (bank deposits) desirable?

Two social benefits are worth considering. One is that it will help control the government's deficit financing better. For a part of the government's borrowing from the R.B.I. will be replaced by its borrowing from the public. For an economy which is subject to continuous inflationary pressures arising from excess deficit financing, this is no mean gain. Second, this will free the R.B.I.'s open market operations as an instrument of monetary policy, for more than one reason. Firstly, as we have seen above, at present open market operations are dominated by considerations of debt management. The growth of the public's demand for treasury bills will take away a part of the pressure on the R.B.I. and the long end of the market in government securities. Secondly, the development of the market for treasury bills will open up the short end of the government securities market for the Bank's open market operations. At present these operations are limited to the long end of the market. This has restricted the effectiveness of whatever open market operations the R.B.I. is able to conduct. Open market operations in treasury bills, when feasible, will allow the R.B.I. to control the liquidity and the cost of credit in the economy better.

One more beneficial effect may also be mentioned. The diversion of funds from bank deposits to treasury bills will act as a pressure on banks to accelerate their efforts at deposit mobilization. To the extent the direct investment by the non-bank public in treasury bills reduces the excess supply of H and so of bank reserves, this pressure on banks to try harder at deposit mobilization will increase further. This will improve banking in the country.

CHAPTER 7

VARIATIONS IN RESERVE REQUIREMENTS

7.1 Cash Reserves of Banks

Banks always keep a certain proportion of their total assets in the form of cash, partly to meet the statutory reserve requirements and partly to meet their own day-to-day needs for making cash payments. Cash is held partly in the form of 'cash on hand' and partly in the form of 'balances with the R.B.I.' All such cash is called cash reserves of banks (R), and is a part of H. 'Current account balances with other banks' are not a part of H, and are not included in R.

The reserves of banks are usually divided under two heads: (a) required reserves and (b) excess reserves. Required reserves are reserves which banks are required statutorily to hold *with the R.B.I.* All other reserves are excess reserves, whether they are held as cash on hand or as balances with the R.B.I.

Every scheduled bank is required by law to maintain all its required reserves as balances with the R.B.I. These reserves bear a specified relation with the bank's demand and time liabilities. This relation itself can be varied from time to time and within limits specified by law. It is this authority of the R.B.I. to vary the minimum statutory reserve ratio which makes the variable reserve ratio a tool of monetary control.

A scheduled bank is one which has been included in the second schedule of the Reserve Bank of India Act, 1934. It must have a paid-up capital and reserves of an aggregate value of not less than Rs 5 lakhs and it must satisfy the R.B.I. that its affairs are not conducted in a manner detrimental to the interests of its depositors. On the last Friday of March 1976, there were 96 scheduled banks, 14 of which were state co-operative banks (though the total number of reporting state co-operative banks was 25) and the rest 82 commercial banks. Among the latter, 14 were foreign banks and the remaining 68 were Indian banks. There were only 8 reporting non-scheduled banks with

aggregate deposits of Rs 25 crores, whereas the net aggregate deposits of the 82 scheduled commercial banks were Rs 14,155 crores, i.e. 99.82 per cent of the aggregate deposits of all commercial banks. Thus scheduled commercial banks cover practically the entire commercial banking industry, and, henceforth, we shall talk only about them.

Initially, when the R.B.I. was set up in 1935, it was not given the authority to vary the statutory reserve ratio. The ratio itself was fixed by law at 5 per cent for demand liabilities and 2 per cent for time liabilities. It was in 1956 that, for the first time, the R.B.I. was empowered to vary the ratio—between 5 and 20 per cent for demand liabilities and between 2 and 8 per cent for time liabilities. Besides, subject to these maximum limits, the R.B.I. was also given authority to require scheduled banks to maintain with it additional cash reserves in a specified proportion to additional liabilities after a specified date. The incremental reserve ratio cannot exceed 100 per cent. The R.B.I. is allowed to pay interest on the additional required reserves over and above the minimum required reserves, provided a bank maintains the whole of the statutory balance required of it.

In September 1962 the distinction between demand and time liabilities for the purpose of reserve requirements was removed and a uniform minimum reserve requirement of 3 per cent of the aggregate of demand and time liabilities of banks was statutorily laid down. Also, the R.B.I. was empowered to vary the minimum reserve ratio between 3 and 15 per cent. The incremental reserve requirement authority of the Bank has been amended accordingly, so that the maximum reserve requirement of banks can, at no time, exceed 15 per cent. Since 1956 the minimum reserve requirement relates to the *average daily balance* of banks with the R.B.I., i.e. the average of the balances held at the close of business on each day of the week Saturday to Friday.

Besides required reserves, banks also hold excess reserves, which are reserves held in excess of the required reserves. It is only these (excess) reserves which banks as a whole can use to meet their currency drains (i.e. *net* withdrawal of currency by their depositors) as well as clearing drains (i.e. *net* loss of cash due to cross-clearing of cheques among banks). A large part of the excess reserves banks hold in the form of 'cash on hand' or 'vault cash' with themselves. The remaining small part they hold as excess balances with the R.B.I. For individual banks, their current-account balances with other

banks also serve the same function as cash. But, as said earlier, for the banking system as a whole (outside the R.B.I.), inter-bank current-account balances (demand deposits) are not cash.

For statutory reserve requirements, the demand and time liabilities of a bank comprise the following: (1) demand and time deposits—from the public and other banks; (2) borrowings—from the public and banks other than the R.B.I., the Industrial Development Bank of India, and the Agricultural Refinance and Development Corporation; and (3) other demand and time liabilities. Net worth of banks, such as their paid-up capital and reserves, and contingent liabilities of banks, such as bills rediscounted by banks with non-bank financial institutions, are not included in the definition of demand and time liabilities. Deposits from the public constitute the bulk of the demand and time liabilities of banks. Over the period 1961–2 to 1976–7, for scheduled commercial banks, the average ratio of deposits of the public to total demand and time liabilities was 92 per cent. For banks as a whole, inter-bank deposits and inter-bank borrowings do not add to their total investible or loanable funds. They only redistribute funds among individual banks for better utilization.

Since excess reserves are the only disposable cash for banks, they always desire to hold some excess reserves. In other words, we can speak of the desired excess reserves of banks or of the banks' demand function for excess reserves or cash or of their liquidity preference, just as we speak of the demand function for cash balances of other economic units, whether households or firms. Similarly, we can speak of the transactions, precautionary, and speculative demand for cash balances of banks. The essential point to note is that the excess-reserves-holding behaviour of banks can be given a rational economic explanation—a point which has not been fully appreciated by several analysts of the Indian monetary scene, and a point which is of substantial importance for the formulation of monetary-control policy.

As a behavioural variable, we would expect the demand for excess reserves to be an increasing function of the total liabilities as well as of the ratio of demand liabilities to time liabilities and a decreasing function of the weighted advance rate of banks and/or of the marginal cost of borrowed reserves or of the weighted rate of interest on investment and of the demand for bank loans and advances (normalized by some appropriate scale factor) as measured by, say, the ratio of bank credit (to the commercial sector) to liabilities. (For

empirical evidence on these hypotheses, see Appendix F.) We would also expect the demand for excess reserves, holding other things constant, to be a decreasing function of such institutional improvements as would reduce the liquidity requirements of banks, e.g. the strengthening of the banking system through liquidation and amalgamation of weaker units, better supervision by the R.B.I., deposit insurance and nationalization of banks which have practically eliminated the fear of 'run' on banks, enlarged inter-bank call money market, easier access to the R.B.I. for loans, etc. Swamy (1975, Chapters 5 and 6) has enquired into all these factors at some length for the period 1951–2 to 1970–1 (for a summary of her findings, see Appendix D). Though she has looked at the total reserves behaviour of banks, her empirical findings are of much relevance for their excess reserves behaviour as well, as the observed variations in total reserves over the sample period were mainly due to variations in excess reserves.

The most interesting thing to note about the excess reserves–liabilities ratio of banks is that, after declining continuously over the period of the fifties from the high of 6.84 in 1950–1 to the low of 2.91 in 1960–1, it stabilized around the mean value of 2.73, with only minor fluctuations, over the period 1960–1 to 1973–4. It fell continuously over the next three years—from 2.58 in 1973–4 to 1.97 in 1976–7. (For annual data on excess reserves held by scheduled commercial banks, see Appendix G.) Swamy (1975, Chapter 6) had found that even the seasonal variations in the reserves–deposits ratio were rather small.

Thus, the evidence on excess-reserves ratio suggests that since 1960–1 variations in the money multiplier due to variations in this ratio have been rather small. Reductions in the value of the ratio over the period 1973–4 to 1976–7 have already brought it to a sufficiently low level (about 2 per cent), leaving very little scope for much further reduction. This would mean that the money-supply impact of any further increases in the statutory reserve requirement cannot be easily counteracted by banks by reducing excess reserves. This provides sharper teeth to the policy of increased statutory-reserves requirement to contain the excess expansion of money supply.

7.2 The Uses of the Variable Reserve Ratio Measure by the R.B.I.

Ever since 1956 the R.B.I. has had the power to use the variable reserve ratio as a method of monetary-credit control, but the measure

has been used very sparingly: once in 1960, then in 1973, and there-after in 1974, 1976 and 1977. These variations have been applied only to scheduled commercial banks. All these years, the statutory reserve ratio for the state co-operative banks has been kept constant at 3 per cent.

The 1960 experiment was for a brief period of about 10 months from March 1960 to January 1961. On 3 March 1960 banks were asked to maintain additional balances with the R.B.I. amounting to 25 per cent of the *increase* in their total liabilities since 11 March 1960. On 5 May 1960 the banks were asked to maintain additional balances with the R.B.I. amounting to 50 per cent of the increase in their liabilities since 6 May 1960. The Bank withdrew in two stages this additional reserve requirement: effective from 11 November 1960, further impounding of reserves for increments to liability over the level of 11 November was suspended, and about half of the reserves already impounded amounting to Rs 13 crores was released by refixing the additional reserve requirement at 25 per cent of the increase between 11 March and 11 November. Subsequently, the additional reserve requirement was completely revoked with effect from 13 January 1961, releasing another Rs 13 crores of reserves to banks. (See R.B.I., *Report on Currency and Finance, 1960–1*, p. 43.)

The measure was taken to check the sharp increase in the aggregate monetary demand for output and prices. This was soon given up, because according to the R.B.I.'s reckoning 'this had only a limited success since [(a)] *the banks managed to minimize its impact on credit largely by recourse to borrowings from the Reserve Bank* and [(b)] *partly by liquidating Government securities*' (R.B.I., 1970, p. 52, my italics). We shall discuss the two phenomena (a) and (b) mentioned in this statement in Section 7.4 of this chapter.

The next use of the variable reserve ratio was made during 1973. First, the minimum reserve ratio was raised from 3 to 5 per cent for a period of one year beginning with 29 June 1973. The ratio was further revised upward in two stages—once from 5 to 6 per cent for one year with effect from 8 September 1973 and then from 6 to 7 per cent for one year with effect from 22 September 1973. The banks were paid interest by the R.B.I. at the rate of 4.75 per cent on additional required reserves above 3 per cent of their demand and time liabilities. Thus, within a short period of three months (July–September 1973), the minimum reserve ratio was more than doubled from 3 to 7 per cent. The first additional cash reserve requirement of 2 per cent

introduced in June 1973 was allowed to expire on 28 June 1974.[1] But the second additional cash reserve requirement of 2 per cent introduced in September 1973 was renewed in September 1974 for a further period of one year. This policy, however, was soon reversed. The required reserve ratio was reduced from 5 to 4 per cent of the total demand and time liabilities—the reduction was 0.5 per cent with effect from 14 December 1974, and a further 0.5 per cent with effect from 28 December 1974. As a result, about Rs 120 crores of additional reserves were released to banks. This was done 'to enable banks to meet the genuine requirements of additional credit during the *busy season*'. But the operation of the measure was not restricted to the duration of the busy season. The 4 per cent reserve ratio was allowed to be operative till the end of August 1976. Excessive expansion of money supply and credit compelled the R.B.I. to raise again the statutory reserve ratio of banks, first from 4 to 5 per cent with effect from 4 September 1976 and further to 6 per cent from 13 November 1976. From 14 January 1977 the banks were further required to deposit with the R.B.I. 10 per cent of their incremental demand and time liabilities over and above their cash reserves requirement of 6 per cent. On the additionally impounded reserves (that is the required reserves in excess of 3 per cent), the R.B.I. pays interest to banks at the rate of 5.5 per cent per annum.

7.3 The Theory and Working of the Variable
Reserve Ratio Measure

The control measure of variable reserve ratio attempts to affect the stock of money via the impounding or release of bank reserves or *H*. When the reserve ratio is revised upward, banks are required to hold larger reserves or balances with the R.B.I. than before for the same amount of deposits. This amounts to leaving the required reserve ratio unchanged but the R.B.I.'s impounding additional reserves. Since reserves are a part of *H*, this amounts to a *virtual* withdrawal of a part of *H* from the public equal to the amount of additional reserves impounded.

[1] In view of the continuing strong and accelerating inflationary pressures in the economy at that time (June 1974) and the package of anti-inflationary measures announced by the government in early July 1974 in the form of compulsory deposits from the public, this relaxation in the cash reserve requirement of banks was totally unwarranted and anti-anti-inflationary. It amounted to a substitution of compulsory deposits (of *H*) by the public for compulsory deposits (of *H*) by banks.

The withdrawal of *H* is only virtual and not actual, because, legally as well as for accounting purposes, the amount of impounded reserves continue to be a part of *H* and continue to be measured as such. Therefore, in order to find out the impact of impounded reserves on the supply of money, one standard method of analysis is (*a*) to *assume* the required reserve ratio has remained unchanged, and (*b*) to pick up the effect of the increase in the required reserve ratio by deducting the reserves impounded from the actual supply of *H*. The *H* so adjusted is called the 'adjusted *H*' or the 'extended base' (of the money multiplier) in the literature.

Thus, adjusted *H* is simply actual *H* less the amount of reserves impounded or plus the amount of reserves released by the Central Bank through increase or decrease, respectively, in the required reserve ratio with reference to a given required reserve ratio. It is this adjusted *H* which serves as the base of the unchanged money-multiplier. The money-multiplier itself is left unchanged, because, in our method of analysis, the impact of the change in the required reserve ratio is picked up through the impounding or release of reserves, *assuming* the reserve ratio has remained unchanged.[2] (See Appendix E.) From the change in adjusted *H*, we can estimate the resulting change in *M* (using the multiplier analysis) attributable to the change in the required reserve ratio.

This argument tells us that the essential function of changes in the required reserve ratio is to bring about desired changes in the effective (or adjusted) amount of *H* and through it in the amount of money (and bank credit) and that, in this sense, the method of variable reserve ratio can act both as a supplement and as an alternative to the method of open market operations.

There is one serious misconception in some quarters about the nature and impact of an increase in the required reserve ratio. As we have argued above, this results in an impounding of *reserves*, resulting in a multiple decline in bank deposits as well as money. In some quarters it is carelessly asserted that the increase in the required reserve ratio is for the impounding of *deposits*. Sometimes the impounding of reserves and the impounding of deposits are spoken of interchangeably, as if the two terms mean one and the same thing. But they do not. What is impounded are reserves, not deposits. This is because the additional reserve requirement can be satisfied only by

---

[2] We are also assuming that the desired excess reserve ratio of banks remains unaffected by a change in the required reserve ratio.

the transfer of reserves to the R.B.I., not by the transfer of deposits. The latter will require the R.B.I. to hold deposits with banks, which it does not. Impounding (or freezing or immobilizing) a part of bank deposits is possible only when the public holding them is temporarily debarred from drawing upon them.

The distinction between the impounding of reserves and the impounding of deposits is not purely terminological; it is also substantive—and much more so. The impounding of reserves reduces adjusted H by an equal amount and reduces M and bank deposits by certain multiples given by the respective money and deposit multipliers. And for successful monetary planning, the authorities must be in a position to estimate their respective magnitudes. For example, in order to reduce M by Rs 100 crores, reserves impounding by Rs 50 crores will do if the marginal money-multiplier has the value of 2. In the absence of recognition of this distinction between the impounding of reserves and the impounding of deposits, the authorities, in their ignorance, may impound reserves by a full Rs 100 crores. This will lead to a reduction of Rs 200 crores in M—an excess reduction by a full Rs 100 crores.

Changes in reserve requirement can be applied either to total liabilities or only to incremental liabilities of banks after a specified date. Both kinds of application have been made in India. The use in 1960 was in incremental form; the later uses till 14 January 1977 were in total form. From the latter date, the incremental form has been combined with the total form. The incremental form has two distinct advantages over the total form. Firstly, it is relatively easier on banks to meet the additional reserve requirement from the fresh accrual of primary deposits, for the revised requirement pertains only to incremental liabilities. Secondly, it automatically differentiates among banks on the basis of their gains in deposits. Since each individual bank may not be gaining in deposits equiproportionately with other banks, the hike in *total* reserve requirement tends to penalize banks with a slow rate of growth of deposits more than those with higher rates of growth of deposits. The incremental form of reserve requirement does not suffer from this kind of defect. This form, however, can be used only to curb further expansions of deposits and credit, and not to produce absolute reductions in deposits. In a growing economy either form can subserve the purpose of monetary control, if the increase in H has not been going on at too excessive a rate.

It is commonly alleged that changes in reserve requirement as an instrument of monetary control is inferior to the tool of open market operations in that it makes lumpy and discontinuous changes both in time and amount of reserves and deposits, and produces 'announcement effect', since changes in reserve requirement are newsworthy. This is true. But too much should not be made of this argument. Banks can be given advance notice of changes and the changes can be introduced in stages so that banks have enough time to adjust their portfolios accordingly. Then, in a situation of accelerating or continuing inflation, H and R would normally be growing rapidly, and it would not be too hard on banks to meet a higher reserve requirement, if they want to co-operate with the monetary authority in checking excessive expansion of money supply. Further, since the R.B.I. does not have much freedom to use open market operations for purposes of monetary control (see Section 6.4), changes in reserve requirement have to be resorted to from time to time, as the situation demands, if monetary stability is valued as a goal of economic policy.

7.4 Leakages

As a control measure, the method of variable reserve ratio is not absolutely foolproof. It has its own leakages, some of which are common to other measures, especially the method of open market operations. For successful monetary management, it is essential that the authorities understand the true nature and working of these leakages correctly and do not get unduly perturbed at their presence. Instead, they should try their best to plug or offset these leakages as far as possible through other measures at their disposal. This only shows that the variable reserve ratio is, by itself, not a sufficient method of monetary control; it needs to be supplemented by other measures to make it effective.

When the required reserve ratio of banks is revised upward to impound bank reserves, which are a part of H, a part of the impounded H may leak back into the economy through the following actions:

1. non-compliance or incomplete compliance of banks with the higher or additional reserve requirement;
2. increased or compensatory borrowing by banks from the R.B.I.; and

3. increased or compensatory sale of government securities by banks to the R.B.I.

The first source of leakage arises because, at present, the law permits banks to default for a limited period on payment of a nominal fine. In our view, such defaults should be totally disallowed by law. There is no reason why banks cannot comply with the statutory reserve requirement on the daily average basis over a week, if they so desire. Or, if the authorities are serious about the use of the reserve ratio as a tool of monetary control, it does not make sense simultaneously to allow banks not to observe the statutory reserve requirement, and that, too, on easy terms. And the leakage through non-compliance is not something purely imaginary that we are talking about, but something which has actually taken place. Further, none of the foreign banks is known to have defaulted in matters of statutory reserves. The defaulters were only among Indian banks, when about 90 per cent of the Indian commercial banking industry is in the hands of nationalized banks. The relevant data for scheduled commercial banks for the period 1973–4 to 1976–7 are given in Table 7.1.

TABLE 7.1

STATUTORY RESERVES OF SCHEDULED COMMERCIAL BANKS
(1973–4 to 1976–7)

(*Rs crores*)

Year	Required	Actual	Shortfall (1) − (2)	Impounded	Percentage of shortfall to impounded
	(1)	(2)	(3)	(4)	(5)
1973–4	589	569	20	258	7.8
1974–5	617	565	51	195	26.2
1975–6	568	543	25	118	21.2
1976–7	893	815	78	272	28.7

In the table, by statutory reserves we mean balances with the R.B.I. The data relate to averages of Friday figures for the years 1973–4 and 1974–5 and 'last Friday of the month' figures for the years 1975–6 and 1976–7. The statutory reserve requirements for these years have already been detailed above in Section 2. Column 1 gives the average

annual figures for statutorily required minimum reserves for scheduled commercial banks. Column 2 gives the annual average values of balances these banks actually held with the R.B.I. Column 3 gives the extent of shortfall in required reserves. Reserves impounded (in column 4) are the excess of actual statutory reserves, i.e. balances with the R.B.I. (column 2) over the statutory reserves required of banks if the minimum statutory reserve ratio had been kept fixed at 3 per cent of total demand and time liabilities of banks. Column 5 simply expresses the extent of shortfall in statutory reserves (column 3) as the percentage of reserves actually impounded (column 4). This is one possible measure of the relative size of annual leakage due to non-compliance with the statutory reserve requirements we have been discussing in this section.

Next, we consider the other two actions of banks. Before we discuss remedies for them, we must try to understand and appreciate their logic, i.e. why banks tend to behave in the manner they do. The simple fact is that when the required reserve ratio of banks is revised upward, other things remaining the same, the banks lose excess or disposable reserves and, consequently, are able to support a smaller amount of deposit liabilities as well as earning assets than before. Therefore, they are forced to adjust and make all-round changes in their balance sheets—asset portfolios as well as liabilities. On the asset side, they try to reduce the ratios of their investments in government securities and of loans and advances to the commercial sector to their total deposits; on the liabilities side, they try to borrow reserves from the R.B.I. All these are necessary consequences of the control measure undertaken—of the increase in the required reserve ratio. And, therefore, the authorities must be prepared to face them. Of course, in a growing system, when fresh deposit accretion is regularly taking place as a consequence of continuous increases in H and the spread of banking habits in the economy, the banks are not greatly constrained to make absolute reductions in either investments or loans and advances, and can meet the higher reserve requirement through a mere reduction in the growth rate of their investments and loans and advances. But both the government and private borrowers may be unhappy at it, i.e. at not getting as much additional credit from banks as they had expected to get previously. Therefore, banks may be under pressure to borrow more from the R.B.I. to meet the increased credit demand of their customers. In such a situation, it is the further duty of the R.B.I. to see that it does not give away to

banks with one hand (through increased lending to them) what it takes away with the other (through a higher required reserve ratio), if it means business about checking the growth rate of money supply. The supplementary measures which it can and should take relate to the tightening up of its lending to banks. We shall discuss these measures in the next chapter.

Liquidation or open market sale of government securities is another method whereby banks try to make up for the loss of reserves impounded by the R.B.I. through upward revision of the statutory reserve ratio. The general pressure to do so is the same that impels banks to increased borrowing from the R.B.I.—to restore balance to their balance sheets and to meet better the demand for credit from the more attractive section of their customers—the commercial sector. This often results in portfolio switches by banks—from investments in government securities to loans and advances. The incentive for such switches is heightened by the need for increasing income relative to liquidity as the increased reserve requirement disturbs the old balance between income and liquidity. The R.B.I. certainly pays interest on additional reserves impounded. But this interest is much smaller than what banks can earn on their loans and advances. Therefore, if no portfolio switches are made, the banks' income per rupee of deposits will go down. To make up for this loss of income, banks are induced to sacrifice some liquidity represented by their investments in government securities, and switch out of them into more paying, but less liquid, loans and advances. Such asset switches are further encouraged by the increased interest-rate differentials between government bonds and loans and advances which emerge in the market for loanable funds during periods of tighter bank credit and the increased demand for bank credit from commercial borrowers. This is almost a universal phenomenon.

But there are two special features of the Indian situation which are noteworthy. One arises from the operation of the statutory liquidity requirement, which requires banks to maintain a certain minimum investment–liquidity ratio. We shall devote Chapter 9 to the operation and role of this requirement, and not discuss it any further here. We only note that for banks to be in a position to liquidate government securities, they must be carrying an excess liquidity position, i.e. an excess of government and 'other approved' securities over the statutorily required minimum, or they might be violating the minimum liquidity requirement. For some time in 1973 banks did enjoy

9

a position of excess liquidity, so that they could afford to switch over from government securities to loans and advances while fulfilling the statutory liquidity requirement. But, after the statutory reserve ratio and the statutory liquidity ratio had been hiked up during the second half of 1973, some banks did fail to meet even the statutory liquidity requirement (in addition to the statutory reserve requirement), as admitted by the R.B.I. in its *Report on Currency and Finance, 1973–4*, p. 96. If banks are allowed non-compliance with the minimum reserve requirement as well as with the statutory liquidity requirement on one pretext or the other, it is more the authorities that are to blame for any lack of success of the control measures adopted rather than the measures *per se*.

The second feature of the Indian situation is specially important in making liquidation of government securities a successful method of gaining reserves, whenever required. When banks liquidate government securities, they are generally bought by the R.B.I. and not by other financial institutions or the public. The latter does so under its well-established policy of over-all support to the government bond market (see Chapter 8). The R.B.I.'s support policy and the high proportion of short-maturity government securities in the investment portfolio of banks minimize any discouragement to banks to liquidate their surplus government securities for fear of capital loss by minimizing such losses. When the R.B.I. buys bonds from the banks, this directly increases H and reserves of banks, which makes good a part of the loss of adjusted H and reserves engineered through the increase in the required reserve ratio. If the R.B.I. holds back and lets the banks sell the government securities to others, it will not undo by its own action a part of the reduction in adjusted H and reserves that the increase in the required reserve ratio brings about.[3]

We do not want to suggest that the R.B.I. should give up altogether its support policy to the government-bond market. That is a separate issue. Here, we are only pointing out the consequences for the working of the policy of monetary control and the need for the use of supplementary measures to reinforce the policy of variable reserve requirement in the special circumstances prevailing in India. Specifically, if the authorities desire that all the portfolio adjustments necessitated by the upward revision of the minimum reserve ratio

[3] We are neglecting here any possible effect of the purchase of government securities by the public from banks on the money multiplier (m).

should be at the cost of loans and advances, and that the investment–deposit ratio should not fall or that banks should not liquidate a part of their holdings of government securities, they should (a) appropriately hike up the statutory liquidity requirement to mop up any surplus liquidity banks might have (see Chapter 9), and (b) enforce the statutory liquidity requirement on banks strictly.

Another kind of leakage which may reduce the efficiency of increases in reserve requirement as a monetary control measure is the compensating reduction in excess reserves which banks voluntarily hold to meet their day-to-day needs for making cash payment. If this happens, the amount of adjusted H would remain unaffected, but the value of the money multiplier, other things being the same, would go up. And this would reduce to some extent the effectiveness of the restrictive measure taken. The motive for reducing excess reserves would, again, be provided by the need to bring about a better balance between liquidity and income, the higher opportunity cost of holding cash (excess reserves), represented by higher market rates of interest which are likely to accompany a restrictive monetary policy, and greater pressure from borrowers for credit.

All this is, no doubt, plausible. But, as already noted in the opening section of this chapter, on account of the very low value of the excess reserves–liabilities ratio already attained (1.97 per cent in 1976–7), there is very little scope left for further (absolute) reduction in the value of this ratio. So any significant leakage through this source need not be a cause for worry for anti-inflationary monetary policy.

7.5 Policy Implications

We are of the view that, in the particular set of conditions prevailing in India, the R.B.I. should make greater use of the variable reserve ratio than it has done in the past. Of late the R.B.I. also seems to have realized it, though only half-heartedly. We have already noted in our discussion so far (1) that the R.B.I. does not have any direct control on the increase in H coming through deficit spending of the government; (2) that there may be both regular and emergency pressures under which the government may choose to indulge in 'excess' deficit financing, and (3) that the R.B.I. cannot undo much of the adverse effect of excessive deficit financing on the expansion of money supply by open market sales operations. In such a context, increases in the statutory reserve ratio to the desired extent, subject, of course, to the statutory maximum, is one of the

things the R.B.I. can do to reduce the supply of adjusted H, provided the leakages from it discussed above are carefully plugged by a judicious combination of supplementary measures. If during any year the government is hard pressed for funds and resorts to excessive deficit financing causing excessive increase in H, the R.B.I. can successfully undo its expansionary effects on M and bank deposits, up to a point, by raising quickly the required reserve ratio and impounding the surplus reserves flowing into banks. How far the R.B.I. can go will depend upon the several magnitudes and parameters involved.

It should, however, be clear to the government that the R.B.I. cannot go on revising upward the statutory reserve ratio year after year. At most, it can keep this ratio at the maximum permissible level till such time as the government continues to indulge in excessive deficit financing on an increasing scale. If the excess deficit financing exceeds the level at which even the maximum impounding of reserves by the R.B.I. does not undo the entire excess ΔH, inflation will be inevitable. Such a situation was never reached in India over the period 1950–77—the period covered in this book. This implies that if the R.B.I. had used only one single tool of the variable cash reserve ratio at its disposal intelligently and boldly, the inflationary effects of actual excessive deficit financing by the government via the supply of money could have been completely avoided.

All along we are assuming that the government would not take any more undue advantage of the powers of the R.B.I. to change the cash reserve ratio of banks than it would if the reserve ratio is kept at its minimum. If the government learns from experience that by jacking up the reserve requirement of banks the limit of non-inflationary deficit financing can be enhanced, it may lose further fiscal discipline and begin to incur much larger deficits than before. This will gradually dry up the monetary-credit control power of the R.B.I. through upward revision of the reserve ratio of banks, unless, simultaneously, the maximum of this ratio is also revised upward from the current 15 per cent. But there is a limit to the latter course, whereas there is no limit to excessive deficit financing. That is, the power of the government to inject inflation into the economy (under the present-day paper currency regime) is truly unlimited! If it is bent upon pursuing an inflationary policy, all our suggestions regarding a non-inflationary monetary-credit policy become totally irrelevant. This, however, will be against the basic presumption of this work.

CHAPTER 8
RESERVE BANK CREDIT TO BANKS

8.1 Introduction

One important source of change in H is the Reserve Bank credit (R.B.C.) to scheduled banks. In recent years it has tended to be excessive, contributing significantly to excessive increases in the supply of money. Since October 1960 the conditions governing its cost and availability have not been the simple affair of the traditional bank rate theory. They have had a vast array of superimpositions, exemptions, and special concessions, varied from time to time. This has made the short history of the working of the R.B.C. arrangement to banks highly complicated.

The R.B.I. makes credit available to banks—only scheduled banks—in the following two forms:

1. as advances against eligible security, and
2. as rediscounts of eligible bills.

What security or bills are made eligible by the R.B.I. for its accommodation is important, because, other things being the same, banks prefer those security/bills as their earning assets which are acceptable to the R.B.I. as collateral or for rediscounting. In turn, the sectors/parties producing these earning assets for banks have an advantage over others in claiming credit from banks.

The advances are made against a wide variety of paper, which include Central Government securities, other approved securities, promissory notes of scheduled banks supported by export bills, other eligible bills or documents or usance promissory notes of banks' constituents (under the Bill Market Scheme during 1952–73).

Rediscounting (of eligible usance bills) has been undertaken by the R.B.I. only recently under its Bills Rediscounting Scheme of November 1970. Earlier to this, the Bill Market Scheme of 1952 had provided only for advances from the R.B.I. on the lodgement of bills as security and not for their rediscount. This Scheme was replaced by

the aforesaid Bills Rediscounting Scheme in November 1970.[1] Technically, rediscounting involves purchase of bills by the R.B.I.; therefore the R.B.I. does not treat it as borrowing by banks. Also, since technically the bills rediscounted by the R.B.I. represent its claims on the commercial sector, in the official data classification they are shown as such, and not counted as a part of the R.B.C. to banks who get the bills rediscounted in the first instance. For reasons already discussed (see Section 4.3), we do not consider this to be a correct view: rediscounting and advances are merely two different methods of providing refinance to banks, hence we are in favour of combining rediscounts with advances to banks and discussing them together.[2] This is also the common practice in other countries, where rediscounting is treated as a method of providing borrowed reserves to banks.

Till November 1973, the R.B.I. tried to control its credit to banks mainly by manipulating the *cost* of it. Only since then has the Bank thought fit to control directly the *availability* of its credit by bringing in a degree of discretionary control on its quantum. The cost of credit, though linked to the bank rate, was provided on a graduated scale, first through the Quota-cum-Slab System (1960–4) and then through the Net Liquidity Ratio (N.L.R.) of banks (1964–73). Further efforts were made to influence the borrowings of banks and their sectoral credit allocation through variations in the special refinance borrowings (and rediscounts under its Bills Rediscounting Scheme) by introducing and varying exemptions from the N.L.R. requirement and interest-rate discounts for bank loans to designated priority sectors. Since November 1975, with the direct control of the availability of the R.B.I. accommodation to banks, its cost is also fixed by the R.B.I. at its own discretion, though within a given range. Each of these developments will be reviewed briefly in this chapter.

8.2 Why Does the R.B.I. Lend to Banks?

Before reviewing the several measures adopted by the R.B.I. from time to time to control its credit to banks, let us ask a basic question:

---

[1] However, advances under the old Scheme continued to be made till November 1973 in respect of food procurement credit provided by scheduled banks.

[2] Without prejudice to the technical distinction between advances and rediscounts, we shall feel free to use the common word 'borrowings' of banks for the R.B.I. advances and rediscounts to them.

why does the R.B.I. lend to banks? The answer will throw light on the essentiality of such lending.

The R.B.I. lends to banks partly in fulfilment of the traditional central banking functions and partly for promoting certain new policy objectives. Under the former, we may place the 'lender of last resort' function and the provision of 'busy season' finance; under the latter, we may place refinance facilities and rediscounting under its Bills Rediscounting Scheme.

Three different interpretations of the 'lender of last resort' argument may be distinguished here. According to the standard one, a Central Bank should always stand ready to come to the rescue of a bank or banks in temporary need of cash when other sources of raising cash are practically closed or have become prohibitively costly. Such extreme situations arise especially during financial crises or panics, when there may be a run on a bank or banks. Such extreme situations are, however, things of the past. With the nationalization of major banks, strengthening of the non-nationalized banks through amalgamation and liquidation, close supervision and inspection of banks by the R.B.I., strengthening of the paid-up capital requirement of banks, deposit insurance, etc., the Indian banking system has been made panic-proof for all practical purposes. Moreover, the true safeguard against banking panics lies in the internal health and strength of individual banks, and not in the availability of last-minute borrowing opportunities. For despite the R.B.I.'s presence and its 'lender of last resort' facility, bank failures in the past could not be helped when they arose due to the inherent weaknesses of banks.

A softer version of this argument would be that, short of banking panics, situations can also arise when individual banks are subjected to excessive currency and clearing drains. The R.B.I. must then come to their rescue. Banks as a whole can also be victims of substantial loss of reserves, if there is a big enough shift in the asset preferences of the public from bank deposits to currency. Taking the latter argument first, we note that such shifts, outside of panic situations, are usually slow. Therefore, normally, they should not require any rescue operations on the part of the R.B.I.—the banks themselves should be able to handle them. Some individual banks, however, can be subject to further drains of cash, i.e. clearing drains, to other banks within the system. Normally, so long as the total reserve position of banks as a whole is not excessively tight, individual banks

should be in a position to meet their needs for cash in the inter-bank call-money market. The sole function of this market is to redistribute call money from surplus banks to deficit banks. Deficit banks, however, may find that this money is costlier than borrowings from the R.B.I. But that is a different argument—that of cost rather than availability of temporary accommodation. There seems no valid reason why the R.B.I. should subsidize borrowings of banks in temporary need of funds.

What however if the general reserve position is tight? We have already dealt with such a situation arising from the shift of the public from deposits to currency. We shall discuss it again below in the context of seasonal fluctuations. The more common source of reserve tightness may be the R.B.I.'s policy of monetary restraint in the face of excessive expansion of the demand for credit. In such cases reserve deficiencies will be more frequent, more acute, and more widespread. It may be argued that this is a fit case for the R.B.I. lending to banks and loosening the pressure on reserves. But if this suggestion is accepted, it will negate the very policy of monetary restraint the R.B.I. had thought fit to adopt. The R.B.I. cannot both adopt a policy of monetary restraint and be liberal in its lending operations.

The third argument is technical. Since reserve needs are estimated in advance and required reserves are calculated after the event, shortfalls in statutory reserves held with the R.B.I. can arise from time to time. A fine is paid by the bank which is short of reserves for the duration of the shortfall. In addition, the shortfall has to be made good. For this, the borrowing facilities at the R.B.I. are useful. But there are also other ways of making up reserve deficiencies open to individual banks, e.g. the opportunities offered by the inter-bank call-money market. Therefore, the borrowing facilities provided by the R.B.I. on this ground are not an essential either.

The paradoxical phenomenon is that, with the decreasing importance of 'the lender of last resort' function, the R.B.I. has been converted more and more into 'the lender of regular resort' as it has come to use its lending power to serve other ends as well. We shall now make a brief study of such lending.

The R.B.I. lends (or has lent in the past) to banks to help them provide 'busy-season' finance to the economy. Any flexible monetary system should adequately meet such seasonal expansion in the demand for funds, arising from any genuine seasonal expansion in

real economic activity, provided there is not already a plethora of funds carried over from the 'slack season'.

There are two chief methods whereby the R.B.I. can meet the busy-season expansion in the demand for funds, and therefore *H*. One is the method of open market purchase; the other is that of increased lending to banks. If the R.B.I. were free to conduct its open market operations for monetary policy purposes and were not under obligation to support the government-bond market, open market purchases would be the best way of meeting the busy-season needs of the system for a larger quantity of *H*. For then the initiative would lie with the R.B.I., and it would decide how much additional *H* is required for the seasonal expansion of credit, and therefore, given the expansion of *H* from other sources, how much additional open market purchase to undertake. Similarly, it would have the initiative in forcing slack-season contraction in credit (relative to the trend) by conducting open market sales of government securities. But, as we know, this option is not really open to the R.B.I. (see Chapter 6). Therefore, the R.B.I. resorts to the second-best solution —that of lending to banks.

Lending to banks can be made an effective tool of controlled seasonal expansion of credit (in an inflationary climate) only if the R.B.I. has complete control over the amount of its lending, and not merely over the terms on which advances are made. For if the R.B.I. specifies merely the terms on which it is willing to lend to banks, the amount of the borrowings comes to be determined by banks, and the R.B.I. thereby loses control over the course of *H*. The past history of the R.B.I.'s lending operations to banks shows clearly how the Bank has been forced to shift from one improvisation to another to be able to control its loans to banks.

Before 1951 banks did not make much use of the credit facilities of the R.B.I. In the post-war years they preferred to sell government securities (accumulated heavily during the war period) in a fully-supported government-bond market to meet their busy-season and other demands for funds. The R.B.I., too, under its 'full support policy' to the government-bond market, stood ready to buy whatever government securities were offered to it for sale. In November 1951 the R.B.I. announced a change in policy. It declared that, instead of buying outright government securities from banks, it would prefer banks to borrow from it on the strength of these securities as collateral. This was done so as to make the bank rate weapon of monetary

control effective, and to discourage banks from unloading government securities from their portfolios. As a further inducement to
banks to borrow from the R.B.I., the latter introduced in January
1952 additional borrowing facilities under its Bill Market Scheme.

All this has not however discouraged banks from switching out of
government securities during the busy season, mainly because the
R.B.I. has continued to support the government-bond market. And
it is hard to say with confidence that R.B.I. purchases are open
market purchases made at the initiative of the R.B.I., and not purchases made passively by it, the initiative resting with banks as
sellers. To gain further initiative, banks have altered greatly the
maturity distribution of their securities portfolio in favour of the
short-dateds and very short-dateds, thereby reducing substantially
the risk of capital loss from their sale during the busy season. All this
has resulted in a situation contrary to what the R.B.I. has presumably
desired. The disinvestment of government securities, instead of
decreasing, has accounted for a rising proportion over time of the
seasonal expansion in bank credit (see Swamy, 1975, pp. 187–92).
In addition, the borrowings of banks from the R.B.I. have also been
increasing over time. The cost of borrowing, manipulated through
the bank rate policy and the net liquidity ratio (discussed later in the
chapter), did not deter banks from increased borrowing, largely
because the lending rates of banks also increased to cover more than
adequately their increased cost of borrowing. Therefore the R.B.I.
has been forced to resort increasingly to discretionary control over
its lending to banks—a point we shall discuss further later in the
chapter.

The R.B.I. also uses (or has used) its lending power to banks
(*a*) to influence their credit allocation and (*b*) to develop a genuine
bill market in India. It does the former under its refinance facilities
to banks and the latter under its Bills Rediscounting Scheme. We
examine briefly the implications of this promotional use of a traditional control measure for the success of monetary control. For this
purpose, both the promotional uses may be studied together.

At this stage we do not question the desirability of the two objectives stated above, namely, influencing the credit allocation of banks
and the development of a bill market in India. To attain these
objectives, the R.B.I. has offered borrowing facilities to banks at
concessional rates. This combines two things: (1) a quantum of
loans, decided largely by banks, and (2) an interest-rate subsidy.

Through the former, the R.B.I. loses a part of the control over H to banks, for, given the terms of borrowing fixed by the R.B.I., it is the banks who determine the quantum of loans they would take from it, and, therefore, a part of the change in H. It is this factor which, in recent years, had eroded further whatever control the R.B.I. has enjoyed over money supply, and has compelled the R.B.I. to make frequent changes in its policy postures, and, finally, come to exercise almost discretionary control over its credit to banks.

The lesson to be drawn from the R.B.I.'s credit facilities to banks is that it should not leave them the right to determine the quantum of loans it should make to them. For a successful monetary policy, it is essential that the additional H be provided to the economy at the initiative of the R.B.I. rather than in response to the demand for such loans by banks. This would require practically closing down the R.B.I.'s loan window to banks for promotional purposes.

The logic of this recommendation should be made clear. One fundamental fact of life should be firmly understood—that though the R.B.I. and banks can increase the *nominal* amount of credit to any extent they like, they have no power to so increase the *real* amount of credit, which is ultimately determined by the asset preferences of the public (see Chapter 2). Therefore, assuming that the R.B.I. pursues a neutral money policy, its freedom to increase H becomes constrained by this objective. Then the deficit financing of the government, over which the R.B.I. has no control, further eats into this freedom or power. It is therefore in no position to keep an open loan window for banks, unless it stops caring for price stability. Once this is realized, the illusion about the R.B.I.'s unlimited power to lend, arising from the widespread failure to distinguish between nominal and real credit, can be discarded, together with the policies based on this illusion.

What about the interest-rate subsidy the R.B.I. has offered to banks in the form of lower interest rates on its refinance facilities and on loans made under the Bills Rediscounting Scheme? The interest-rate subsidy does not conflict directly with the exercise of monetary control, as does the amount of loans made. Therefore, inasmuch as the interest-rate subsidy is desired to be used as an inducement factor for influencing either the allocation of credit or the development of the bill market, it can as well be used without combining it with loans from the R.B.I. The R.B.I. can announce ground rules for the distribution of the subsidy, and individual

banks can be asked to provide information, along with documentary evidence, for the actual distribution of the subsidy. The R.B.I. should finance the payment of subsidy from its profits, which will, no doubt, reduce its net profits, but will also force both it and the government to consider if the subsidy to banks is worth it. Under the present arrangement, the subsidy question does not come to the forefront, as it is not distributed openly, and the R.B.I. earns increased nominal profits on its increased lending operations, though at the cost of monetary stability.

8.3 Bank Rate Policy

Formally, the bank rate is the rate at which the R.B.I. is prepared to buy or rediscount eligible bills of exchange or other commercial paper. Since the bill market is not well developed in India and since the R.B.I. does make advances to borrowers in other forms, the bank rate has come to form the basis for the rates at which the R.B.I. makes advances to various types of borrowers.

In the initial years of its establishment in 1935, the Bank used to provide all accommodation uniformly at the bank rate, except its ways and means advances to Central and provincial governments which used to be made at one per cent below the bank rate. Subsequently, agriculture was offered credit at concessional rates, and recently, credit at concessional rates has also been offered to other priority sectors, like exports. Further, till recently, the lending rate to banks varied according to their net liquidity ratios, which we shall study later in the chapter. The main point to note here is that there is no longer one single rate of interest at which the R.B.I. extends accommodation to its borrowers, but that there is a multiplicity of rates, most of which are closely linked with the bank rate.

The theory of the bank rate is divisible into two parts. The first is concerned with the operation of the bank rate as a weapon of monetary control of money supply. The second is concerned with the further effects of bank rate changes on the level of economic activity and the balance of payments of a country via changes in the level and structure of the domestic rates of interest. Briefly, the full theory of the bank rate states that an increase in the bank rate, other things being the same, would discourage borrowings of banks from the Central Bank and thereby the expansion of H and so of M, and lead to increases in the market rates of interest (more so in the short-term than in the long-term rates), which would exert downward pressures

on the aggregate demand and induce capital movements into the country, both the latter factors resulting in improvement in the country's balance of payments. The reverse is supposed to happen if the bank rate is reduced. Since we are concerned here only with questions of monetary control (narrowly defined), our attention will be devoted mainly to the effect of bank rate changes only on the borrowings of banks. We shall deal only briefly with the much wider second part of the bank rate theory.

According to the bank rate theory one immediate consequence of an increase in the bank rate is for the borrowings of banks. It is hypothesized that an increase in the cost of borrowed reserves, represented by an increased bank rate, the market rates of interest (including the lending rates of banks) and other factors remaining the same, would reduce the borrowings of banks, as they would now find it profitable to do so on a smaller amount of borrowings. This would dampen the expansion of H and so of M, assuming the money multiplier to remain unchanged.

In actual practice, however, it is extremely difficult to predict precisely the effect of a change in the bank rate on the amount of bank borrowings, let alone on M. For this effect will depend on several factors, such as (1) the degree of banks' dependence on borrowed reserves, (2) the sensitivity of the banks' demand for borrowed reserves to the differential between their lending rates and borrowing rates, (3) the extent to which the other rates of interest have already changed or change subsequently, (4) the state of demand for loans and the supply of funds from other sources, etc. Much will also depend on the refinance facilities made available by the R.B.I. at concessional rates, and the extent to which borrowing by banks is treated as a right, not a privilege, freely available to banks on specified terms.

The experience in India and most other countries is that even as an instrument for controlling only the amount of bank borrowings, the bank rate is not very efficient. The most important reason is that by varying merely the bank rate, the R.B.I. cannot vary the interest-rate differential between the lending rates of banks and the cost of borrowed reserves—the factor which determines the extent of profitability to banks from borrowing. This is because the R.B.I. has no control over the market rates of interest with which the lending rates of banks have a close relation. So if, with a rise in the market rates of interest, the banks can hike up their lending rates and thereby

more than cover their increased cost of borrowing without losing business, an increase in the bank rate would not discourage them from borrowing. The market, in turn, may be in a position to support a higher level of interest rates, if, under the impact of inflationary expectations generated by an on-going inflation, it expects much higher nominal rates of return from the use of borrowed funds.

Further, in order even to maintain a given control over the borrowings of banks, in a period of rising market rates and the lending rates of banks, the bank rate must also be increased continuously in step. But the bank rate is, usually, much more sticky than other rates, and changes in it are always discontinuous. Since bank rate changes have 'announcement effects' (i.e. effects or market reactions produced by the mere announcement of a change in the bank rate), Central Banks avoid making frequent changes in their bank rates even though changing conditions may warrant them.[3] Another defect of the bank rate policy of monetary control is that under it the initiative lies with banks. The banks determine what funds they would like to borrow at a given bank rate. Consequently, the R.B.I. loses control over the amount of borrowed reserves, and so of H and M. To overcome such a situation, the Bank has been compelled to take additional measures of various kinds, which we shall discuss later in this chapter.

The other part of the bank rate theory, or what may even be called the alternative theory of the bank rate, relates to the effect of bank rate changes on the domestic level and structure of interest rates, and thereby on the level of economic activity and the balance of payments of the country. An increase in the bank rate is supposed to be followed by a rise in the market rates of interest all along the line—more so and rapidly on the short end than on the long end of the interest-rate spectrum. This happens because the lending rates of banks are likely to be revised upward, partly to absorb the higher cost of borrowed reserves and partly to take in the slack in their lending rates which, being sticky, might have become lower than what the market could pay, and because the banks' supply of credit tends to be reduced consequent on their reduced borrowing from the Central Bank. The other market rates rise in sympathy or as the effect of costlier as well as tighter bank credit spreads through the market for loanable funds. The 'announcement effect' of changes in

[3] In India, up to a point, considerations of public debt management also inhibit the R.B.I. from raising the bank rate too much.

the bank rate is supposed to hasten the spread process, as the market has come to interpret an increase in the bank rate as the official signal for the onset of a period of relatively dearer as well as tighter money, and the reverse in the case of a reduction in the bank rate.

In the U.K., the bank rate (known as the discount rate) does undoubtedly constitute the king-pin of the interest-rate structure, especially on the short end. There the other market rates are adjusted fairly closely to this rate, so that a change in it does lead to a change in the entire rate structure in the same direction, as hypothesized in the theory. The relationship is not as tight elsewhere. Moreover, neither in the U.K. nor elsewhere can it be said that market rates do not vary independently of the bank rate. On the contrary, quite often, it is the case that market rates have gone up or down due to the operation of any number of forces impinging on them, and changes in the bank rate are a delayed recognition of such market changes, or a lagged adjustment to them. In such events, changes in the bank rate do not play the initiating role assigned to them in the theory. In India this has often been the case.

Bank rate changes in India have been relatively infrequent. The course of the bank rate soon after the establishment of the R.B.I. in April 1935 is given in Table 8.1. The weighted average advance

TABLE 8.1

BANK RATE IN INDIA

Period	Number of months	Bank rate (percentage)
(1)	(2)	(3)
November 1935—November 1951	192	3.0
December 1951—May 1957	66	3.5
June 1957—December 1962	67	4.0
January 1963—September 1964	21	4.5
October 1964—February 1965	5	5.0
March 1965—February 1968	36	6.0
March 1968—December 1970	34	5.0
January 1971—May 1973	29	6.0
June 1973—July 1974	14	7.0
August 1974—		9.0

Source: R.B.I. (1970), p. 49; R.B.I., *Report on Currency and Finance, 1973–4*, p. 56.

rate of the R.B.I. for scheduled commercial banks is given in Appendix G.

8.4 Supplementary Measures

We have noted above that the R.B.I. is inhibited in the full use of the bank rate as a weapon of monetary and credit control for discouraging excessive bank borrowings from it through a sufficient increase in the bank rate, as it would have an adverse effect on the gilt-edged market. Further, in the general inflationary climate which has prevailed in the economy since the mid-sixties and the consequent excess demand for bank funds (most of the time) at rates of interest which have not risen fully to allow for the expected rate of inflation, mild increases in the bank rate still leave it low enough to encourage banks to borrow excessively from the R.B.I. By itself, therefore, the bank rate weapon has not been as effective in discouraging banks from borrowing excessively from the R.B.I. and thereby checking the 'passive' expansion of H, as has been warranted by the requirements of monetary control for price stability. The R.B.I. has therefore been compelled to supplement the bank rate weapon with a system of differential lending rates of one sort or another, with or without discretionary control of its credit to banks and ceiling on the lending rates of banks. We discuss each of these measures in the next four sections.

8.5 The Quota-cum-Slab System (1960–4)

This system operated for four years from October 1960 to September 1964. It ushered in for the first time the system of differential lending rates at which the R.B.C. was made available to banks. They were allowed borrowing quotas, divided into slabs chargeable at different rates of interest. The sizes of the quota slabs were linked to the statutory reserve requirements of individual banks. The slab-rates of interest were linked to the bank rate. The sizes of different quotas, the number and sizes of slabs, and the rates of interest charged on them were varied from time to time.

To begin with, from 1 October 1960, a three-slab system was introduced. Banks were given a basic quota (of the R.B.C.) equal to 50 per cent of the average of the statutory cash reserves required to be maintained by a bank during each week of the previous quarter. Up to this quota, the banks could borrow from the R.B.I. at the prevailing bank rate. An additional quota (slab of borrowing) equal

to the basic quota was made available at 1 per cent above the bank rate. Borrowings above this limit were made chargeable at 2 per cent above the bank rate.

This system continued till July 1962, when a four-slab system was substituted in its place. The first slab chargeable at the bank rate was reduced to the sum equal to 25 per cent (instead of the previous 50 per cent) of the acquired reserves; the next slab, equal to the first slab, was charged at 1 per cent above the bank rate; the third slab, equal to 50 per cent of the required reserves, carried a charge of 2 per cent above the bank rate; and the rest was chargeable at 2.5 per cent above the bank rate.

A few months later, the R.B.I. reverted to the three-slab system by abolishing the fourth slab and charging all borrowings above 50 per cent of the value of required reserves 2 per cent above the bank rate.

In January 1963, the bank rate was raised from 4 per cent to 4.5 per cent, and the three-slab system was reduced to a simpler two-slab system. The first slab, equal to 50 per cent of the required reserves, was made available at the bank rate. Any further borrowing beyond this carried a charge only 1 per cent higher than the bank rate.

This was changed again in October 1963. The three-slab system was brought in again. Now, the first slab of borrowings available at the bank rate was made equal to 75 per cent of the required reserves. An equal amount was made available at 6 per cent rate of interest. Borrowings beyond this were charged at 6.5 per cent.

Thus, frequent changes were made in slabs and rates, creating an illusion of 'doing something'. But the effect was insignificant. The average ratio of borrowed reserves to required reserves of scheduled commercial banks for the 5-year period 1960–5 at 38.4 per cent was higher than the average of the previous two years 1958–60 at 32.8 per cent.

Through the quota-cum-slab system the R.B.I. was only tinkering with the problem of excess borrowings of banks from the R.B.I., without coming to grips with it. Fundamentally, the system suffered from the limitations of the bank rate policy. On the R.B.I.'s own admission (1970, p. 53), the system was defective as, under it, 'the rise in the average cost of borrowing would be small and gradual and banks could pass on the higher cost to their customers in the form

10

of higher lending rates'. Additionally, 'it did not take into account the differences in the banks' assets distribution'.

So, after four years of operation, the system was given up in favour of the 'net liquidity ratio' system, which was supposed to remedy both these defects.

Two additional measures were adopted during this period, but without much success. Since October 1962 'excess borrowing' in the highest slab has been allowed only at the discretion of the R.B.I. That is, an element of quantitative control of bank borrowings was admitted into the system. However, no information is available regarding the actual exercise of this discretion by the R.B.I.

Secondly, in July 1962, banks were asked to enforce higher minimum lending rates than before on all advances, excluding inter-bank advances.

8.6 The Net Liquidity Ratio (N.L.R.) System (1964–75)

The N.L.R. system was introduced in September 1964 and given up in November 1975. Under it, borrowing banks were charged interest rates for their borrowings from the R.B.I. on a sliding scale based on their net liquidity ratios. The N.L.R. of a bank was defined as the ratio of its net liquid assets to the sum of its demand and time liabilities. Thus,

$$NLR = \frac{R + CB + I - B}{L}$$

where

R = total reserves,
CB = current-account balances with other banks,
I = investment in government and 'other approved securities',
B = borrowings from the R.B.I., the State Bank of India, the Industrial Development Bank of India, and the Agricultural Refinance and Development Corporation, and
L = total demand and time liabilities.

Total reserves of a bank are defined as the sum of its cash on hand and balances with the R.B.I. Investments in government securities are investments (at book value) in Central and state government securities, including treasury bills, treasury deposit receipts, treasury savings deposit certificates, and postal obligations, such as national plan certificates, national savings certificates, etc. 'Other approved securities' are securities of state-associated bodies such as electricity

boards, housing boards, etc., and corporate bonds which are treated as approved securities under Section 5(*a*) of the Banking Companies Act (formerly, Banking Regulation Act), 1949. The numerator of the ratio gives a bank's net liquidity.

The minimum N.L.R. and the sliding scale of interest rates related to it were varied from time to time. When the N.L.R. system was introduced in September 1964, it was fixed at 28 per cent. It was progressively raised over the years till it reached the peak of 40 per cent in September 1973. It was reduced to 39 per cent in December 1974. The system was abandoned in November 1975. So long as the N.L.R. of a borrowing bank was above or equal to the minimum N.L.R. specified, the R.B.I. used to lend at the going bank rate (for non-priority sectors). For any 'excess borrowing', i.e. borrowing with the N.L.R. below the prescribed minimum, the rate of interest charged by the R.B.I. used to be progressively higher according to a prescribed formula. The usual formula was that the rate of interest payable by a borrowing bank would rise by one percentage point above the bank rate for every drop of one percentage point or a fraction thereof in the actual N.L.R., subject to a specified maximum of the penal rate. Initially, the penal rate was applicable to total borrowing of a bank from the R.B.I. Soon after, it was modified to apply only to additional borrowings. The maximum chargeable rate of interest was varied from time to time, too. From 23 July 1974 onwards, it was pitched at 18 per cent per annum, while the bank rate was hiked from 7 to 9 per cent. Recourse to refinance facilities from the R.B.I. within the N.L.R. system was free only till November 1973, when it was made discretionary for the R.B.I. Ultimately, the system was totally scrapped two years later.

Under the N.L.R. system the supply curve of borrowed reserves faced by a bank became a rising step function, instead of being perfectly elastic at the going bank rate. The height of the first step was given by the going bank rate. Subsequent steps were higher by one percentage point each. At the highest step, given by the maximum rate of interest, the supply curve became perfectly elastic. The width of the first step was given by the excess of 'net liquidity' of a bank over its minimum net liquidity, where net liquidity $= NLR \times L$. At any time, subsequent steps (except the last) were of equal width, given by 1 per cent of L of a bank. Thus, the R.B.C. available to each bank at any rate of interest varied positively with the amount of L of a bank.

Policy variations in the minimum N.L.R., bank rate, and the maximum rate of interest affected the position of the curve, shifting it mostly upwards. The widths of individual steps were mostly affected by variations in the excess of net liquidity positions and the liabilities of individual banks.

The N.L.R. system was devised to perform two special functions which the ordinary bank rate policy was incapable of performing:

1. The major function was to discourage 'excess' borrowings by banks by adding teeth to the bank rate policy. The latter, in its ordinary form, had become blunted in the inflationary climate and under the added responsibility of the R.B.I. to keep the interest cost of market borrowings of the government as low as possible. The new system permitted penalizing excess borrowings of banks by raising their cost of borrowing in a graduated manner, while keeping the bank rate unchanged and thus allowing the cost of market borrowings to the government to be kept low.

2. The second (as well as secondary) function was to discourage portfolio switches by banks from governments (and other approved securities) into loans and advances. One common problem faced by every Central Bank is such switches whenever it tries to control excessive expansion of bank credit to the commercial sector. Under the N.L.R. system, if a bank was already operating at or near the minimum of the N.L.R., any switching out of governments (or other approved securities) raised the marginal cost of borrowing—and the greater the switching the higher was this marginal cost. This, other things being the same, was supposed to act as a disincentive against switching.

But the new system did not really fulfil expectations either. Several factors conspired for its failure. The system had too many escape routes in the form of special refinancing exempt from N.L.R. obligations, which we discuss in the next section. Then, as pointed out in connection with the bank rate (Section 3), the higher borrowing cost *per se* does not reduce actual borrowing (or switching) if the lending rates of banks go up equally or more. This suggests the need for direct control of bank borrowings and statutory restrictions on switchings. The latter will be discussed in Chapter 9. The former seems to be the current policy of the R.B.I., adopted since December 1973. We shall discuss it later in this chapter.

8.7 Special Refinance and Exemptions from the N.L.R. System

The system of differential cost of borrowing from the R.B.I. linked with the N.L.R. of banks was not applied to all kinds of finance made available by the R.B.I. to banks. There were two important exemptions. One was the refinance made available in respect of bank advances to 'priority sectors', viz. credit for exports, agriculture, small-scale industries, food procurement, etc. The other was with respect to the refinance provided since June 1971 under the 'Bills Rediscounting Scheme' (introduced in November 1970).

The following special features of these exemptions are worth noting:

1. The *cost* of the refinance made available under both these schemes was independent of the N.L.R.s of banks. Most of it was provided at the going bank rate, whatever the N.L.R. of the borrowing/rediscounting bank. Some of it was provided even at concessional rates below the bank rate. For example, till July 1973 refinance up to 10 per cent of the annual average export credit of the previous year used to be made available at a rate $1\frac{1}{2}$ per cent below the bank rate. Similarly, concessional refinance at $\frac{1}{2}$ per cent below the bank rate was made available in respect of banks' short-term direct advances to agriculture and small-scale industries covered by the guarantee of the Credit Guarantee Organization.

2. The *proportion* of bank advances that could be refinanced from the R.B.I. at or below the bank rate was varied from time to time and from sector to sector. For example, till 17 February 1970 *full* refinance (i.e. up to an amount equal to the total of a bank's advances outstanding) was available to banks in respect of their short-term direct advances to agriculture and small-scale industries covered by the guarantee of the Credit Guarantee Organization. From February 1970 refinance was restricted to only *increases* in such credit over a prescribed base period (usually the immediately previous year). Concessional refinance for export credit has never been full. It has varied between 10 per cent and 20 per cent. Similarly, the extent of refinance for food-procurement advances has also been varied from time to time.

3. The list of *special refinance sectors* has been varied from time to time. At the time of the institution of the N.L.R. system in September 1964, bank advances to the following sectors were made eligible for the special refinance facilities of the R.B.I., independently of the borrowing banks' N.L.R.s: (*i*) exports, (*ii*) agriculture, (*iii*) small-

scale industries, and (*iv*) loans under the Bill Market Scheme. From time to time such facilities have been extended for varying periods in respect of bank advances for other purposes as well, such as food procurement by public agencies, defence packing-cum-supply credit, credit to oil companies and public-sector undertakings. The special refinance facility of the Bill Market Scheme, 1952 has been extended to the Bills Rediscounting Scheme (also known as the New Bill Market Scheme), introduced in November 1970.

4. The provisions about the impact of borrowing by banks under the special refinance facilities from the R.B.I. on their N.L.R.s have also been varied from time to time. Thus, initially, refinance for export credit did *not impair the N.L.R.* of banks. Later on, only 20 per cent of such refinance was allowed this status. After July 1973 the whole of the refinance against export credit was counted as borrowing from the R.B.I. for purposes of computing the N.L.R. and thus impaired 'fully' the N.L.R.s of banks. All refinance under the old Bill Market Scheme was supposed to impair fully the N.L.R. But under the new scheme, since the R.B.I. rediscounts (i.e. purchases) eligible usance bills from banks, the refinance made available under this head is not even treated as borrowing from the R.B.I., and, as such, it was not taken into account in the computation of the N.L.R.

Whether a particular item of refinance impaired or did not impair the N.L.R. was important, because, by affecting the N.L.R., it affected the cost of other kinds of borrowing.

5. To ensure that the cost advantage of special refinance facilities was passed on by banks to their respective borrowers, the R.B.I. had also specified *maximum lending rates of banks* to these sectors. Thus in February 1970, the maximum rate of interest chargeable by banks on all kinds of export credit, whether refinance was utilized for it or not, was fixed at 6 per cent. Of course, this rate was revised upward from time to time as the cost of R.B.I. refinance had gone up.

Thus R.B.I. policy concerning its refinance facilities to banks over the years had become very complicated. It was no longer the simple traditional bank rate policy, in which the bank rate is the only weapon of monetary control used. Even the N.L.R. policy involving a system of differential rates linked to the N.L.R.s of banks had been modified in numerous ways through several other qualifications and concessions attached to special refinance facilities. This had happened because the R.B.I. had unwittingly sought to use what was essentially an aggregative control measure as a method of affecting the sectoral allocation of bank credit. In the bargain, it definitely lost control of the aggregate supply of money and credit. Whether it has gained much in terms of sectoral allocation of credit, which could not be gained through alternative simpler measures, is a much harder question to answer. It requires much more detailed work than can be attempted in the present state of data availability. The necessary data are not published by the R.B.I. Even publication of information on the weighted average cost of borrowed reserves of scheduled commercial banks, which the R.B.I. used to issue regularly in its (monthly) *Bulletin* (Table entitled 'Borrowings By Scheduled Commercial Banks From The Reserve Bank Of India At Various Rates of Interest') was given up after 1969–70. And the period since then has seen heavy borrowing by these banks from the R.B.I. in the face of several manipulations of the N.L.R. system and hiking up of the bank rate and the R.B.I.'s maximum advance rate. For a proper evaluation of the N.L.R. system and the behaviour of the nationalized banking system, it is essential that the R.B.I. release all the relevant data in full detail.

In the absence of any quantitative information, we fall back upon a purely theoretical analysis in terms of the step supply curve of borrowed reserves of the N.L.R. system (discussed in the previous section). From the point of view of aggregate monetary control, various features of the special refinance facilities can be seen to affect the N.L.R. system in any one or more of the following three ways:

1. all refinance at the going bank rate merely widened the first step of the supply of borrowed reserves curve;

2. all refinance at rates below the bank rate added steps at the beginning of the supply of borrowed reserves curve; the heights of the new steps were determined by the R.B.I., but their widths were determined jointly by the borrowing public in the privileged sectors, the banks, and the R.B.I., which determined, from time to time, the proportion of the bank advances eligible for concessional refinance;

3. the R.B.I. decision to allow certain refinance not to impair the N.L.R. of banks was equivalent to a reduction in the minimum N.L.R. The extent of the reduction was given by the ratio of the 'non-impairing' refinance to the total amount of demand and time liabilities of a bank.

In each of these three cases the extent of the change in the supply of borrowed reserves curve depended upon the amount of refinance in each category availed of by individual banks. Thus, apart from differences in the initial net liquidity ratios of banks, the refinance facilities availed of by individual banks was a further source of difference in the shape and position of the 'supply of borrowed reserves' curve facing individual banks. More importantly, an individual bank was in a position to twist this supply curve (within limits, of course) to suit its needs. It was this feature of refinance facilities which made the R.B.I. share its powers of monetary control with banks.

8.8 New Refinance (or Basic Quota-cum-Discretion) Policy

Since the N.L.R. system, in view of the refinance/rediscounting facilities open to banks, was not found sufficiently effective in keeping the borrowings of banks within acceptable limits, and since inflation in the country was fast getting out of hand, the R.B.I. was forced to bring in some kind of quantitative control on its loans to banks in December 1973, further revised in November 1975.

The main features of the new refinance policy are summed up below:

1. *Basic Quotas.* Under the new refinance policy, banks are allowed basic borrowing limits. These limits relate to the total demand and time liabilities of banks as of a particular date. Starting with 1.5 per cent of such liabilities, they were raised to 2 per cent for a short period. Since 19 April 1974 they have remained fixed at 1 per cent of total liabilities. The reference date for such liabilities is progressively shifted forward to allow banks a larger absolute amount of 'basic' borrowing facilities as their total liabilities grow over time. The declared purpose of allowing banks this facility is to enable them to meet day-to-day clearing and other operational needs, and not to augment their lending resources.

2. *N.L.R.* The N.L.R. system was abandoned in November 1975, till when it had continued to govern the cost of R.B.I. accommodation. This cost is now fixed directly by the R.B.I. For 1977–8, the basic borrowing facility was made available at a rate of interest of 10 per cent per annum, while the bank rate continued to rule at 9 per cent.

3. *Special Refinance.* The categories as well as the eligible amounts of special refinance (over and above the basic quotas) have been severely limited. Such refinance has been continued mainly for 'public food-procurement' credit and export credit, both of which

have however been progressively tightened. For example, for the period November 1974 to October 1975, the refinance for public food-procurement was limited to 50 per cent of the excess over Rs 300 crores (and full refinance over Rs 450 crores of credit out-standing). By 1 June 1977 the base of internal finance by banks had been raised from Rs 300 crores to Rs 1,500 crores outstanding. Only credit in excess of the latter figure was eligible for 50 per cent refinance. The rate of interest charged was 10 per cent per annum. Refinance for export credit for 1977–8 was fixed at 50 per cent of the increment in export credit of a bank over the annual average of 1976.

4. *Discretionary Refinance.* All other refinance in regard to quan-tum, duration, and the rate of interest is entirely at the discretion of the R.B.I. Such discretionary accommodation is supposed to be determined on the basis of several criteria, such as the banks' general compliance with policy objectives, their credit–deposit ratios, sec-toral deployment of credit, and performance of individual banks in the field of export credit. During 1977–8 the cost of discretionary refinance ranged from 11.5 to 18 per cent.

5. *Bill Rediscounting.* From the end of December 1974 the new policy has been extended to the rediscounting of bills as well. The basic quota for the rediscounting of bills had been fixed at 10 per cent of the total inland bills purchased and discounted as of a specified date (varied from time to time). Rediscounting in excess of this was allowed at the R.B.I.'s discretion, not only in regard to amount but in respect of rates of interest also. The interest rates charged ranged between 11.5 per cent and 18 per cent for the busy season of 1975–6 and between 10 and 12 per cent during 1976–7. From the end of June 1977 this basic rediscount quota (of the total inland bills purchased and discounted) available on an automatic basis was withdrawn. Instead, all rediscount was placed at the discretion of the R.B.I.

6. *Seasonal Finance.* In September 1976 the R.B.I. announced a major departure from its long-established tradition when it declared that henceforth instead of looking at the credit situation in terms of busy and slack seasons, the credit policy would be formulated on an annual basis and subjected to review every quarter, as the seasonal distinction had lost much of its meaning.

The R.B.I., in its new refinance policy, has rightly given up the illusion that the borrowings of banks can be effectively controlled merely by manipulating the cost of its credit. So the adoption of quantity controls is a step in the right direction. But the new policy needs to be strengthened further along the following lines:

(*a*) Special and discretionary refinance needs to be completely given up. For such escape routes have a tendency to grow bigger and frustrate monetary planning in the name of flexibility. If credit to particular sectors is thought to be of prime social importance, appropriate guidelines can be issued to banks, consortia arrangements can be worked out, and other administrative arrangements made. In place of discretionary lending by the R.B.I., banks should be made to depend more and more on the call money market. Measures should also be taken to strengthen the banking system's capacity for quick redeployment of credit according to changing social needs and priorities.

(*b*) The basic quota approach deserves reconsideration. Why should the call money market not perform the task the basic quotas are supposed to perform? However, so long as they are there, it must be ensured that banks do not use them as another way of augmenting their lending capacities, but use them only temporarily to meet their unforeseen day-to-day needs. Further, the implications of basic quotas (plus special and discretionary refinance) for monetary planning should be clearly taken into account. They mean that a certain part of the neutral increase in H (see Chapter 5) gets allocated as the R.B.C. to banks. Therefore, this amount would not be available for deficit financing of the government or for other sources of change in H. While drawing incremental H budget for a period, the R.B.I. must take due cognizance of it. If the R.B.I. finds that other sources of change in H, including deficit financing of the government, are not manipulable, and there is a danger of excess increase in H, then *it must make a compensatory increase in the statutory reserve ratio of banks*. In fact, if the R.B.I. wishes to stick to its new refinance policy and estimates that basic quotas (for ordinary borrowing as well as rediscounting) plus special and discretionary refinance will amount to (say) 2 per cent of the total demand and time liabilities of banks, it should raise the statutory reserve ratio of banks by another 2 percentage points and thereby augment its own real lending capacity. The extra reserves can serve as the common contingency fund for banks. Also, the R.B.I. can use a part of it at its discretion.

8.9 Policy Achievements

What achievements have there been of all the policy manipulations since 1960? How far has the R.B.I. been successful in keeping the borrowings of scheduled commercial banks under control? In the inflationary climate since the mid-fifties, the problem has not been one of encouraging these banks to borrow from the R.B.I., but of keeping their borrowings under control. Such control is essential for over-all monetary-credit control, since the R.B.C. to banks is an important source of increase in H.

The R.B.I.'s record on this score has not been praiseworthy. Regarding the quantum of their borrowings, scheduled commercial banks have called the tune, not the R.B.I. This is understandable when borrowings are low, for the R.B.I. cannot compel banks to borrow more from it, but 'excess' borrowings must be interpreted to mean that the R.B.I. has been unsuccessful in keeping its credit to banks under check.

What is our criterion for excess borrowings? While none can be scientifically derived, two can be fruitfully improvised. In terms of our neutral H approach of Chapter 5, monetary planning would require preparation of an incremental H budget, giving absolute shares of various sources of change in H in the planned incremental H. While deciding upon such an allocation, all the claims of competing sectors and other relevant factors would be considered. This would provide a (rough) bench mark for neutral R.B.C. to banks. The actual R.B.C. to them can then be compared with it to arrive at excess R.B.C. to banks. We do not however propose to go into such a hypothetical exercise.

We follow a simple alternative to arrive at a broad qualitative judgement (Table 8.2).

The data used in Table 8.2 are annual averages of Friday figures up to 1974–5 and averages of 'last Friday of the month' figures thereafter. Borrowings by commercial banks from the R.B.I. became important only after the policy change of November 1951 mentioned in Section 8.2. Therefore, we have left out the year 1950–1. The data on borrowed reserves (BR) from 1970–1 onwards includes the R.B.C. made available to banks through rediscounting/purchase of inland commercial bills by the R.B.I. under its Bills Rediscounting Scheme introduced in November 1970.

What Table 8.2 reveals is interesting. Even when we leave out three exceptional years (1956–7, 1970–1 and 1976–7) of very high values of

156   *Monetary Planning for India*

TABLE 8.2

Ratio of Borrowed Reserves (*BR*) to Required Reserves (*RR*) of
Scheduled Commercial Banks (1951–2 to 1976–7)

Year	*BR/RR* (percentage)	Year	*BR/RR* (percentage)
(1)	(2)	(1)	(2)
1951–2	39.2	1964–5	47.7
1952–3	33.5	1965–6	53.8
1953–4	31.9	1966–7	29.7
1954–5	42.6	1967–8	20.4
1955–6	63.5	1968–9	62.0
1956–7	152.3	1969–70	69.2
1957–8	92.0	1970–1	148.4
1958–9	32.8	1971–2	74.0
1959–60	32.8	1972–3	16.3
1960–1	51.4	1973–4	34.9
1961–2	33.2	1974–5	73.8
1962–3	28.1	1975–6	84.3
1963–4	31.4	1976–7	125.7

Average (excluding 1956–7, 1970–1 and 1976–7) 46.9

Source: Appendix G.

the *BR/RR* ratio, the average *BR/RR* over the period covered is about 47 per cent. This means, on average, an effective cutting into (roughly) half the statutory reserve requirement for banks. In addition, the years during which the R.B.I. has tried to control excess expansion of *H* (and bank reserves) by hiking up the statutory reserve requirement, viz. 1960–1, and the four years 1973–7, have also been among the years of higher-than-average *BR/RR* except for the year 1973–4. And the value of *BR/RR* for the three years 1974–7 have been quite high—more than 100 per cent for the year 1976–7. A better comparison on this score is provided by Table 8.3.

In Table 8.3, column 2 gives average reserves actually impounded (*RR*$_i$) through changes in statutory reserve requirement over basic reserve requirement. Column 3 gives additional average *BR* over the previous year (*ΔBR*). Note the very high value of *ΔBR/RR*$_i$ for the year 1976–7.

From Table 8.3 it is not clear what the R.B.I. has tried to accomplish through impounding reserves on the one hand and simultaneous release of almost the whole of, or even more than, this

TABLE 8.3

RESERVES IMPOUNDED AND INCREMENTAL BORROWED RESERVES
OF SCHEDULED COMMERCIAL BANKS

(Selected Years)

Year	Reserves Impounded	Incremental *BR* (Rs crores)	$\Delta BR/RR_i$ [(3) ÷ (2)] (percentage)
(1)	(2)	(3)	(4)
1960–1	25	24	96
1973–4	258	157	61
1974–5	194	212	109
1975–6	118	48	41
1976–7	272	566	208

Sources: Table 7.1 and Appendix G.

amount through the widening of its loan/discount window on the other hand. And note that the high values of BR/RR or $\Delta BR/RR_i$ for the year 1976–7 relate to the first full year of the new discretionary refinance policy launched by the R.B.I. in November 1975.

The results of regression analysis of the empirical evidence on the borrowed reserves of scheduled commercial banks over the period 1950–1 to 1976–7 tell a more interesting story (see Appendix F, Section F.3). They show that the demand of such banks for borrowed reserves has not been affected significantly by either the bank rate of the R.B.I. (weighted average bank rate up to the year 1960–70 for which period such data are available), or the weighted average advance rate of banks, or the excess of the latter over the former. The two most important determinants of borrowed reserves have been the demand for loans and advances, as measured by the credit–liabilities ratio, and required reserves of banks, each one exerting a positive effect on borrowed reserves. A 1 per cent increase in required reserves has led, on average, to an increase of 0.53 per cent in borrowed reserves, whereas the elasticity of demand for borrowed reserves with respect to the credit–liability ratio was estimated at about 5.7. They show the ineffectiveness of the bank rate policy even when administered differentially, partial neutralization of variable reserve ratio policy, and strong domination of the demand for loans and advances on the borrowed reserves of banks.

CHAPTER 9

THE STATUTORY LIQUIDITY RATIO

9.1 Introduction

The Statutory Liquidity Ratio (S.L.R.) for banks is yet another tool of monetary control in the hands of the Reserve Bank of India. For aggregative monetary control, it works indirectly rather than directly. Therefore its role as a tool of monetary control is not fully appreciated, or even understood. The chief direct role of the S.L.R. is to govern, howsoever imperfectly, the allocation of total bank credit between the government and the commercial sector. The indirect role of monetary control is played through this direct role.

There are two distinct ways in which the S.L.R. operates as an instrument of monetary control: one is by affecting the borrowings of the government from the R.B.I.; the other is by affecting the freedom of banks to sell government securities or borrow against them from the R.B.I. In both ways the creation of H and thereby variations in the supply of money is affected.

9.2 The S.L.R.

Banks in India are subject not only to a cash reserve requirement; they are also subject to a statutory liquidity requirement. Under the latter, each bank is required statutorily to maintain a prescribed minimum proportion of its daily total demand and time liabilities in the form of designated liquid assets. These liquid assets consist of (a) excess reserves, (b) unencumbered government and 'other approved securities', and (c) current-account balances with other banks. Thus, the statutory liquidity ratio (S.L.R.) of a bank is defined as follows:

$$SLR = \frac{ER + I^* + CB}{L}$$

where

ER = Excess reserves,

$I^* =$ Investment in unencumbered government and 'other approved securities',

$CB =$ Current-account balances with other banks, and

$L =$ Total demand and time liabilities.

Excess reserves are defined as total reserves (cash on hand plus balances with the R.B.I.) minus statutory or required reserves with the R.B.I. Investments in government and 'other approved securities' are as defined for the N.L.R. in Section 8.6. Securities are unencumbered if loans have not been taken against them from the R.B.I.

It is interesting that the presence of inter-bank balances on current account in the definition of the S.L.R. opens a way whereby banks can collude to beat the S.L.R. requirement to some extent. For example, if bank A makes a current-account deposit of Rs 1 crore with bank B in exchange for B's current-account deposit of equal amount with it, the SL as well as L of each bank A and B will increase by Rs 1 crore each. But since the S.L.R. is less than 1, this will necessarily raise the S.L.R. of each bank A and B.

The S.L.R. should be carefully distinguished from the N.L.R. of the previous chapter. In the matter of definition, the two differ in the computation of their numerators—statutory liquidity (SL) and net liquidity (NL). There are only two differences:

1. NL includes the total cash reserves of banks, whereas SL includes only excess reserves; and

2. SL excludes from gross liquidity only borrowings from the R.B.I. against government and other approved securities, whereas NL excludes (from gross liquidity) not only *all* borrowings from the R.B.I., but also borrowings from the State Bank of India, the Industrial Development Bank of India, and the Agricultural Refinance and Development Corporation.

The S.L.R. (of 20 per cent) was first imposed on banks under the Banking Regulation Act 1949. Statutory liquidity was defined to include, among other liquid assets, total reserves of banks and not merely their excess reserves. The present formulation of the S.L.R. given above was enacted in September 1962 and made effective from 16 September 1964. The change from total reserves to excess reserves was introduced to prevent banks from offsetting the impact of variable reserve requirements by liquidating their government security holdings. Also, the S.L.R. was revised upward to 25 per cent.

The S.L.R. as a policy tool has been used mainly during the seventies. It has been revised upward from time to time. (The state co-operative banks have been exempted from the higher S.L.R., which for them continues to be 25 per cent.) The brief history of the uses of the S.L.R. for commercial banks is summed up in Table 9.1.

TABLE 9.1

S.L.R. FOR COMMERCIAL BANKS

(Since 16 September 1964)

With effect from	S.L.R. (percentage)
(1)	(2)
16 September 1964	25
5 March 1970	26
24 April 1970	27
28 August 1970	28
4 August 1972	29
17 November 1972	30
8 December 1973	32
29 June 1974	33

In July 1978, the S.L.R. continued to be 33 per cent. It is not known what the actual value of the liquidity ratio (*LR*) of banks has been over the years or how far banks have observed the stipulated S.L.R. The R.B.I. does not publish any data on it, or on its components. Specifically, it does not publish what part of the government and other approved securities held by banks are encumbered at any time. It is thus not possible to compute on our own the actual *LR* of banks, the extent of shortfall or excess of actual liquidity of banks over the stipulated *SL*, or the voluntary demand of banks for government securities. The R.B.I. should fill this lacuna and publish the missing information on the actual *SL* of banks for all the previous years and as a regular feature in future. Only then can the working of the S.L.R. system be evaluated intelligently.

9.3 S.L.R. and Government Share in Bank Credit

The chief direct role of the S.L.R. is presumably to ensure a certain minimum share of bank credit to the government. In this sense it is the chief instrument by which the R.B.I. can govern the allocation of total bank credit between the government and the rest of the economy. The tool, however, does not work perfectly. It suffers from certain defects, all of which arise because of components other than investment in unencumbered government securities in the definition of *SL*. If the chief objective of the S.L.R. is to ensure a certain minimum proportion of bank resources to the government, it will be most efficient to stipulate the requirement directly in terms of the proportion of total liabilities or deposits to be invested in unencumbered government securities, in place of the present S.L.R.

Of the other components of *SL*, the chief competition for investment in government securities has come from investment in 'other approved securities'. Over the 13-year period 1964–77, the ratio of inter-bank current-account balances to liabilities (*CB/L*) has averaged only 1 per cent. The ratio of excess reserves to liabilities (*ER/L*) averaged 2.71 per cent over 1964–74, with small year-to-year fluctuations. Over the four years 1973–7, this ratio has fallen continuously and sharply—from 2.58 in 1973–4 to 1.97 in 1976–7. The absolute decline in the ratio is still small. Nevertheless, the gainer from this fall has been the investment component of the S.L.R. But when we come to the 'investment–liability ratio' component of the S.L.R. and examine the composition of the investment portfolio of banks, we notice an important development. In 1966–7 (the first year for which such data are available), investments in 'other approved securities' were about 12 per cent of total investments and the rest were investments in government securities. Ever since, the former have been growing relatively to the latter year after year, so that in 1976–7 about 29 per cent of total investments of scheduled commercial banks were in 'other approved securities' and 71 per cent (in place of 88 per cent in 1966–7) in government securities. Consequently, the ratio of investment in government securities to the aggregate deposits of banks shows a declining trend. The upward revisions of the S.L.R. have reversed this trend only temporarily. The relevant information is summed up in Table 9.2.[1]

No official policy statement on these developments is available. Nor is the composition of 'other approved securities', especially the share of corporate bonds in them, known. For rational credit

---

[1] All the ratios in this chapter have been calculated from annual data which are averages of Friday figures till 1974–5 and averages of 'last Friday of the month' figures thereafter.

162 *Monetary Planning for India*

TABLE 9.2
S.L.R. and Ratio of Investment (in Government Securities) to Liabilities of Scheduled Commercial Banks

Year	S.L.R. (percentage)	Investment–Liabilities Ratio (percentage)
(1)	(2)	(3)
1965–6	25	26.3
1970–1	26–8	21.8
1971–2	28	21.6
1972–3	28–30	23.4
1973–4	30–2	22.2
1974–5	32–3	21.8
1975–6	33	21.7
1976–7	33	21.2

planning, the subject deserves careful examination and conscious policy-decisions. We would suggest replacing the present S.L.R. system by a system of statutory investment–liability ratios separately for unencumbered government securities and quasi-government securities. The alternative system will be operationally neat, efficient, and without leakages. It will strengthen fiscal, monetary, and credit planning in the economy.

In fiscal terms, the 'statutory investment ratio for government securities', called S.I.R.(G.S.) hereafter, will ensure a growing captive market of banks for such securities, and at a low enough interest cost to the government.[2] This will help control deficit financing of the government better, because government borrowing from the market (including banks) is not counted as a part of deficit financing. This is important for monetary planning, because containing 'excess' deficit financing will help contain 'excess' generation of money supply. As explained elsewhere (Section 3.5), Reserve Bank credit is fundamentally different from commercial bank credit. The former is the most important determinant of the latter. When the government borrows from the R.B.I., it increases H and thereby the total supply of money as well as total bank credit, given stable

[2] This should not be interpreted to mean that we are giving unqualified support to the low-interest-rate policy for government bonds. We are simply not examining this question.

money and credit multipliers. But when the government borrows from commercial banks instead, other things being the same, it merely reallocates total bank credit as between the government and the commercial sector, without affecting the total amount of money/ bank credit. This distinction between the two kinds of borrowing (credit) is of great practical importance. The rest of the discussion in this section is based on this distinction.

The policy implication of the distinction is clear: if the government honestly wants to avoid any 'excess' increase in the supply of money, it should meet government deficit entirely from the commercial bank credit, and not from the R.B.I. credit. It will be recalled (see Chapter 5) that we are using the term 'excess' deficit in the sense of government deficit in excess of the 'neutral' deficit required to increase actively the amount of H to meet the growing demand for money in a growing economy in the climate of monetary stability. Normally, in arriving at the figure for 'excess' deficit, account will already have been taken on the side of capital receipts through market borrowings of the additional funds which will be invested by banks in new government securities in the normal course under existing institutional arrangements. Therefore in order that the 'excess' deficit may also be absorbed entirely by banks, special measures will need to be taken. It is here that the S.L.R., or better, S.I.R.(G.S.), policy can be brought into action, if the rate of interest on government bonds is not to be allowed to go up.

Unless banks are already holding undesired excess investment in government securities, an increase in the S.I.R.(G.S.) will force them to invest a larger proportion of their total resources in government securities. Therefore, given the size of the excess deficit, the expected average amount of total deposits of banks over the year when the average amount of H is the 'optimal' amount, and given the excess liquidity of banks, the S.I.R.(G.S.) can be revised upward suitably to yield enough extra investment by banks in government securities to fill up its 'excess' deficit fully. It follows that the R.B.I. must be ready to raise S.I.R.(G.S.) substantially, if it is serious about maintaining monetary stability, and the government insists on having too large an excess deficit. The only alternative is the present policy of drift, wherein the excess deficit is met from excess borrowings from the R.B.I., resulting in excess creation of H and M, leading to inflation.

One implication of the variable S.I.R.(G.S.) (or S.L.R.) policy recommended above should be clear. Given the total bank credit, controlled through a rigorous control over H, increased bank credit to the government will automatically mean reduced bank credit to the commercial sector. Neither the government, nor banks, nor commercial borrowers are likely to take kindly to such a situation. Arguments would be put forward to the effect that credit restriction to the commercial sector would hurt production as well as investment and profits of banks, and so must be relaxed (see Gupta, 1978a). Pressure would also be brought to bear on the government and the R.B.I. for giving greater credit to the commercial sector. Capitulation to such arguments and pressure is a sure way to inflation. This has happened in the past and is likely to happen in the future as well, unless the importance of monetary stability and the sources of monetary disequilibria in the economy are correctly recognized. Once the objective of monetary stability is fully accepted and the illusory policy of forced saving through inflation is honestly rejected as either unworkable or counter-productive or socially undesirable, the ceiling on additional bank credit must also be accepted as a necessary corollary. Then the government must consciously decide how this additional bank credit must be apportioned between the government and the commercial sector. The government budget is an instrument for implementing government policy and plans. Therefore, if it wants relatively more bank credit to flow to the commercial sector, it must be satisfied with a smaller share of it for itself. Alternatively, if it chooses itself to borrow more from banks, it must be prepared for curtailment of credit to commercial borrowers.

9.4 S.L.R. and Portfolio Switches

A related function of the S.L.R. policy is to control 'excessive' creation of credit by banks for the commercial sector through portfolio switches. In countries like the U.S.A. and Canada, which do not have S.L.R.-type secondary reserve requirements, it is a standing problem that during periods of business expansion banks frustrate restrictive policy measures adopted by the Central Bank, by portfolio switches from government securities into loans and advances. Thus the commercial sector is not starved of bank credit and the boom continues.[3] This has been the experience in India as well.

[3] The 'availability doctrine' of Rosa (1951) goes against the above widely-held view by suggesting that banks will desist from such portfolio switches, because

Broadly speaking, a bank's portfolio of government securities acts as a kind of shock absorber. Fluctuations in the demand for loans (at given rates of interest) are absorbed through opposite variations in the investment–liability ratio for government securities. In all this, banks are guided by profit considerations and not by considerations of monetary stability. In a regime of S.I.R.(G.S.), in normal times banks would carry some excess of government securities over the minimum required, either because, given the prevailing *net* rates of return from lending and investing,[4] the demand for loans from 'acceptable' customers, and the state-of-market uncertainty, the unconstrained optimal investment–deposit ratio for government securities may turn out to be higher than the S.I.R.(G.S.), or because government securities act as a good substitute for excess reserves to meet the unexpected currency and clearing drains.[5] Required reserves are available to meet these demands only for a short duration of the intra-reserve-period.[6] Excess reserves carry perfect liquidity, but no profitability. They involve an opportunity cost. Therefore, banks try to economize on them. One way of doing so is to hold assets which are highly liquid and earn some return. Call loans and investments in government securities are examples of such assets. Government securities can be used to borrow funds from the R.B.I. if need be, they can be sold without much fear of a big capital loss in a market well supported by the R.B.I. This is particularly true of treasury bills and other government securities of short maturity. Therefore government securities act as a good-enough substitute for excess reserves. But, with S.I.R.(G.S.), it is not all government securities but only the securities in excess of the statutorily required

otherwise they will have to incur capital losses on the government securities they sell. We do not go into an evaluation of this argument, as enough literature is available on it. We only note that the empirical evidence does not lend support to Rosa's hypothesis.

[4] Net of the cost of servicing lending and investing and of the associated risk premia. The gross rates of interest on both lending and investing are 'controlled' by the R.B.I.

[5] Under the current S.L.R. system it is not easy to define the quantum of the statutorily required minimum of government securities for banks. Hence our argument in the present section can be adapted to the S.L.R. system only in broad qualitative terms, and not in quantitative terms.

[6] Since 1956 the reserve period has been one week. The minimum reserve requirement is related to the *average daily balance* of banks with the R.B.I. over the week from Saturday to Friday.

minimum that would be available either for sale or as collateral against borrowing. Therefore, normally, banks would carry a cushion of 'excess' government securities. It is only these excess securities which would provide a margin of substitution between them and loans and advances, or a scope for portfolio switches. The greater, therefore, the 'excess' of government securities which banks are holding at any point of time, the greater the danger of portfolio switches. The extent of portfolio switches will, of course, depend upon the relative net rates of return from investing and lending and the demand for loans in the event of externally-controlled lending rates of banks.

There is one immediate policy implication of this analysis. If banks are carrying 'too much' excess investment in government securities, there would be a constant danger of above-normal expansion of loans and advances through portfolio switches as soon as the demand for bank loans picks up. A more rigorous way of saying the same thing would be the following: that the demand for 'excess' government securities from banks would be an increasing function of the rate of interest on government securities and a decreasing function of the rate of interest on loans, the bank rate, and the demand for loans. Other things being the same, therefore, as the demand for loans goes up, the demand for 'excess' government securities (along with the demand for excess reserves) will go down. This means that a part of the hitherto desired 'excess' government securities will become undesired and, in order to move back into portfolio equilibrium, banks will try to move out of government securities into loans and advances.

In such a situation, the monetary authority must first decide whether such portfolio switches and the consequent expansion of bank credit to the commercial sector would be inflationary and to what extent. It must then decide and act upon a suitable package of corrective measures. One of these measures can be an adequate temporary upward revision of the S.I.R.(G.S.), so as to lessen substantially the possible switching operations by banks. Of course, it will be important not only to push up the S.I.R.(G.S.) on paper, but also to enforce it strictly. In recent years banks have not been observing fully the higher S.L.R. or the higher statutory reserve requirement.

The idea is that the R.B.I. should minimize the 'passive' creation of 'excess' high-powered money, and through it 'excess' generation of *M*. Undesired excess government securities have (in the past) entitled banks to get reserves from the R.B.I. through sale of such securities or borrowing against them. These reserves, then, serve as the basis for the 'unplanned' creation of credit. The N.L.R. System, with special refinance and rediscounts as escape routes, was a weak instrument for discouraging borrowing by banks (Sections 8.6 and 8.7). In comparison, the S.L.R. is a much stronger instrument— at least, potentially so—because, if revised upward adequately, it could restrict directly the borrowing capacity of banks to any extent. With discretionary control over the borrowings of banks under the New Refinance Policy (Section 8.8), such borrowings can now be controlled much more easily as well as directly, without manipulating the S.L.R., though the actual control over total borrowings of banks from the R.B.I. leaves much to be desired. The problem of outright sale of government securities by banks in the market supported by the R.B.I. still remains. This can be tackled successfully by the manipulation of the suggested S.I.R.(G.S.).

CHAPTER 10

RESERVE BANK CREDIT TO
DEVELOPMENT BANKS

10.1 Introduction

According to R.B.I. terminology, this chapter should have been titled 'Reserve Bank Credit to the Commercial Sector'. We have done otherwise because, in our opinion, the latter title is misleading. For the R.B.I. does not extend any credit directly to the commercial sector. Whatever credit it wishes to direct specifically to this sector is routed through other financial institutions—whether commercial and state co-operative banks, or development banks. For reasons given elsewhere (see Section 4.5), it is advisable, both for analytical and for policy purposes, to recognize the existence and role of these other financial institutions in channeling R.B.C. to the ultimate deficit spenders, whether the commercial sector or the government. For the same reason and contrary to R.B.I. practice, we have counted the 'bills rediscounted and purchased' by the R.B.I. as the 'R.B.C. to banks' and not as the 'R.B.C. to the commercial sector' (see Section 4.3). This is only consistent with R.B.I. practice elsewhere. For example, the R.B.I. makes large sums of credit available to state governments and state co-operative banks for further channeling for agricultural purposes. But the R.B.I. does not classify such credit as credit to the commercial sector. Instead, loans made to state governments are classified as the R.B.C. to the government; the loans and advances made to the state co-operative banks are also shown as such in most statements of the R.B.I. Perhaps only in its table entitled 'Factors Affecting Money Supply', because of peculiar (and unwarranted) consolidation of the balance sheets of the banking system as a whole, does the R.B.C. to banks get neglected.

We now come to the main subject of this chapter. Apart from its traditional central-banking functions, the R.B.I. also has a variety of developmental and promotional functions. In this new role the

R.B.I. has helped in the establishment and progress of several new specialized financing agencies, called development banks. This has meant not only initial subscription to the share capital of some of these institutions by the R.B.I., but also regular provision of funds to them through loans and advances, and subscription to their bonds/debentures for financing their lending operations. This has resulted in the creation of an additional source of increase in high-powered money (H). For monetary planning, it is this fact which must be taken fully into account.

10.2 The Reserve Bank and Development Banks

Separate development banks have been set up in the country for industry and agriculture.

In the field of industrial-development banking, the Industrial Development Bank of India (I.D.B.I.) is the apex institution. It was set up in 1964 as a wholly-owned subsidiary of the R.B.I., but was made an autonomous corporation with effect from 16 February 1976. The I.D.B.I. is empowered to finance all types of industrial concerns engaged (or planning to be engaged) in the manufacturing or processing of goods, or in mining, transport, generation and distribution of power, etc., both in the public and in the private sectors. It provides direct financial assistance to industrial concerns in the form of direct loans and underwriting of, and direct subscriptions to, their shares and debentures. It provides indirect financial assistance to industrial units by providing refinance to eligible financial institutions (state financial corporations and licensed scheduled commercial banks/state co-operative banks) in respect of industrial term loans and by rediscounting bills/promissory notes arising out of sales of indigenous machinery on a deferred payment basis. It also gives direct loans to industrial concerns for exports and refinance to eligible banks against the medium-term export credit granted by them to exporters of capital and other engineering goods. Finally, as the apex bank in the field of industrial-development banking, it subscribes to the shares and bonds of other financial institutions in the field.

The R.B.I. has played a leading role in the growth of the I.D.B.I. It has been the principal source of funds: it has provided the entire initial paid-up capital of Rs 10 crores, and it also gives loans and advances (which stood at Rs 526 crores at the end of June 1977). These loans are made from the National Industrial Credit (Long-

Term Operations) Fund of the R.B.I., which was set up in July 1964 along with the setting up of the I.D.B.I. Started with an initial contribution of Rs 10 crores, the Fund had grown to Rs 715 crores by the end of June 1977, through annual contributions by the R.B.I. from its profits.

Other industrial development banks in *the public sector* are: (1) Industrial Finance Corporation of India (I.F.C.I.), (2) Industrial Reconstruction Corporation of India (I.R.C.I.), (3) State Financial Corporations (S.F.C.s), and (4) State Industrial Development Corporations (S.I.D.C.s).

All these term-lending institutions have been set up at the initiative of the R.B.I. The first one to be established was the I.F.C.I., in 1948, followed by S.F.C.s and S.I.D.C.s at state levels. The I.R.C.I. was set up in 1971. The R.B.I. has provided them with funds by subscribing to their share capital and/or bonds/debentures and by making loans and advances. With the establishment of the I.D.B.I. in 1964, all the shares held by the R.B.I. were transferred to the former. The I.D.B.I. extends refinance loans to these institutions and also subscribes to their bonds/debentures. We have already said that the R.B.I. continues to be the principal source of funds to the I.D.B.I. Thus, the R.B.I. credit gets channelled to these institutions both directly and (mainly) through the I.D.B.I. The latter also subscribes to the bonds/debentures of the only industrial development bank in *the private sector*, namely, the Industrial Credit and Investment Corporation of India (I.C.I.C.I.), established in 1955.

It may be mentioned briefly that the R.B.I. also played an active role in the establishment of the Unit Trust of India (U.T.I.) in February 1964 and supplied half of its share capital. The U.T.I. is also empowered to borrow from the R.B.I. The U.T.I. raises the bulk of its funds from the investing public by selling them 'units'. Its assets consist almost entirely of investments in the shares and debentures of industrial companies which it also underwrites.

Similarly, the R.B.I. has provided share capital for the Deposit Insurance Corporation—its wholly-owned subsidiary, set up in 1962.

The R.B.I. provides credit to agricultural development banks too. The all-India institution in the field is the Agricultural Refinance and Development Corporation (A.R.D.C.—formerly the Agricultural Refinance Corporation). At the regional levels in the states are central land development banks (also known as central land mortgage banks). These financial institutions provide medium and long-term finance for agriculture. The A.R.D.C. was established on 1 July 1963. It provides refinance mainly to the state co-operative banks, central land development banks, and the scheduled commercial banks which are its shareholders. It does so by way of loans and advances and by making investments in the debentures of eligible institutions.

At the end of June 1977 the total refinance outstanding of the A.R.D.C. was about Rs 722 crores. Of this, Rs 525 crores was in the hands of state/central land development banks (in the form of debentures), Rs 186 crores was given in the form of refinance loans to scheduled commercial banks, and only Rs 11 crores to state co-operative banks.

The R.B.I. has made a major contribution to the share capital (of Rs 25 crores) of the A.R.D.C. It also gives it loans and advances. At the end of June 1977 these loans and advances stood at Rs 173 crores. The R.B.I. also extends direct credit to central land development banks by investing in their debentures. At the end of June 1977 these investments amounted to Rs 8.6 crores.

For providing term finance for agriculture (through appropriate agencies) the R.B.I. had set up in 1956 the National Agricultural Credit (Long-Term Operations) Fund. Started with an initial contribution of Rs 10 crores, the Fund had grown to Rs 495 crores by the end of June 1977 through annual contributions from its profits by the R.B.I.

The common feature of financial institutions like the I.D.B.I., the A.R.D.C., the L.D.B.s, etc. should be clear by now. They are development and not commercial banks. The latter accept demand deposits, which the former do not. The main source of funds of development banks is not deposits of the public but their share capital, reserves, and borrowings (through the issue of bonds or debentures or otherwise) from the government, the R.B.I., and others. As the name suggests, the I.D.B.I. specializes in the promotion of industrial development by providing finance (primarily long-term, but also medium- and short-term) directly as well as through the I.F.C.I., the S.F.C.s, etc. Similarly, the A.R.D.C. and the L.D.B.s specialize in providing finance for the development of agriculture. Thus the R.B.I. uses these several agencies to channelize its credit into the two most important sectors of the economy—an important promotional activity.

10.3 The Growth of R.B.C. to Development Banks

The R.B.C. to development banks as a source of change in high-powered money (H) became important only after the establishment of the I.D.B.I. in 1964, or even much later, from 1970–1 onwards. At the end of March 1951 this kind of credit outstanding was only Rs 1.2 crores; over the next five years it had increased to only Rs 6 crores. Another five years later, at the end of March 1961, it stood at only Rs 9 crores; but by March end of 1966 it had increased to Rs 47 crores. During the seventies this credit has grown rapidly. The annual average value of it for 1976–7 stood at Rs 653 crores. For further details, reference may be made to Tables 4.1, 4.2, and 4.3.

10.4 Monetary Planning and Reserve Bank Credit to Development Banks

For monetary planning it is important to remember that the net R.B.C. to whomsoever given, when adjusted for a sector's due share in the net non-monetary liabilities of the R.B.I. (see Section 4.8), causes a change in H. This is equally true of the R.B.C. to development banks.

We recall our discussion of a related point in Section 4.8, about the R.B.M. effect of the R.B.C. to development banks. The R.B.I. makes this credit available from its accumulated surpluses held in the form of two national funds, viz. the National Industrial Credit (Long-Term Operations) Fund and the National Agricultural Credit (Long-Term Operations) Fund. From this, it may be inferred that any loans or investments made by the R.B.I. from these owned funds would not affect the R.B.M., which is true in an accounting sense. But, analytically, *all* R.B.C. is financed partly from the monetary and partly from the net non-monetary liabilities of the R.B.I. Therefore, whatever the accounting practice and the institutional arrangement supporting it, from the economic point of view the R.B.C. to development banks, too, is financed partly from the monetary and only partly from the net non-monetary liabilities of the R.B.I. Thus the R.B.C. to development banks also adds to the stock of H.

Granting that the R.B.C. to development banks results in the creation of H, what attitude should we have towards it? Should it differ from that towards other sources of increase in H? The answer is 'no'. And the explanation is quite general. While the productivity or growth-promoting quality of particular kinds of credit is surely an important consideration, it should be taken into account at the stage of deciding about allocation of credit. This productivity will, then, reflect itself in the expected rate of growth of real income and thereby in the expected rate of growth of the demand for real cash balances. But, once all this has been taken into account and the 'optimal' ('neutral' in our view) growth rate of the supply of money determined (see Chapter 2), the optimal rate of increase in H will also be determined (see Chapter 5). Therefore, there is no scope left for any special treatment of a particular component of R.B.C.

We can restate this argument in different terms: once the objectives of price stability and maximum feasible output have been accepted (see Chapters 1 and 2), the new amount of H the R.B.I. can afford to inject into the economy will be determined by the incremental demand for H, given by the incremental demand of the public to hold currency plus the incremental demand for reserves (required plus excess) of banks, associated with the planned 'neutral' increase in M. This 'neutral' ΔH in real terms will represent the amount of real savings of the public the R.B.I. can appropriate through the issue of new H. It is only this part of the real savings of the public which the R.B.I. can divide among competing claimants.

This argument clearly implies that development banks have to compete for R.B.C. with the government, the commercial and state co-operative banks, and the accumulation of foreign exchange by the R.B.I. Under optimal allocation, the marginal social productivity of the various uses of the R.B.C. must be equal. The application of this rule will require much careful research and analysis into the social productivity of the various uses of R.B.C.

One point, however, is clear. Since 1970–1 the R.B.C. to development banks has been expanding fast (see Table 4.1). Consequently, it has become an important source of change (excessive increase) in H (see Table 4.3). We shall have to be watchful of its future rate of expansion, if the 'neutral money' policy is to be implemented seriously.

The control problem in this case, at least on the surface, is rather easy. Credit offered to development banks is entirely at the discretion of the R.B.I. Even the 'lender of last resort' argument supposedly relevant for credit to commercial banks is not applicable to the development banks.

But at deeper level, the problem of resources available to development banks to perform their development banking role must be squarely faced. The answer, in our view, does not lie in continued and increasing dependence on the R.B.I. for funds, but on building up the capacity of these institutions to raise funds on their own in the market. This will require several measures, the chief among which will be briefly stated here. One, and the foremost, is the interest-rate weapon which must be unfrozen. This ties in with the whole interest-rate policy of the government and the R.B.I., the key feature of which is the authorities' effort to keep the interest rate on government bonds as low as possible. This has placed too low a ceiling on the interest rate development banks can offer on their bonds/debentures. In the inflationary climate that has prevailed in the country ever since the mid-fifties, and more so since the mid-sixties, this has restricted the growth of the bond market in India. By allowing the bond rates of interest to go up gradually, this market must be allowed to expand more rapidly and attract funds from various sources all over the country (see Chapter 1).

Another measure urgently needed is the expansion and strengthening of the internal working of development banks. What is required is a detailed and in-depth study of various investment projects and careful selection of them before funds are committed to them, and full follow-up action. In equity-type investments by the I.D.B.I. and its associates, it is all the more necessary to pay careful attention to the expected profitability of the investments undertaken. The developmental and promotional role of these banks should not be misinterpreted to mean extending support to low-profitability investment projects. A sound and healthy asset portfolio built by these banks will, on the one hand, inspire confidence in the minds of financial investors in their bonds, and, on the other, generate internal funds for re-investment.

THE DEMAND FOR MONEY IN INDIA

The importance of the demand for money for monetary planning
has already been emphasized in Chapter 2. There, we had also
reported an empirically-estimated demand function for money in
India for the period 1950–1 to 1975–6. Theoretically, the demand for
money is generally hypothesized to be an increasing function of
some measure of income or wealth (as a scale variable), a declining
function of the rate or rates of return from alternative non-money
assets (as opportunity-cost variables), and some other variables re-
presenting the structural composition of the economy. We now
discuss what we consider to be the key problems concerning the
empirical estimation of the demand function for money in India and
some empirical results on the function. Khusro (1976), Lahiri (1977),
Vasudevan (1977), among others, give a survey of the statistical
demand functions for money for India, and Laidler (1972), an auth-
oritative overall discussion of the subject.

A.1 The Empirical Definition of M^1

The key problem concerning the narrow measure of M as the
sum of currency and demand deposits of banks held by the public,
concerns the treatment of savings deposits of banks. Should they
be treated as demand deposits, as time deposits, or partly as demand
and partly as time deposits? If the latter, in what proportions and
how can one decide on those proportions? A way out was found as
a by-product of the administration of the statutory reserve requirements imposed by the R.B.I. on banks. Before September 1962
scheduled banks were statutorily required to hold with the R.B.I.
cash reserves at a minimum of 5 per cent of their demand liabilities
and 2 per cent of their time liabilities. It was therefore of some importance to banks how their savings deposits were divided between
demand and time deposits. Under the Scheduled Banks' Regula-
tions, 1951, framed by the R.B.I., banks were advised to classify
that portion of savings deposits with them which could be withdrawn

[1] Discussion under this subhead draws heavily on the R.B.I., 1977, pp. 84–5.

without notice as demand deposits, and the rest as time deposits. This arrangement has continued ever since. Accordingly, this classification is done twice a year by each bank—once for the last Friday of June and again for that of December. The proportion so obtained at each bank branch-level is used for apportioning savings deposits to the demand and time deposits for the following weeks/months. The resulting information has also been used for measuring money.

The significant feature of this method is that the partitioning of savings deposits is decided by individual banks and not by the depositors themselves. This offers opportunities for arbitrariness, application of rule-of-thumb practices, or changes in the partitioning of savings deposits that are unconnected with the 'moneyness' or the 'demand deposit character' of savings deposits as perceived by their holders. It has resulted in rather sharp fluctuations in the measured demand deposit portion of savings deposits, which cannot be justified by referring purely to changes in the rules of withdrawals. For what matters is not only the existence of these rules, but also how far they are enforced in actual practice, and also (and more important, too) how the holders of savings deposits view the withdrawal restrictions/facilities governed by these rules.

On these matters, the following facts pointed out by the R.B.I. (1977, pp. 84–5) should be noted:

1. 'In practice, the savings deposits are operated without any withdrawal restrictions.'

2. 'An analysis of data of the individual banks reveals that the demand liability portion of savings deposit balances differs widely from bank to bank, ranging from 90 per cent to 68 per cent. A part of the explanation for this is to be found in the bank-wise differences in the size-wise differences in savings deposits, the proportion of demand liability portion being low in those banks which have a larger portion of big-size deposits.'

3. 'With the unification of the cash reserve ratio in September 1962 (at 3 per cent for both time and demand liabilities against 2 per cent and 5 per cent, respectively), the scheduled commercial banks had resorted to competitive liberalization of their deposit rules since April 1963. Consequently, the demand liability portion of saving deposits of all scheduled commercial banks had risen rather sharply from 64.3 per cent at the end of March 1963 to 86.9 per cent at the end of March 1964. . . . Subsequently, again with the stipulation that interest rate paid on deposits for periods of less than

15 days should not exceed the rate allowed on current accounts, the short notice deposits were converted into demand deposits.'

With continued competitive liberalization in savings deposit rules, the measured demand liability portion increased steadily from 86.9 per cent in March 1964 to 93.2 per cent in March 1968. Thereafter, under the Inter-Bank Agreement on Deposit Rates, withdrawal facilities were tightened. As a result, the measured demand liability portion fell sharply to 84.5 per cent in March 1969. Since then this portion has averaged about 85 per cent.

In the circumstances, it seems best to treat all savings deposits of banks as demand deposits for purposes of measuring M. Such treatment will rid the time series on M of measurement errors introduced by arbitrary classificatory changes. The R.B.I. need not commit itself officially to the new measure of M; all that is required of the R.B.I. is to admit one more plausible measure of M, publish at least the data on it for the past years since 1950–1 and regularly for the current year thereafter, to allow researchers to try out the revised series on M in their research work.

A.2 Which Income Measure to Use?

Once it is decided to use income as a scale variable in the demand function for money, it must next be decided which of the several alternative measures of income to use. Effectively, the choice has to be made

1. between total income and monetized income and
2. between net or gross national income at factor cost or at market prices.

We discuss below the two choices.

A.2.1 Monetized Income (Y_m) or Total Income?

Some economists, notably Prasad (1969) and Bhattacharya (1975), have taken the view that it is monetized, and not total, income that should enter the demand function for money. Monetized income is not rigorously defined. The practical test used for distinguishing between monetized and non-monetized income is whether final income is received and disposed of in cash or kind. Most non-monetized income is known to originate in the agricultural sector, owing to the existence of a large number of subsistence farmers, and the partial prevalence of barter in agricultural transactions. Thus, non-monetized income is defined as that part of the net agricultural produce (mainly food) which the farmer and his family consume themselves (imputed income) and which is paid in kind as wages to workers and as rent to the landowner. (Madalgi [1976] also includes seed and feed in his measure of non-monetized income. This is unwarranted, because seed and feed are not a part of the N.N.P.) Monetized income is simply total national income less non-monetized income.

There are several shortcomings of the monetized income (Y_m) approach to the demand for money:

1. It links the demand for money too closely to only the transactions demand for it, to the total neglect of the asset demand for money for precautionary, speculative, and finance motives. It does not even mention the asset demand for money, much less explain why such demand will be a function of Y_m rather than total income (Y).

2. The link between the transactions demand for money and Y_m is assumed to be obvious. No logical explanation of the assumed link is offered. The best construction that can be put on the implied explanation is that since imputed and barter transactions, by definition, do not make use of money, non-monetized income does not generate any (transactions) demand for money. This is not necessarily true. For payments made to others (farm hands and landowners) in kind, there is no guarantee that foodgrains so received will all be consumed by the recipient families and not sold for money in the market.[2] In addition, farm households are both consuming units and producing enterprises. Their transactions demand for money arises in both capacities. Of course, domestic retention of food output for family consumption is partly in payment of wages for family labour used on and off the farm. But there are other market-purchased inputs (for which money is used as the means of payment) even for output directly consumed by the producer households. Thus, looked at purely from the consumption angle, imputed income does not require any money; but, from the production side, the transactions associated with it do, in general, require some use of money as the medium of exchange. Therefore, it is dangerous to

[2] This argument is not applicable to Bhattacharya (1975) who looks at monetized consumption expenditure and other components of monetized expenditure to arrive at total monetized expenditure and money income. The argument, however, applies to Madalgi (1976).

assume that the so-called non-monetized income does not generate any transactions demand for money.

3. The Y_m approach is an illegitimate cross between the transactions approach of the long-discarded old Quantity Theory of Money and the income approach of the new monetary theory, whether of the Quantity Theory of Money variety or the Keynesian variety. In the transactions approach to the old Quantity Theory of Money, Fisher (1911) had taken the value of total market transactions mediated through money as the appropriate scale variable for the demand for money. Concentrating on money as the medium of exchange, this was interpreted to give the total amount of work to be done by a given stock of money per unit of time. Assuming constant transactions-velocity of money, it is, then, simple to arrive at the technical requirement (not behavioural demand) of money as a function of the total money value of monetary transactions of all kinds. The larger the latter, the greater the demand for money.

The theory of the demand for money has advanced greatly since. The demand for money is now no longer linked to the value of monetary transactions. Instead, income or wealth is regarded as the appropriate scale variable. Correspondingly, the mechanical approach of the transactions version has given place to the behavioural approach of the simple Cambridge Cash-Balance Equation (see Friedman, 1968), or of the Keynesian theory (Keynes, 1936), or of the new Quantity Theory of Money (Friedman, 1956). In the now popular alternative approach, the emphasis is on the demand for money as an asset in an efficient asset portfolio; and income is chosen as a scale variable as a proxy for the wealth variable. When it is argued that the transactions demand for money is more a function of income than of wealth, it must be implied that the total volume of monetary transactions is stably related to income. The concept of income chosen, then, should hinge, not on whether individual components of it are themselves monetized or not in any of the senses discussed above, but on what concept of income would give the most stable relation between it and the total volume of monetary transactions. The latter, it need hardly be emphasized, include not only final monetary transactions in the components of net value added, but also monetary transactions in all intermediate goods, old or second-hand goods, and financial transactions of all kinds.

4. If the 'demand for money' function is used to explain the role of

changes in money supply in money-income changes and for designing a suitable monetary policy to influence the course of money income, the appropriate income concept to be used in the demand function for money would also be Y and not Y_m.

For all these reasons, we have thought it best to stick to total income and eschew monetized income in all our discussions involving the use of some measure of income.

A.2.2 Net or Gross National Income at Factor Cost or at Market Prices?

There is no hard-and-fast criterion regarding this choice problem. Empirically, each of the alternative income measures seems to work very well. Yet, if income is to act not only for itself but also as a proxy for wealth in the demand function for money, net income should be clearly preferable to gross income. For what matters for asset choice is net wealth and not the gross wealth of the public. The choice of gross over net income on the ground that 'there is a transactions demand for money corresponding to depreciation expenditure' makes it liable to the defects of the 'monetized income' approach discussed in the previous sub-section. The behavioural-choice approach would also suggest that net national income at market prices should be preferable to that at factor cost. For indirect taxes less subsidies, which represent the difference between the two income measures, are fully a part and parcel of net income as viewed by the public. The public, obviously, has the option to spend it at the going market prices.

This approach, when taken to its logical conclusion, would dictate that for the demand for money held by the *public* what should matter is not the total net national income but only that part of it which is at the disposal of the *public*. The latter is a broader concept than personal disposable income, for it would exclude only direct taxes and net income of departmental undertakings of the government. The retained earnings of all corporate firms, whether in the private or the public sector, would be included in the disposable income of the 'public', for the cash balances held by these firms also get included in the money held by the 'public'. However, this kind of logical purity has a cost attached to it. Knowledge of the demand function for money is desired not for its own sake but for the use that can be made of it in explaining and predicting, say, changes in money income consequent on changes in the supply of money. At this juncture, we are interested in the behaviour of total income and not of some narrow measure or a part of this income. This important consideration has made us stick to the measure of total income. However, as a compromise, we tried out a new variable, the ratio of disposable income of the public to net national income, along with other standard variables, in the demand function for money. Our results for the period 1950–1 to 1975–6 for the new variable were uniformly poor. The reason may lie in the time profile of the new variable, which, over the period covered, has shown very small year-to-year variations in its values.

A.3 Real or Nominal?

It is a matter for theory to decide whether the demand for money relation should be specified in real or in nominal terms. The assumption of rationality dictates that the public be viewed as demanding a certain stock of real cash balances to hold, given the values of real income (or real wealth) and of other arguments entering the demand function for money. The rationale is that the public demands money not for its own sake but for the real services it yields to its holder and the value of these services per rupee depends upon the general price level. Thus, in standard monetary theory, whereas the monetary authority is supposed to control the nominal stock of money the public is seen as determining the stock of real money it wishes to hold. It is the discrepancy between the two at the going price level and the values of other determinants of the real demand for money which lead to portfolio switches and the consequent changes in asset prices, and to changes in expenditure flows.

It can happen that the real demand for money function is of unitary real-income elasticity. Then, provided the P (the general price level) used for converting nominal income into real income is the same as that used for deflating M (nominal money) to arrive at M/P (real money), algebraically, the demand function in real values will be the same as that in nominal values. But normally the two Ps are different: real-income measurement involves the use of the appropriate implicit price deflator; for deflating M, the use of the wholesale price index number is more popular. More important, the unitary real-income elasticity of the real demand for money is a particular case. This should not be used as a justification for a general switch-over from real variables to nominal variables. For if we relate any two nominal variables and the observations on them are drawn from a period in which P has been changing significantly, the effect of changing P on both the nominal variables will tend to produce a positive correlation between them even where none exists between the underlying real variables—a case of spurious correlation. Deflation by P will tend to remove this sort of spurious correlation. (See Laidler, 1972, p. 104, fn. 12.)

One misconception about the consequence of deflation of nominal variables by P should be dispelled. If alongside real (or deflated) variables P is not entered as an independent argument in the usual linear in logs real demand for money function, it does imply the assumption or the 'maintained hypothesis' that the real demand for money is homogeneous of degree zero in P (see Laidler, 1972, pp. 103–5). But this is neither necessary, nor generally warranted (see Gupta, 1972). The homogeneity assumption can and had better be treated as a testable hypothesis. We can do so by introducing P as an independent variable in the real demand for money function and setting up the null hypothesis that its co-efficient is equal to zero. We have tried it in our empirical work (see Section A.7 below).

Then, there are tasks for which the real and not the nominal demand function for money is of the essence. One such case is of monetary planning for price stability—the main concern of this work. For our purposes, we want to know how the real demand for money is likely to behave over time, so that changes in the nominal stock of money are adapted to match the growing real demand at constant prices.

A.4 Which Rate of Interest?

There is a wide variety of assets each of which competes with money, closely or from a distance, in the asset portfolio of the public. Correspondingly, there is a wide variety of rates of return on these assets, which serve as gross opportunity costs for holding money. Only on the convenient, but highly unrealistic, assumption of a perfect capital market is it possible to assume that the pure rates of return on all these assets tend to equality, so that we can speak of the (common) rate of interest on all non-money assets. In actual practice, the recorded rates of interest differ a good deal among themselves. Then, there are rates of interest charged and paid in unorganized markets on which no reliable data are available. No satisfactory method is known whereby the rates of risk premia on several risky assets can be computed to arrive at the pure rates of interest dictated by the theory of the demand for money. Differential tax treatment of interest income from various classes of non-money assets further complicates the problem.

What can the practical researcher do in the circumstances? Entering simultaneously several recorded rates of interest in the statistical demand-function for money creates problems of multi-collinearity and loss of degrees of freedom. It is also inelegant theoretically. Trying some of these rates singly or together is, therefore, common practice, the choice of individual rates varying from researcher to researcher. The underlying choice criteria, in several cases, are highly questionable.

The non-money assets chosen should be close substitutes for money. They should be broadly representative of such assets held by the public and should carry high enough weights among such assets. Reliable data on their rates of interest must of course be available. Against these criteria, time deposits of banks and post office savings deposits are very strong candidates. Other non-money assets, such as equities, are relatively distant substitutes for money. They compete more with other non-money assets than with money. A large part of government bonds (and treasury bills) is held by the banking system, which is not part of the 'public'. Other main holders of government bonds (L.I.C., Provident Funds, G.I.C. and its subsidiaries), though part of the 'public', do not constitute a large enough part of it from the point of the aggregate demand for money to hold. Also, the holdings of government bonds by these financial institutions are mainly governed by statutory investment requirements imposed on them by the government and not by voluntary choice or interest-rate considerations. Even as a government-bond rate, the rate of interest on the 3 per cent Conversion Loan (1986 or later) used by some researchers, is highly unrepresentative, since the proportion of such undated securities in total rupee (Government of India) securities has declined from 17.9 per cent at the end of March 1951 to only 3.2 per cent at the end of March 1977. Also, the rate of interest on such securities has been kept fixed by the R.B.I. at 5 per cent per year since 1969–70, whereas the average redemption yield on government securities of over 15 years' maturity has varied between 5.11 per cent during 1969–70 to 6.27 per cent during 1975–6.

Neither does sticking to the time deposits of banks alone solve the problem. For these deposits are not simply one asset, but many. They differ according to the period of maturity and the associated rate of interest. Most of the time, several time-deposit rates move together, generating multi-collinearity. One good way out would be to construct a weighted average time-deposit rate, using the ratio of time deposits in a particular maturity to the total stock of time deposits as the weight for the associated rate of interest. The weights may vary from year to year, and they are found to have so varied when we look at data for the years for which they are available. However, there are data gaps due to which a complete time series beginning (say) from 1950–1 cannot be constructed, although the R.B.I. might have the requisite information. Using this information, the R.B.I. should come forward with a time series on the weighted average time-deposit rate of banks and publish it regularly. In the absence of this series, in our empirical work we have used the 12-month time-deposit rate as representative of several time-deposit rates. We have preferred it to the alternative procedure of constructing a weighted average time-deposit rate selecting a few maturities and using constant arbitrary weights. Such a weighted average cannot be claimed as the true weighted average. It also introduces arbitrariness of an unknown magnitude in the measure. This will apply *a fortiori* to any other weighted average of interest rates, constructed by using constant arbitrary weights. Besides, the demand for money cannot be assumed to be equally responsive to an equal absolute (or proportionate) change in every rate of interest entering the latter weighted average.

A point of considerable importance regarding the interest-elasticity of the demand for money in India, not yet recognized by researchers, arises from the presence of interest-bearing 'demand liability portion' of savings deposits. This means that the stock of money as currently measured in India is not altogether non-interest-bearing. The weighted average rate of interest on money is given by the rate on savings deposits weighted by the ratio of the demand liability portion of savings deposits to total money supply (narrowly defined). This means that the appropriate interest-rate variable will be given by the difference between the rate of interest on a non-money asset (say, time deposits) and the weighted average rate of interest on money. We have not used such a variable because, in the absence of information on the demand liability portion of savings deposits, it is not feasible to construct the variable. This is an additional reason for the R.B.I. to make public the data on the demand liability portion of savings deposits. (For another reason, see Chapter A.1.)

In periods of significant and continuous inflation, the expected rate of inflation has presumably also affected negatively the real demand for money. Researchers have not however been successful in showing this rate to be a significant independent variable over the sample period (e.g. see Lahiri, 1977, pp. 102–3). This is not surprising. For a large part of the inflationary-expectations effect seems to have been picked up by the upward movement of money rates of interest (say, r_{12}) which are included as arguments in the demand-for-money function. In the relatively mild inflationary experience of India, the residual effect of inflationary expectations should be rather small.

A.5 The Ratio of Agricultural Income (at Current Prices) to Net National Income (at Current Prices)

Changes in the distribution of income among income classes or among sectors, such as between the household and the business sectors, or within the business sector, between the rural–urban or agricultural–non-agricultural sectors, can also influence the aggregate demand for money, provided (1) the sectoral demands for money with respect to income (along any of the sectoral classifications) differ significantly from each other, (2) there is significant variation in the intersectoral income distribution, and (3) the sectors chosen have significant weights in the aggregate of national income as well as the amount of money held. One such sectoral-income distribution which has been studied by researchers in India (e.g. Biswas, 1962; Rangarajan, 1965; Pandit, 1977; Lahiri, 1977) is that between the agricultural and the non-agricultural sectors. This also acts as a proxy for the rural–urban income distribution, for which data are not available.

The agricultural–non-agricultural income distribution as an argument in the demand function for money easily satisfies the last two of the three desiderata of the previous paragraph for including the argument in the function. The underlying hypothesis that both the average and the marginal propensity to hold money with respect to income in the two sectors differ significantly as between sectors, rests on a combination of the following two factors: (1) a lower degree of monetization of the rural (agricultural) economy, and (2) greater rural (agricultural) poverty, allowing only a very simple economic life-pattern. These factors generate relatively lower demand for money (per rupee of income), both as a medium of exchange and as a store of value.

The form in which sectoral incomes should be included in the demand function for money is a problem in empirical estimation. The two kinds of income are highly correlated, so their simultaneous inclusion as two independent variables is known to have seriously created the problem of multi-collinearity (see Biswas, 1962; Lahiri, 1977, p. 96). Therefore the ratio form of the distribution variable, along with a separate income variable, is usually tried. The new variable is also usually defined as the ratio of agricultural income (at current prices) to net national income (at current prices). An alternative form can take non-agricultural income (at current prices) as the denominator of the ratio.

Some researchers have computed the ratio at constant prices. This is indefensible, because the sectoral income-distribution can change not only because of differences in the rates of growth of sectoral output, but also because of changes in the inter-sectoral terms of trade, represented in the above ratio by the ratio of agricultural prices to the implicit price deflator.

Another measurement problem arises when we have to decide between national income at factor cost and national income at market prices. The usual practice is to choose the former in the form of the ratio of net domestic product from agriculture and allied activities (at factor cost) at current prices to net domestic product (at factor cost) at current prices. The switch from net national product (N.N.P.) to net domestic product (N.D.P.) in both the numerator and the denominator of the ratio is dictated by the difficulty in partitioning 'net factor income from abroad'—the item which stands between N.N.P. and N.D.P.—between agriculture and the rest. If it is sensible to assume that agriculture's imputed share in net factor income from abroad is nil, the ratio can be taken as N.D.P. from agriculture/N.N.P. Given the relatively small size of the net factor income from abroad (negative for all years except 1956-7), which has been only a fraction of 1 per cent of N.N.P., the point involved is of very minor statistical importance. So we ignore it.

The truly important problem concerns the choice of factor cost rather than market prices as the basis of income computations. The difference, as is well known, arises from the neglect of 'indirect taxes less subsidies' under the former and their inclusion under the latter. The choice of factor cost measures in the ratio implies the assumption that 'indirect taxes less subsidies' are borne by the agricultural sector in the same proportion as given by 'N.D.P. from agriculture (at factor cost)/N.D.P. (at factor cost)'. Reliable data on the subject are not available. But as a matter of empirical judgement, such an assumption cannot be true. The agricultural sector presumably bears a much smaller proportion of the burden of *net* indirect taxes (i.e. indirect taxes less subsidies). This makes the aforesaid measure of the sectoral distribution of income, denoted hereafter by Za/Z, positively suspect.

What is the alternative? Using our empirical judgement and simple rule-of-thumb practice, we have tried to apportion *net* indirect taxes to agriculture. The improvised formula is:

$$(Ta/T)_t = (Za/Z)_t . A_t,$$

where t is annual time subscript, $Ta/T =$ the proportion of net indirect taxes borne by agriculture, Za/Z is already defined, and A_t is given arbitrary values of 0.3 for each year from 1950–1 to 1965–6, and 0.31, 0.32, . . . , 0.40 for 1966–7 onwards. Increasing values of A_t from 1966–7 onwards or from the beginning of the Green Revolution were chosen on the presumption that the incidence of net indirect taxes on agriculture might be on the increase since then. In the formula, this increase is, to varying extents, undone by the change in the value of Za/Z. By applying the computed value of $(Ta/T)_t$ to total net indirect taxes, the absolute share of agriculture in net indirect taxes was arrived at. When added to N.D.P. from agriculture at factor cost at current prices, and imputing all the 'net factor income from abroad' to the non-agricultural sector, the N.N.P. from agriculture at market prices at current prices was arrived at. When divided by the total N.N.P. at market prices at current prices, we get an alternative series on the distribution variable, denoted by Ya/Y. We have used this series in arriving at our empirical results reported below. The series itself is given in Appendix G.

A conceptual decision problem still remains. Even if the new variable Ya/Y gives statistically significant results and its co-efficient in the estimated demand function for money has the 'right' sign, must we always use it as an explanatory variable? We have deliberately kept it out from the demand for money function reported in Chapter 2. What is the rationale?

It is generally agreed that statistical considerations alone do not dictate the specification of a behavioural function—theoretical considerations are paramount. Theoretically, a distribution variable should definitely be included, provided the desiderata for its inclusion (already specified above) are fulfilled. But its presence does create a problem for the income variable. What meaning should one attach to the income co-efficient? Suppose the fitted demand function is linear in logs of all the variables included. In a multiple regression equation, the income co-efficient would, then, give the *partial* income-elasticity of demand for money, holding all other variables, including the sectoral distribution of income, constant. For monetary analysis and planning, is this the kind of partial income-elasticity of demand for money we need? Holding all non-income variables constant is not the point at issue: what makes the difference is the sectoral composition of income. When monetary theory and policy refer to the income elasticity of demand for money, the reference is to the elasticity of the demand for money with respect to total income, *whatever the sectoral composition of the total.* That is, the said elasticity is to be estimated without holding constant the sectoral composition of income. Obviously, such an elasticity co-efficient cannot be estimated by a regression equation in which the distribution variable appears as one of the variables. No transformation of variables made possible by the logarithmic form of the equation can get rid of the problem faced by us. For example, consider the following regression equation in nominal magnitudes:

$$\log M = a_1 \log Y - a_2 \log Ya/Y. \tag{A}$$

This can be rewritten as

$$\log M = (a_1 + a_2) \log Y - a_2 \log Ya. \tag{B}$$

The 'income-composition constant' restriction is present in both equations (A) and (B). Hence neither a_1 alone nor $(a_1 + a_2)$ yields the desired aggregate income-elasticity of demand for money, whatever the composition of income. The specification of money and total income in the function in real terms and the measurement of Ya and Y (for the ratio Ya/Y) at current prices creates further problems when we move from an equation like (A) to an equation like (B). We do not pursue them here. This discussion should be enough to explain our main point: that it is also the use we want to make of our results that matters in choosing from among alternative specifications, provided the regression results are broadly similar. We shall have occasion to draw upon the role of Ya/Y variable in another context discussed in Appendix B.

A.6 Average versus One-Day Stock Figures

Money is a stock variable. (So are all prices and rates of interest per unit time.) For such variables, an average over-the-unit period (say, a year) is always better than a one-day figure, for the former is more representative of the variable than the latter and has less random noise in it. One-day figures may suffer from 'window-dressing'. Among averages, the average of daily stock figures is the first best, average of weekly (Friday) figures for money is the second best, average of 'last Friday of the month' figures is the third best, while one-day, 'last Friday of March', figures are the worst. Unfortunately, the R.B.I. specializes in purveying one-day figures on money stock and its components. This promotes the use of the 'worst' monetary data by lax researchers and writers, and imposes unnecessary research costs of data gathering and data processing on others. The situation has progressively deteriorated on this front. In general, the R.B.I. has been switching over from average stock figures to one-day figures, a move which should be stopped. One-day stock figures are no substitute for average figures. As in the past (during the fifties and early sixties), the R.B.I. should publish both kinds of data.

The R.B.I. is in the best position to compute and publish average figures on all financial variables: it is the primary or main source of such data and their revision; it has adequate computational facilities, not available to individual researchers; it has vehicles for distributing information regularly in the form of its monthly *Bulletin* and other periodic publications. The data published by the R.B.I. have the stamp of authority. Centralization of the work of averaging stock figures will save 'duplication' of effort by individual researchers.

All estimates of sectoral demand functions for money are clearly suspect, as they are necessarily based on one-day cross-section data. At best, they are second-best demand functions.

A.7 Some Empirical Results

We have experimented with alternative specifications of the demand function for money for India for the period 1950–1 to 1975–6 (annual data). The better ones are reported in Table A.1.

Figures within parentheses are t-values of the estimated coefficients above them. y stands for real net national income (at market prices). All other variables are as defined already. $\bar{R}^2$ is coefficient of determination adjusted for degrees of freedom. d gives

the value of the Durbin–Watson statistic for the first-order serial
correlation among residuals.

TABLE A.1

DEPENDENT VARIABLE: LOG $(M/P)^d$

Intercept	Independent variables			$\bar{R}^2$	d	Eq. no.
−1.680	+1.019 log y	−0.119 log P	−0.026 r_{12}			
(−1.390)	(7.620)	(−1.697)	(−1.077)	0.939	1.455	(A.1)
1.710	+0.918 log y	−0.610 log Ya/Y				
(0.982)	(7.232)	(−2.491)				
	−0.043 r_{12}	−0.058 log P				
	(−1.867)	(−0.852)		0.951	1.259	(A.2)
0.802	+0.969 log y	−0.506 log Ya/Y				
(0.379)	(5.457)	(−2.075)				
	−0.112 log r_{12}	−0.143 log P				
	(−1.326)	(2.436)		0.947	1.210	(A.3)

The results are very much the same if y in the above regressions is
replaced by real net national income *at factor cost* (y_{fc}). We shall
report the actual results later. First, the main findings from the group
of regression equations using log y will be discussed.

For the theoretical reasons given earlier, we have tried only the
real demand for money functions. Such demand functions in
logarithmic form (except for interest-rate variables) are seen to give
better results than the ones in simple linear form. The average of the
bazar bill rates for Bombay, Calcutta and Madras as a proxy for
rates of interest in unorganized money markets always gave very
poor results, whether introduced in log or the original form. Therefore, after several trials, it was dropped. The 12-month time-deposit
rate of banks, r_{12}, gives better results when entered in the original
form in a regression equation with log M/P as the dependent variable
than in log form. This means that the interest-rate elasticity of the
demand for real money tends to increase in absolute value as the
value of r_{12} goes up, instead of remaining constant. However, it is
only in equation (A.2) that r_{12} is significant at 5 per cent level of
significance. In equation (A.3) r_{12} is barely significant at only 10 per

cent level of significance. In equation (A.1) r_{12} does not become significant even at 10 per cent level of significance.

Another variable tried and found highly insignificant (with the highest t-value of 0.315 with 22 degrees of freedom) was the ratio of disposable income of the *public* to net national income (both measured at market prices) in log form. The negative sign of its co-efficient in all the three equations fitted also went against the *a priori* expectation of positive sign. The rationale for experimenting with this variable was stated briefly in section A.2.

Yet another new variable we have tried is P. Log P is very significant in equation (A.3), quite significant in equation (A.1) and not significant in equation (A.2) by the usual standards of statistical significance. In all the equations its co-efficient has a negative sign indicating that a rise in the *level* of P lowers the real demand for money. This goes against the usual 'maintained hypothesis' by which it is assumed that the real demand for money is homogeneous of degree zero in P.

In all the equations, multi-collinearity among independent variables might have plagued our results. Thus, for the sample period, the co-efficient of correlation of log y with log P, log r_{12}, and r_{12} is 0.921, 0.968, and 0.963, respectively. The correlation co-efficient between log y and log Ya/y has the value of -0.804. The first three very high correlations might have affected adversely the t-values or the standard errors of the co-efficients of log P and log r_{12} (or r_{12}) in the regressions. However, keeping in view very high t-values of the co-efficients of log y in the fitted equations, any possible effect of multi-collinearity on these co-efficients is not troublesome.

In the last two regression equations, the value of d (Durbin–Watson statistic) lies in the inconclusive range even at 1 per cent level of significance. Therefore, positive first-order auto-correlation among residuals of either equation cannot be ruled out. Interestingly enough, equation (A.1) yields d with a value of 1.455. Therefore, for this equation with 26 observations and 3 explanatory variables, the null hypothesis of no auto-correlation among residuals cannot be rejected at 1 per cent level of significance. Other things being the same, this makes equation (A.1) somewhat better than the other two equations.

But the more important reason for our preference for equation (A.1) lies somewhere else, as already explained in Chapter A.5. We are interested in estimating the real-income elasticity of demand for real money, when the sectoral composition of income is allowed to change with it and is not held constant. A regression equation with log Ya/Y (or Ya/Y) as an explanatory variable cannot give us this value. Therefore, even though the other two equations have somewhat higher $\bar{R}^2$, we prefer equation (A.1). Yet we have reported the other two equations for what they are worth.

The estimated income elasticity of demand for money turns out to be 1.019. This is slightly higher than unity—but, with standard error of the co-efficient being only 0.1337 and 26 observations, even at 10 per cent level of significance for one-tail test, which gives a large enough critical region, the null hypothesis of unitary income elasticity is not rejected.

The regression results for the demand for money when, in the three equations (A.1), (A.2) and (A.3), y is replaced by y_{fc} and Ya/Y by Za/Z, where the latter is the ratio of N.D.P. from agriculture (at factor cost) at current prices to total N.D.P. (at factor cost) at current prices, are given in Table A.2.

Broadly speaking, the regression results of the two alternative sets of equations are similar. Yet, equation for equation, the results of

TABLE A.2

DEPENDENT VARIABLE: LOG $(M/P)^d$

Intercept	Independent variables		$\bar{R}^2$	d	Eq. no.
−2.054 (−1.543)	+1.064 log y_{fc} (7.199)	−0.123 log P (−1.676)			
	−0.020 r_{12} (−0.812)		0.934	1.529	(A.4)
0.023 (0.018)	+1.125 log y_{fc} (8.911)	−0.668 log Za/Z (−3.141)			
	−0.037 r_{12} (−1.706)	−0.103 log P (−1.656)	0.953	1.296	(A.5)
−0.388 (−0.222)	+1.114 log y_{fc} (6.491)	−0.597 log Za/Z (−2.787)			
	−0.091 log r_{12} (−1.112)	−0.171 log P (−3.07)	0.949	1.268	(A.6)

equation (A.1) are slightly better than those of its counterpart equation (A.4), when we compare the several test statistics, such as $\bar{R}^2$, d, and t values of individual co-efficients of the independent variables; hence, even on statistical grounds, our preference for equation (A.1) over equation (A.4). (On the other hand, on the aforesaid criteria, the results of equations (A.5) and (A.6) are somewhat better than those of the comparable equations (A.2) and (A.3), respectively, except for the t-values of the co-efficients of r_{12} and $\log r_{12}$.)

APPENDIX B

THE INCOME VELOCITY OF MONEY
IN INDIA

The fitted demand function for real money (see Appendix A) with real income and other variables as arguments basically picks up the trend relation between real money and real income. It is a linear trend if the regression equation is linear in variables; it is a logarithmic trend, if the regression equation is linear in logarithms of variables. This is because of the strong dominance of trend in the levels of both real money and real income, and high correlation of real income with other explanatory variables tried, viz. $\log r_{12}$ (or r_{12}), $\log P$, and even with $\log Ya/Y$. The statistical solution to the problem of common time trend is to fit a regression equation in first differences of variables. The statistical results were found to be poor.

We take another course as a supplement to our aggregate demand for money analysis of Appendix A. We look at the behaviour of the income velocity of money (V), defined as Y/M, where $Y =$ net national income at current prices. Its reciprocal M/Y, in equilibrium, will be equal to M^d/Y, which gives us the nominal demand for money per rupee of Y. Technically speaking, we have normalized M^d with respect to Y. The use of Y as the normalizing factor reduces substantially the trend factor in M^d/Y, and so in V. We are practically assured of this outcome by the results of our regression equation (A.1). The behaviour of V, therefore, can be expected to highlight the short-run year-to-year fluctuations in its reciprocal M^d/Y. If for longer-term monetary planning, the trend behaviour of the aggregate demand for money is the deciding factor, for short-run stabilization policy, the behaviour of V is of the essence. In this sense, the analysis of V complements the demand for money analysis.

For measuring V, the measure of Y chosen by us is N.N.P. at market prices. (The time profile of V derived by using N.N.P. at factor prices is very much like that given by using N.N.P. at market prices.) The time graph of measured V is given in Figure B.1 and the underlying data in Appendix G.

The dominant feature of the graph is cycles of irregular length and

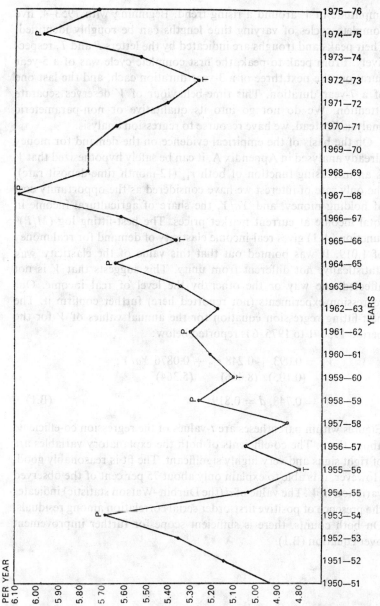

Figure B.1. Income Velocity of Money (*V*) in India, 1950-1 to 1975-6

amplitude in V around a rising trend. Beginning with 1953–4, five complete cycles of varying time lengths can be roughly identified. Their peaks and troughs are indicated by the letters P and T, respectively. From peak to peak, the first complete cycle was of a 5-year duration, the next three of a 3-year duration each, and the last one of a 7-year duration. This time-behaviour of V deserves separate attention. We do not go into its qualitative or non-parameteric analysis; instead, we have recourse to regression analysis.

On the basis of the empirical evidence on the demand for money already analysed in Appendix A, it can be safely hypothesized that V is an increasing function of both r_{12} (12-month time-deposit rate), the only rate of interest we have considered as the opportunity cost of holding money, and Ya/Y, the share of agricultural income in total income at current market prices. The best-fitting log $(M/P)^d$ function (A.1) gives real-income elasticity of demand for real money of 1.019. It was pointed out that this value of the elasticity was, statistically, not different from unity. This suggests that V is not affected one way or the other by the level of real income. Our regression experiments (not reported here) further confirm it. The best-fitting regression equation for the annual values of V for the period 1950–1 to 1975–6 is reported below:

$$V_t = 0.093 + 0.248\,r_{12} + 0.0876\,Ya/Y;$$
$$(0.105)\quad(8.466)\qquad(5.364)$$

$$\bar{R}^2 = 0.748,\ d = 0.819 \qquad\qquad\qquad (B.1)$$

Figures within parentheses are t-values of the regression co-efficients above them. The co-efficients of both the explanatory variables are of right signs and very highly significant. The fit is reasonably good. However, it is able to explain only about 75 per cent of the observed variation in V. The value of d (the Durbin–Watson statistic) indicates the presence of positive first-order serial correlation among residuals. On both counts, there is sufficient scope for further improvement over equation (B.1).

MONEY STOCK MEASURES

Empirically, money is defined as the sum of its constituent assets. Therefore, the key empirical questions are to decide what financial assets are money and how to measure precisely each such asset.

We shall first consider the assets: the chief criterion is that the asset in question should serve as a medium of exchange. This criterion yields what is called the 'narrow' definition of money. 'Broader' definitions of money are based on the 'liquidity' of assets as stores of value. Money is viewed as being perfectly liquid, that is, something fully convertible into the generally accepted media of exchange on demand and without loss of the face value of the asset. At times, the condition of perfect liquidity is relaxed to one of 'very high' liquidity without specifying what degree of liquidity (if measurable) should be treated as very high.

On the 'broader' (liquidity) approach to money, the chief candidates for the money status considered by the R.B.I. are (1) currency, (2) demand deposits of banks, (3) savings deposits of banks, (4) post office savings deposits, (5) time deposits of banks, and (6) time deposits of post offices. The first two are universally regarded as money. Demand deposits (known as current-account deposits in India) are deposits payable on demand, on which cheques can be drawn. Thus they serve as means of payment through cheques. Time deposits (called fixed or term deposits in India) are fixed-term deposits and are not drawable by cheques, but they are easily encashable. Savings deposits are a hybrid: they are partly like demand deposits as they are drawable by cheque and partly like time deposits as the chequing facility is not unrestricted. For example, a certain minimum balance has to be maintained in the account, the account cannot be used for business purposes, etc.

Till March 1977, the R.B.I. used to publish only two alternative measures of money—one 'narrow' and the other 'broader'. We have already discussed (in Chapter 3.2) the constituents of the narrow measure of money. The R.B.I. used to call the broader measure of money 'aggregate monetary resources'. It comprised money narrowly defined, and time deposits of banks. The new measure was introduced in 1964 and the data on it regularly published from 1967–8 onwards.

On the recommendations of its Second Working Group on Money Supply (R.B.I., 1977), the R.B.I. started publishing from the April–May 1977 issue of its monthly *Bulletin* four alternative measures of money supply in place of the old series. The Working Group also presents 'last Friday of the month' figures on these measures since March 1970. These 'new' measures of money supply are discussed below.

The four new measures of money supply are designated M_1, M_2, M_3, and M_4. Their respective definitions are:

$$M_1 \equiv C + DD + OD.$$

The meaning of each of the assets C, DD, and OD has already been explained in Chapter 3.2.

$M_2 \equiv M_1 +$ savings deposits with post office savings banks;

$M_3 \equiv M_1 +$ net time deposits of banks; and

$M_4 \equiv M_3 + total$ deposits with the Post Office Savings Organization (excluding National Savings Certificates). Besides savings deposits, the latter include various other deposits with post offices such as Post Office Time Deposits, Post Office Recurring Deposits and Post Office Cumulative Time Deposits.

We shall now comment briefly on the new and revised measures of money supply and their coverage.

1. M_1 is the revised measure of what the R.B.I. used to call money supply. The new series gives a better coverage of the co-operative banking sector. This sector consists of: state co-operative banks (at the state level), central co-operative banks (at the district level) and a variety of primary co-operative credit societies and banks (at the local level)—agricultural and non-agricultural. Formerly, only the *demand liabilities* of state co-operative banks were included in money supply. Other tiers of the co-operative banking sector were neglected mainly on account of non-availability of data. Further, inter-bank deposits of the central and primary co-operative banks with the state co-operative banks were not excluded because the depositor-wise breakdown of such deposits was not available. The practice at least partly compensated for the total neglect of the net demand

deposits of the central and primary co-operative banks. In the new series net (i.e. excluding inter-bank) demand deposits of state co-operative banks, central co-operative banks, and a segment of primary co-operative banks consisting of (1) urban co-operative banks and (2) salary earners' credit societies are included.

Similarly, M_3 is the revised version of the series on aggregate monetary resources with extended coverage for the co-operative banking sector.

2. For money-supply analysis, savings deposits with banks are not treated as a separate category. Instead, they are divided between demand and time deposits on the basis of withdrawal facilities. The classification is left to banks. We have already argued above that this practice has introduced an element of arbitrariness in the measurement of money stock, and that it would be advisable to treat all the savings deposits of banks as their demand deposits (see Appendix A.1).

3. The new series M_2 and M_4 have been devised to accommodate post office deposits. These deposits are of two broad kinds: (*i*) savings deposits and (*ii*) time deposits. The chequeable portion of the former is negligible. They are mainly drawable by withdrawal slips. Also, the data for them are received after a long time lag, and on a month-end basis. For all these reasons, post office savings deposits are not treated at par with the savings deposits of banks. And a separate 'broader' series M_2 has been constructed incorporating them with M_1.

M_4 is a series broader than M_3. Besides M_3, it includes total deposits of post offices, as already explained in the definition of M_4.

4. The R.B.I. takes the four measures of money stock to represent different degrees of liquidity. It has specified them in descending order of liquidity, M_1 being the most and M_4 the least liquid of the four measures.

But the liquidity measure of money is a difficult one to decide upon. If different assets are assumed to represent different degrees of liquidity, their unweighted total cannot give a correct measure of total liquidity represented by the component assets. And liquidity weights are hard to come by. This should be borne in mind in choosing a measure of money stock on considerations of liquidity.

5. Every measure of money (and its component assets) is supposed to measure money (and its component assets) held by the *public*. We have already explained (in Chapter 3.2) that, for measuring

M_1, the public stands for all the holders of currency and demand deposits of banks except the government and the banking system. The R.B.I. also accepts this definition. The definition holds when we move from M_1 to M_3 or to aggregate monetary resources. When the coverage for measuring money is extended to the lower tiers of the co-operative banking sector, the scope of the banking system is appropriately extended and that of the public correspondingly contracted. The same principle would apply to measurement of M_2 and M_4 as applies to measurement of M_1 and M_3. For measuring M_2 and M_4, the Post Office Savings Organization would have to be excluded from 'the public' and included under the producers of 'money' M_2 and M_4, along with the government and the banking system. This would require that the cash on hand of the Post Office Savings Organization is excluded. This has not been done. In its *Report*, the Second Working Group on Money Supply of the R.B.I. (1977, p. 79) has simply added Post Office savings deposits to M_1 to arrive at M_2 (and added total deposits of the Post Office Savings Organization to M_3 to arrive at M_4), without deducting cash on hand of the said postal organization from M_1 or M_3 respectively. In the *Report*, even the conceptual necessity of doing so has not been recognized. This has resulted in overestimates (of unknown magnitudes) of M_2 and M_4.

Which of the alternative measures of money is more useful? The object of enquiry will decide the issue. Most of the time we are interested in understanding the role of money in the economic system and in using this knowledge to devise monetary policy for the furtherance of policy objectives. In all this, the demand function for money plays the key role. So a major criterion would be to choose that measure of money which gives the best-fitting and most stable demand function for money. This would also suggest what assets the public regards as money in actual practice. Monetary controls should be designed in such a way that the monetary authority can exercise sufficient control over the variations in the monetary aggregate chosen.

THE MONEY MULTIPLIER

This appendix is devoted to a further discussion of the money-multiplier theory of money supply we had stated very briefly in Chapter 3.3. We now state very briefly the structure of the theory and the multiplier, identify the proximate determinants of the latter, examine briefly the empirical behaviour of each of these proximate determinants, and analyse the effect of a change in any one of them on the multiplier.

We hypothesize the following simple asset demand-functions of the public for currency, time deposits, and other deposits, and of banks for reserves, and also a supply function for total liabilities of banks, respectively:

$$C^d = c (\quad) DD \qquad\qquad\qquad \text{(D.1)}$$
$$TD^d = t (\quad) DD \qquad\qquad\qquad \text{(D.2)}$$
$$OD^d = b (\quad) DD \qquad\qquad\qquad \text{(D.3)}$$
$$R^d = r (\quad) L \qquad\qquad\qquad\quad \text{(D.4)}$$
$$L^s = l (\quad) D. \qquad\qquad\qquad\quad \text{(D.5)}$$

In these equations C, DD, TD, D and OD stand for currency, demand deposits, time deposits, total deposits and 'other deposits' with the R.B.I., respectively, held by the public; R and L for cash reserves and total demand and time liabilities of banks respectively; superscripts d and s for the amount demanded and supplied respectively; and c, t, b, r, and l are behavioural parameters. These parameters are assumed to be functions of a few specifiable variables, derivable from standard economic theory. The empty parentheses after each of these parameters indicate the behavioural nature of each and that, at this stage of the analysis, the determinants of these behavioural ratios have been left unspecified. We shall return to the question of the ultimate determinants of each of these ratios after deriving the money-multiplier relation. Therefore, for simplicity we shall henceforth ignore the empty parentheses after each of the ratios.

In this analysis we assume that the statutory reserve ratio for banks is kept unchanged throughout and that the change in r occurs only due to a change in the excess reserve ratio of banks with respect to either their total deposits or total liabilities. How to analyse the effect of a change in the statutory reserve ratio on money supply via a change on the supply side of H and why, will be discussed separately in Appendix E.

We note that by definition,

$$D \equiv DD + TD. \tag{D.6}$$

Using (D.2), (D.6), and (D.5) in (D.4) and simplifying, we may rewrite (D.4) as

$$R^d = r.l(1 + t) DD. \tag{D.7}$$

Now, $H^d = C^d + R^d$

$$= [c + r.l(1 + t)] DD. \tag{D.8}$$

For simplicity, we assume the supply of H to be autonomously given by the monetary authority (see Chapter 4.10), so that

$$H^s = \bar{H}. \tag{D.9}$$

Equilibrium in the market for H requires that

$$H^d = H^s, \tag{D.10}$$

$$\text{or} \quad [c + r.l(1 + t)] DD = \bar{H}. \tag{D.11}$$

From the above equation we have

$$DD = \frac{1}{c + r.l(1 + t)} . \bar{H}. \tag{D.12}$$

Equation (D.12) determines the amount of D and the expression $1/[c + r.l(1 + t)]$ can be called the *demand-deposit multiplier* with respect to H. It should be noted that we have derived it from demand and supply functions (however simple) and a market equilibrium condition. Hence the end product is behavioural.

We continue to define M 'narrowly' as $M \equiv C + DD + OD$.

We assume that the public's demand for currency has the first claim on H, so that it is always fully satisfied, giving us actual $C = C^d$.

Then, $M = C^d + DD + OD$,

or, using equations (D.1) and (D.3) for C^d and OD^d respectively,

$$M = (1 + c + b)\,DD. \qquad (D.13)$$

From equations (D.12) and (D.13) we finally get

$$M = \frac{1 + c + b}{c + r.l\,(1 + t)} \cdot \bar{H}. \qquad (D.14)$$

Equation (D.14) determines the supply of M, given H. The value of the money-multiplier, m, is given by the term multiplying H. Or, we have

$$m = \frac{1 + c + b}{c + r.l\,(1 + t)}. \qquad (D.15)$$

Thus, m is seen to be a well-defined function (of a special form) of five behavioural asset ratios : c, b, t, r, and l. Of these, b and l are peculiar to the Indian monetary system. Following Friedman and Schwartz (1963, Appendix B) and Cagan (1965), we call these five ratios the *proximate determinants* of m. They are not the ultimate determinants of m, because, being behavioural ratios themselves, they are functions of other variables, such as several rates of interest, holdings of black money, the spread of banking facilities in the country, especially rural areas, and such other factors as can be theoretically justified and are found to be empirically significant (see Swamy, 1975). The proximate determinants serve as intermediate stages through which the money-supply mechanism works. They also provide highly useful vantage points from which to observe and analyse the working of the complex of forces that impinge on the behaviour of the money-multiplier.

In a full study of the money-multiplier, one should not stop merely at the derivation of equation (D.14) or (D.15), but study further the determinants and behaviour of each of the ratios entering the multiplier. Swamy (1975) has made such a detailed study for the key ratios (c, t, and r) for India for the period 1951–2 to 1970–1. She has made both qualitative and statistical analyses of the data. We draw upon her work and summarize below her relevant findings (Swamy, 1975, Chapter 7).

(1) c, the currency ratio (C/DD), tended to increase over the period 1951–2 to 1961–2, and declined sharply thereafter. (The decline has contined unabated after 1970–1.) She first adjusted her figures for demand deposits for the change in the classification of

saving deposits by banks in favour of demand deposits since 1962–3 (see R.B.I., 1977, p. 84). For the adjusted currency ratio, using regression analysis, she could explain as much as 95 per cent of the observed change in the ratio in terms of a dummy variable interpreted to represent holdings of black money, the spread of banking facilities in rural areas, and two interest rates—the bazar-bill rate and the 3-month time-deposit rate of banks.

(2) t, the ratio of time deposits to demand deposits (TD/DD), has shown an upward trend over the period. (The upward trend has continued after 1970–1.) She adjusted her figures for the change in the classification of savings deposits into demand and time deposits after 1962–3, and for credits and withdrawals of P.L.480 funds between 1956–7 and 1966–7. She found that for the adjusted ratio, interest-rate factors alone were important. She could statistically explain 91 per cent of the observed change in the adjusted ratio in terms of only two interest-rate factors—the 12-month time-deposit rate of banks and the rate on variable-dividend industrial securities. Of the two, the former turned out to be much more important.

(3) The reserve ratio of banks, defined by her as R/D, declined over the period 1951–2 to 1962–3, and remained quite stable thereafter. After considering both interest-rate factors and several non-interest-rate factors, such as shifts in deposits among scheduled, non-scheduled, and state co-operative banks, structural changes within the scheduled banking sector in terms of the redistribution of total deposits among banks of different sizes, stability in the banking system, liquidations and amalgamations of banks, etc., she made a very interesting finding—that purely institutional factors have been far more important for the observed behaviour of the reserve ratio than the interest-rate factors. In her final regression equation, she was able to explain 84 per cent of the observed change in the ratio in terms of a specially-constructed dummy variable, interpreted by her to represent the increasing stability and strength of the banking system, and the advance rate of banks. The regression co-efficient of the latter was found to be statistically insignificant (with a low t-value of only 0.53).

The reserves of banks are a composite of statutory or required reserves (RR) and excess reserves (ER). The former are not behaviourally determined by banks, the latter are. The R.B.I. has tried to impound/release a part of the reserves of banks by making changes in the statutory reserve ratio. For reasons given elsewhere (see

Appendix E), it is best to pick up the influence of such policy changes by adjusting the amount of H available to the public and banks. So, in analysing the reserves-holding behaviour of banks, we should consider their demand for excess reserves. This demand is best related to total demand and time liabilities (L) of banks, as is the case with their required reserves. The average annual values of the excess reserves–liability ratio (ER/L) of scheduled commercial banks for 1950–1 to 1976–7 are given in Appendix G. They show a continuous decline in the value of the ratio with only a few minor and temporary reversals of this declining trend. The value of the ratio has already fallen from the high of 6.84 in 1950–1 to the low of 1.97 in 1976–7.

(4) The ratios b and l are relatively less important for the observed behaviour of m. b is a small proportion of DD (on average, only 1.9 per cent over the period) and a much smaller proportion of M. Therefore, its capacity to influence m has been negligible. So we need not pay serious attention to b. Moreover, the major holders of OD are a mixed lot, such as the I.M.F., foreign Central Banks, and quasi-government institutions, not amenable to behavioural analysis.

l, the ratio of liabilities to deposits of banks (L/D), has been highly stable. For scheduled commercial banks, for the period 1961–2 to 1976–7, it has averaged around 1.09 with minor year-to-year fluctuations around it on both sides. This, too, need not be pursued any further.

We may now analyse the partial effect of a change in any of the five ratios on m (holding others constant). For this, we recall the equation for m:

$$m = \frac{1 + c + b}{c + r.l(1 + t)}. \tag{D.15}$$

Differentiate m partially with respect to each of the five ratios, one by one. For notational simplification, denote $[c + r.l(1 + t)]^{-2}$ by α. Note that α is necessarily positive. Then, we shall have

$$\frac{\partial m}{\partial c} = -\,[1 + b - r.l(1 + t)]\,\alpha \qquad \begin{aligned} &< 0 \text{ for } r.l(1 + t) \\ &< 1 + b \end{aligned} \qquad \text{(D.16)}$$

$$\frac{\partial m}{\partial t} = -\,r.l(1 + b + c)\,\alpha \qquad\qquad < 0 \qquad\qquad \text{(D.17)}$$

$$\frac{\partial m}{\partial b} = \alpha^{-1} \qquad\qquad\qquad\qquad\quad > 0 \qquad\qquad \text{(D.18)}$$

206   *Appendix D*

$$\frac{\partial m}{\partial r} = - [l(1+t)(1+b+c)]\alpha \quad < 0 \qquad (D.19)$$

$$\frac{\partial m}{\partial l} = - [r(1+t)(1+b+c)]\alpha \quad < 0 \qquad (D.20)$$

Thus, we find that increase in t, r, or l will unambiguously lower the value of m; increase in b unambiguously raise it; and increase in c will lower the value of m so long as $r.l(1+t) < 1+b$ —a condition likely to be satisfied in most actual cases.

The economic rationale of these results is simple. Increases in any of c, r, t, and l represents a greater leakage or drain of H into currency holdings or reserves than before. Therefore, the same amount of H is now able to support a smaller volume of M, which means lower m. Under the narrow definition of money under which demand deposits alone are included in money, reserves held by banks against their time deposits are a pure leakage from the point of view of supporting demand deposits. Therefore, any increase in t must lower m. A *ceteris paribus* increase in l will also require larger reserves to support the same level of deposits than before, hence the negative effect on m. OD do not require any holding of reserves on the part of the R.B.I. So, H remaining the same, if OD go up, M goes up, and so does m.

Armed with this knowledge, if we also know in what direction individual ratios are expected to move or have moved and by how much, we can estimate the partial effect on m of the (expected) change in each one of them and, adding up the several partial effects, the total effect of all the changes. The method of doing so is given below. We know that

$$m = m(c, r, t, b, l). \qquad (D.21)$$

Differentiating m totally, we have

$$dm = \frac{\partial m}{\partial c}.dc + \frac{\partial m}{\partial r}.dr + \frac{\partial m}{\partial t}.dt + \frac{\partial m}{\partial b}.db + \frac{\partial m}{\partial l}.dl. \qquad (D.22)$$

Since economic data are only available in discrete values, we take a discrete approximation of equation (D.22). This gives

$$\Delta m = \frac{\partial m}{\partial c}.\Delta c + \frac{\partial m}{\partial r}.\Delta r + \frac{\partial m}{\partial t}.\Delta t + \frac{\partial m}{\partial b}.\Delta b + \frac{\partial m}{\partial l}.\Delta l + e. \qquad (D.23)$$

where e is the residual or the unexplained part. The residual necessarily arises whenever we take discrete approximations of differential terms. Obviously, the smaller the residual term, the better the approximation.

The first five terms on the right-hand side of equation (D.23) represent the partial contribution to the change in m of the change in each of the five ratios c, r, t, b, and l, respectively. The sum of these terms constitutes the explained part of Δm. The values of partial derivatives in the equation can be calculated from equations (D.16) to (D.20). Δc, Δr, etc. are either observed or predicted. Thus, all the terms on the right-hand side of equation (D.23) can be estimated from the data.

The relative contribution of each of the ratios to the change in m can be found by dividing both sides of equation (D.23) by Δm which yields the desired result:

$$1 = \frac{\partial m}{\partial c} \cdot \frac{\Delta c}{\Delta m} + \frac{\partial m}{\partial r} \cdot \frac{\Delta r}{\Delta m} + \frac{\partial m}{\partial t} \cdot \frac{\Delta t}{\Delta m}$$

$$+ \frac{\partial m}{\partial b} \cdot \frac{\Delta b}{\Delta m} + \frac{\partial m}{\partial l} \cdot \frac{\Delta L}{\Delta m} + \frac{e}{\Delta m}. \tag{D.24}$$

Series Derivation of the Money Multiplier

It will be instructive to derive an expression for the money multiplier from infinite rounds of expansion of deposits initiated by (say) a fresh injection of some ΔH. The whole analysis resembles the well-known Keynesian expenditure-multiplier formulation very closely.

For simplicity, let us assume (a) that all deposits are of only one kind, namely, demand deposits of banks, (b) that all liabilities of banks are the deposits of the public with them. The two assumptions eliminate the need for considering t, b, and l ratios, without affecting our argument qualitatively. We do, of course, retain c and r.

Consider new ΔH in the hands of the public. (We shall look at the introduction of H into the system later.) With the public, it is all ordinary money, M. The public decides to hold a part of it in the form of currency (C) and the rest in the form of bank deposits (D). At the aggregate level, it does not matter what fraction of the public holds all money in the form of currency, and none in the form of deposits. On the simplifying assumption of a constant currency–deposit ratio (c), the public will hold $c/1 + c$ of ΔH in currency and

$1/1 + c$ of ΔH in deposits. Thus, the first-round accretion of deposits to banks will be $1/1 + c.\Delta H$.

Now, further rounds of deposit expansion start. Let us assume banks to hold reserves in the ratio of r per rupee of deposits. They lend or invest the rest, $(1 - r)/(1 + c).\Delta H$ in the present case. The borrowers spend it and the public comes to have this amount of additional money in its hands. Again, the public holds $c(1 - r)/(1 + c)^2.\Delta H$ of it in the form of currency (the currency drain) and the rest, $(1 - r)/(1 + c)^2.\Delta H$, in the form of deposits. This gives us the second-round accretion of deposits of $(1 - r)/(1 + c)^2.\Delta H$.

Similarly, the third and subsequent round accretion of deposits would be $(1 - r)^2/(1 + c)^3.\Delta H$, $(1 - r)^3/(1 + c)^4.\Delta H, \ldots$

Thus the total deposit-expansion would be given by:

$$\Delta D = \Delta H.\left[\frac{1}{1 + c} + \frac{1 - r}{(1 + c)^2} + \frac{(1 - r)^2}{(1 + c)^3} + \frac{(1 - r)^3}{(1 + c)^4} + \cdots\right]$$

$$= \frac{\Delta H}{1 + c}\left[1 + \frac{1 - r}{1 + c} + \frac{(1 - r)^2}{(1 + c)^2} + \frac{(1 - r)^3}{(1 + c)^3} + \cdots\right]$$

$$= \Delta H.1/(c + r) \tag{D.25}$$

where $1/(c + r)$ is the deposit-multiplier of the traditional theory.

It should be noted that the common ratio of the geometric series is $(1 - r)/(1 + c)$, and not $1 - (c + r)$, as one might infer by simply looking at the value of the deposit multiplier. It is obvious that $(1 - r)/(1 - c) < 1$, whatever the (non-negative) value of c. Hence the series necessarily converges.

The incremental accumulation of currency with the public is given by

$$\Delta C = \Delta H\left[\frac{c}{1 + c} + \frac{c(1 - r)}{(1 + c)^2} + \frac{c(1 - r)^2}{(1 + c)^3} + \cdots\right]$$

$$= \Delta H.\frac{c}{1 + c}\left[1 + \frac{1 - r}{1 + c} + \left(\frac{1 - r}{1 + c}\right)^2 + \cdots\right]$$

$$= \Delta H.\frac{c}{c + r} \tag{D.26}$$

since the sum of the convergent infinite geometric series within the square brackets $= (1 + c)/(c + r)$.

The sum of (D.25) and (D.26) gives us

$$\Delta M = \frac{1+c}{c+r} \cdot \Delta H \qquad (D.27)$$

where $(1+c)/(c+r)$ is the money multiplier of the traditional theory.

The way ΔH is introduced into the system makes no difference whatsoever to the money-multiplier analysis, whether (*i*) the government borrows ΔH from the R.B.I. and spends all of it in the form of currency, or (*ii*) the R.B.I. purchases foreign exchange or government securities from the public or banks, or (*iii*) the banks borrow on their own from the R.B.I., etc. In all cases, the public comes into possession of ΔH, when the government or bank borrowers spend their loan proceeds. Deposits do not accrue to banks at all at this stage, but only accrue when the public 'buys' such deposits. Once primary deposits have accrued to banks, the deposit-expansion process starts working, as explained above.

CHANGES IN THE STATUTORY RESERVE RATIO AND ADJUSTED H

What effect does a change in the statutory reserve ratio for banks (call it z) have on money supply M? How can we analyse it? In terms of the money-multiplier theory of money supply discussed in Appendix D, does a *change in z* affect M through a change in m and/or a change in H? What is the meaning and usefulness of the concept of adjusted H (call it H^*) mentioned in Chapter 3.3? These questions are taken up here in the context of the money-supply model of Appendix D. We shall continue to use the notation of the latter.

For a behavioural analysis of money supply, what matters is the amount of *disposable H* rather than total H. The former is that part of H which the public and the banks are free to dispose of as they like. The concept is analogous to that of disposable income. Disposable H is given by total H less statutory reserves. Denoting the former by DH, we can write

$$DH \equiv H - z.l.(1 + t).DD. \tag{E.1}$$

DH is demanded by the public as currency and by banks as excess reserves. Again, using the hypotheses of the simple money-multiplier model of Appendix D, we have

$$DH^d = c.DD + e.(1 + t).l.DD \tag{E.2}$$

where $e \equiv$ the desired excess reserve ratio for banks. We assume it to be independent of z.

For equilibrium in the market for DH, we should have

$$DH^d = DH.$$

Or, from (E.1) and (E.2),

$$DD[c + e.l(1 + t)] = H - z.l(1 + t)DD. \tag{E.3}$$

When solved for DD, this gives

$$DD = \frac{1}{c + l(z + e)(1 + t)} \cdot H \qquad \text{(E.4)}$$

$z + e$ = statutory reserve ratio + the excess reserve ratio
= total reserve ratio (r).

Thus, equation (E.4) above is exactly the same as equation (D.12) in Appendix D. It immediately follows that the money supply equation derived from the DH approach will be identical to equation (D.14) of Appendix D, derived from the total H approach. In this sense the two approaches give identical results. This is because, as it turns out, both z and e enter symmetrically in the deposit-multiplier equation (E.4) above, and would do so for the money-multiplier equation, too. The values of the two multipliers do depend upon the value of z, among other things. Both D and M are seen as functions of H even though we had started with only DH. There is no way to separate the effect of z until we have solved for the equilibrium value of D (or M).

What about the effect of Δz—a change in z? Does this conclusion apply here as well? Can we assess the influence of Δz on M only via a change in m? Or is there an equivalent way of obtaining this influence via appropriate adjustments in measured H? We take up the second route first.

It is very common to say that an increase/decrease in z is a way of impounding/releasing reserves (or H or DH). Most of the time, the R.B.I. also subscribes to this view. Let us analyse its meaning in terms of our money-supply analysis.

Let us take the case of an increase in z. Since we are dealing with stock quantities, we take averages of such quantities over a period (say, a year). Given Δz, the amount of H impounded (HI), for our purposes, will be given by

$$HI = \Delta z \cdot l \cdot D \qquad \text{(E.5)}$$

where HI and D belong to the same period.[1]

---

[1] It may be noted that this HI is not the same as the HI given by the average amount of reserves actually collected by the R.B.I. at a higher z over what it would have collected at a given (lower) z, other things being the same. This alternative measure of HI, denoted by $HI(A)$, will be given by

$$HI(A) = \Delta z \cdot l \cdot D - l \cdot \Delta D(z + \Delta z). \qquad \text{(E.6)}$$

This is different from the HI of (E.5) by the second term. The latter carries a negative sign, because, given H and other things, a higher z will reduce D and L. By itself, this will reduce the required-reserve liability of banks at the current

Let d stand for the total-deposit multiplier at the initial value of z. (Since total deposits $= (1 + t) . DD$, the total-deposit multiplier will be $(1 + t)$ times the multiplier for DD, as derived in equation (D.12) of Appendix D.) Then, under the 'adjusted H' approach, D will be equal to $d . H^*$, so that (E.5) can be rewritten as

$$HI = \Delta z . l . d . H^*. \tag{E.7}$$

Define a new variable 'adjusted H' as

$$H^* \equiv H - HI. \tag{E.8}$$

Using (E.7) in (E.8) we have

$$H^* = H - \Delta z . l . d . H^*,$$

or

$$H^* = \frac{1}{1 + \Delta z . l . d} . H. \tag{E.9}$$

The 'adjusted H' proposition, then, says that, in the face of a change in z, when we use H^* in place of H and keep m unchanged, the supply of M given by the multiplier equation will be the same as that given by the equation using H and the adjusted value of m.

The first part of the proposition can be stated thus:

$$M^* = m . H^* \tag{E.10}$$

where the star on M is used to emphasize that, in fact, $\Delta z \neq 0$.

Using (E.9) in (E.10), we have

$$M^* = m . \frac{1}{1 + \Delta z . l . d} . H,$$

or

$$M^* = m^* . H, \tag{E.11}$$

---

required-reserve ratio of $z + \Delta z$. (E.6) takes care of it, which (E.5) neglects. (E.6) would give the correct measure of HI if we were interested in HI for its own sake, or if the problem were to solve for Δz that will give us a target HI. We are not interested in anything of the sort. Our interest is only to see if, for explaining money-supply changes, the influence of Δz can be correctly captured by making appropriate adjustments only in measured H. The adjustment is made on the assumption that the amount of H supporting the observed M and D has gone down by the extra required reserves at the observed D (and L), whenever z is raised. The correct measure of this extra required reserves is given by HI of (E.5), not by $HI(A)$ of (E.6).

where

$$m^* = m/(1 + \Delta z . l . d).$$

But the above equation represents the second part of the 'adjusted *H*' proposition, and it is equivalent to equation (E.10). Hence, the 'adjusted H' proposition is true. The multiplicative adjustment factor $1/(1 + \Delta z . l . d)$ can be applied either to *H* to yield *H** (as in equation (E.10)) or to *m* to yield *m** (as in equation (E.11)). This is an interesting result.

It is interesting for three reasons. One, it validates the view that what Δz does essentially is to impound or release reserves or *H*. This explains the true nature of the Δz measure. Second, as a corollary, it helps separate the 'policy-controlled' from the 'policy-autonomous' in the determination of money supply. As an empirical matter, *m* is *largely* policy-autonomous—it is a function of the decisions of the public and banks—and *H** *largely* a policy-controlled variable. The above result helps preserve this separation. Third, a large variation in *z* will produce a sizeable change in *measured m*, given by the ratio of *M* to *H*. This will give the wrong impression that *true m* giving the relation of *M* to *H** is also unstable and, therefore, the money-multiplier theory of money supply an unreliable basis for predicting money-supply behaviour and for monetary-policy formulation.

The result in (E.10) can also be derived with the help of our analysis of *m* in the previous appendix. There, we had

$$m = \frac{1 + c + b}{c + r . l (1 + t)}. \tag{E.12}$$

Recalling that $r = z + e$ and holding other things constant, the effect of a small change in *z* (*dz*) on *m* is given by

$$dm = \frac{\partial m}{\partial z} . dz$$

$$= - \frac{(1 + c + b)(1 + t) . l}{[c + r . l (1 + t)]^2} . dz. \tag{E.13}$$

In real-life situations, the change in *z* is not infinitesimally small, but discrete. Then, the use of (E.13) can give us only an approximation of Δm due to Δz. Still we have to face the problem of evaluating the partial derivative in equation (E.13), namely, whether it should be evaluated at the initial value of *r* (denoted by r_0) or at the new value of r (denoted by r_1), corresponding to the initial and new values of z, respectively. Perhaps the simplest way out is to use both the values in the following manner.

Factor out the right-hand side of (E.13) thus:

$$dm = -\frac{(1 + c + b)}{c + r \cdot l(1 + t)} \cdot \frac{(1 + t)}{c + r \cdot l \cdot (1 + t)} \cdot l \cdot dz.$$

$$(E.14)$$

In (E.14) we have two factors involving r. Evaluate one of them at r_1 and the other at r_0 when we go to find out Δm due to Δz. This gives

$$\Delta m = -\frac{(1 + c + b)}{c + r_1 \cdot l(1 + t)} \cdot \frac{(1 + t)}{c + r_0 \cdot l(1 + t)} \cdot l \cdot \Delta z$$

$$= - m^* \cdot d \cdot l \cdot \Delta z \qquad (E.15)$$

where the star on m indicates that it has been evaluated at the new value of z.

Now,

$$m^* = m + \Delta m$$

$$= m - m^* \cdot d \cdot l \cdot \Delta z. \qquad \text{(from E.15)}$$

Or

$$m^* = m/(1 + \Delta z \cdot l \cdot d).$$

This is the same as the result arrived at in (E.11), when we had started out by interpreting Δz as a method of impounding/releasing reserves (or H).

Hence, it is fully consistent with the money-multiplier theory to use H^* (in place of H) to allow for changes in z, while keeping m constant.

MONEY SUPPLY AND OTHER EMPIRICAL FUNCTIONS

F.1 The Supply of Money (M^S)

The theory of money supply has been discussed in Chapter 3 and Appendices D and E. Here, we look at the related empirical evidence for the period 1950-1 to 1975-6 (annual data). We experimented with several alternative specifications, and the best-fitting regression equation for M^S is given below:

$$M^S = -11.6 \quad -1568.7Z \quad + \quad 0.993H^*$$
$$t \text{ values:} \quad (-0.08) \, (- \quad 10.05) \quad (10.65)$$

$$+ \; 0.616ZH^* + 114.88r_{adv} \, ;$$
$$(7.49) \qquad (4.64)$$

$$\bar{R}^2 = 0.999, \quad d = 1.81 . \tag{F.1.1}$$

For definitions of M, H^* and r_{adv} and the data, see Appendix G. Z is a dummy variable, taking the value of 1 for 1962-3 and every following year and the value of zero for every preceding year. The qualitative evidence on the behaviour of the proximate determinants of m assembled and examined by Swamy (1975), some of which has already been summed up in Appendix D, and the time graph of m (defined as M/H^*) suggested that a structural shift in the relation between M and H^* had occurred around the year 1961-2. The shift was presumably both in the intercept and the slope co-efficient of H^*. On this ground an intercept dummy variable in the form of z and a slope dummy variable in the form of ZH^* were introduced. The slope co-efficient of r_{adv} was constrained to stay unchanged throughout the period. So there is no dummy variable involving r_{adv}.

The fit given by equation (F.1.1) is excellent. It explains 99.9 per cent of the observed variation in M. The estimated value of d shows that the fit is free from any first-order serial correlation in residuals. The t-values of all the estimated co-efficients (except that for the constant term) are highly significant. The results support the hypothesis of structural shift.

For the period 1950–1 to 1961–2, Z was assigned the value of zero. Therefore in the fitted equation the terms for Z as well as ZH^* disappear. Since for this period the intercept term is not significantly different from zero, the value of the average money multiplier is the same as that of the marginal money multiplier (with respect to H^*), holding r_{adv} constant.

For the period 1962–3 to 1975–6, with $Z = 1$, equation (F.1.1) is reduced to:

$$M^S = (-11.6 - 1568.7) + (0.993 + 0.616)H^*$$
$$+ 114.88r_{adv};$$
$$(4.64)$$
$$\bar{R}^2 = 0.999; \quad d = 1.81. \tag{F.1.2}$$

In this equation, we have left out t-values of the co-efficients for the constant term and for H^*, because they are not known. Yet the knowledge of equation (F.1.1) fortifies us in saying that each estimate is statistically significant. The marginal money multiplier (with respect to H^*), for this period, has increased substantially in value from 0.993 to 1.609. That is, holding r_{adv} constant, an additional rupee of H^* has tended, on average, to increase M^S by Rs 1.609. The negative value of the intercept says that, with r_{adv} constant, the value of the average money multiplier has been increasing with increase in H^*.

The co-efficient of r_{adv} in the equation is rightly signed, because the theory of money supply suggests that the partial effect of an increase in r_{adv} would be to raise M^S. Over the full period, an increase of one percentage point in r_{adv}, holding other things constant, has led, on average, to an increase of Rs 114.88 crores in the supply of money. At the mean values of M and r_{adv} for the full period, this gives an interest rate (r_{adv}) elasticity of money supply of the value of 0.018.

In other regression equations fitted but not reported here, we tried two additional rates of interest, namely, the 12-month time-deposit rate of scheduled commercial banks r_{12} and the bazar-bill rate r_{bz} (see Appendix G for their definitions and the data). They were entered singly and along with other rates of interest. The results for r_{bz} were always highly insignificant. r_{12}, when entered without the dummy variables, always came out with a highly significant negative co-efficient. The negative sign is what we would also expect theoretically, because a rise in r_{12} will tend to shift the public out of money into time deposits, lead to relative expansion of such deposits, and diversion of some reserves of banks to support time deposits, which are not included in M. However, all such equations gave a low value of d indicating the presence of positive autocorrelation in them. When r_{12} was entered along with the dummy variables, its co-efficient retained its negative sign, but turned statistically insignificant. Hence it was dropped. Thus from among all the fitted regression equations equation (F.1.1) was chosen as the best.

F.2 The Demand for Excess Reserves (ER^d)

In Chapter 7.1, several hypotheses regarding the demand for excess reserves of scheduled commercial banks were made out. We have tested them with the help of annual data for the period 1950–1 to 1974–5/1976–7 (see Appendix G). For this, alternative regression equations were fitted. Equations involving the ratio of demand liabilities to time liabilities of scheduled commercial banks (DL/TL) as a variable covered the period only up to 1974–5, because the data on this variable beyond this year have not been published by the R.B.I. For specifications not containing this variable, we could extend the period up to 1976–7. The best-fitting regression equation for ER^d is given below:

$$ER^d = 41.16 + 0.026L + 0.0902DL/TL$$
$$t \text{ values:} \quad (3.14) \quad (28.68) \quad (2.046)$$

$$- 8.105r_{RBI};$$
$$(-3.268)$$

$$\bar{R}^2 = 0.990, \quad d = 1.83. \tag{F.2.1}$$

For definitions of the variables used and the data, see Appendix G. The fit given by equation (F.2.1) is very good. It explains 99 per cent of the observed variation in the ER of scheduled commercial banks over the period 1950–1 to 1974–5. The estimated value of d shows that the equation is free from any first-order serial correlation in residuals. The estimated co-efficients are statistically significant and of 'right' signs. The co-efficient of L is very highly significant. The partial R^2 for this variable in the equation is 0.975. The results confirm the hypotheses that ER^d is an increasing function of both L and DL/TL and a decreasing function of r_{RBI}.

What about the influence of other variables? Two other rates of interest r_{adv} and r_{call}, in company with L and DL/TL, did not give

218 *Appendix F*

equally good results when entered with r_{RBI} or in place of the latter. In the presence of r_{RBI}, the other two rates of interest, together or individually, came out with negative (right) signs, but insignificant t-values of their co-efficients. This might be due to multi-collinearity among the three rates of interest. When tried in place of r_{RBI}, either rate was statistically significant and of negative sign. But the value of d deteriorated to take it in the inconclusive range, so that first-order positive serial correlation among residuals could not be ruled out.

All these experiments were repeated with intercept and slope dummy variables Z and ZL on the lines of equation (F.1.1). In each case each of the two dummy variables turned out to be statistically insignificant. Invariably, their presence affected adversely the t-values of the co-efficients of other variables. Most of the time, except for L, other variables were rendered statistically insignificant. Therefore, all such equations were rejected along with the hypothesis of a structural shift in the ER^d function around the year 1961–2.

Finally, we give a brief account of the outcome of replacing DL/TL by Cr/L, the credit–liabilities ratio (see next section and Appendix G), keeping other variables in alternative specifications unchanged. The results were uniformly poorer: the $\bar{R}^2$ did not suffer much in value, hovering around 0.975, but every time the value of d was low enough to indicate the presence of first-order positive serial correlation among residuals. The new variable Cr/L, interpreted to represent the demand for bank credit normalized for total liabilities, always turned out to be statistically insignificant. So did the two interest-rate variables r_{adv} and r_{call}. Their co-efficients also showed wrong (positive) signs. The r_{RBI} did come out with correct (negative) sign of its co-efficient, but with very poor statistical significance.

F.3 The Demand for Borrowed Reserves (BR^d)

In Chapter 8 we discussed the theory and institutional arrangements concerning the borrowed reserves of scheduled commercial banks. Here, we look at the related empirical evidence for the period 1950–1 to 1976–7 (annual data). The regression results of selected alternative specifications for the BR^d function are reported in Table F.1.

Figures within parentheses are t-values of the regression co-efficients above them. For definitions of the variables used and the data, see Appendix G.

TABLE F.1

DEPENDENT VARIABLE: log BR^d

Intercept	Independent variables	$\bar{R}^2$	d	Eq. no.
0.234 (0.063)	0.107 Cr/L (4.457) +2.071 log RR (2.225)			
	−1.707 log L (−1.584) +0.225 r_{adv} (0.991)			
	−0.206 r_{RBI} (−0.849) −0.00066 r_{call} (0.0052)	0.853	0.810	(F.3.1)
0.180 (0.072)	0.107 Cr/L (4.867) +2.094 log RR (3.714)			
	−1.701 log L (−2.648) +0.226 $(r_{adv}-r_{RBI})$ (1.286)	0.866	0.818	(F.3.2)
−4.934 (−4.18)	0.088 Cr/L (4.474) +0.534 log RR (2.625) +0.117 r_{call} (1.764)	0.850	0.813	(F.3.3)

Each of the rates of interest tried in equation (F.3.1) is statistically insignificant. However, r_{adv} and r_{RBI} enter with right signs. r_{call} enters with wrong sign, but is very highly insignificant. To avoid multi-collinearity among these rates, only the difference between r_{adv} and r_{RBI} was entered in equation (F.3.2) and only r_{call} in equation (F.3.3). Both these modifications were an improvement to some extent, but not wholly for $(r_{adv} - r_{RBI})$. Its co-efficient, though rightly signed, continues to be insignificant. Only the co-efficient of r_{call} in equation (F.3.3) is rightly signed and also significant at 5 per cent level of significance. In its place $(r_{adv} - r_{RBI})$ had turned out insignificant.

Of the two scale variables RR and L, the former is the truly significant one. Log L is not significant in equation (F.3.1). It was also found to be insignificant when entered alone, i.e. without log RR (results not reported here). On the other hand, log RR is significant in all the three equations. Further, both in equations (F.3.1) and (F.3.2) log L enters with a negative sign. This is contrary to *a priori* expectations, because as a scale variable, L should exert a positive, and not a negative, effect on BR^d. What reason can there be for the wrong sign of log L? We note that the co-efficient of correlation between log RR and log L has a very high value of 0.984, and the resultant multi-collinearity might have spoiled the result. This is confirmed by other regression equations (not reported here) wherein log L, when entered as the only scale variable, came out with positive sign, though with statistically insignificant value of its co-efficient. Again, to avoid multi-collinearity, log L was also dropped, and equation (F.3.3) fitted. A comparison of the value of the regression co-efficient of log RR (0.534) in this equation with the values of its regression co-efficients in the other two equations shows how the simultaneous presence of log L in the other two equations had inflated the value of this co-efficient.

The co-efficient of Cr/L is rightly signed and very highly significant in all the equations. It shows the importance of the demand for loans and advances (as measured by Cr/L) in determining BR^d.

It should be noted that all the equations are semi-logarithmic. Therefore, the co-efficients of individual independent variables have to be interpreted with care. Thus, in equation (F.3.3), with the value of 0.088 for the co-efficient of Cr/L and the mean value of 64.33 per cent for this variable, the elasticity of BR^d with respect to Cr/L at the latter's mean value comes to 5.66. Further, this elasticity will vary in the same direction in which the value of Cr/L varies.

For the reasons discussed earlier, we prefer equation (F.3.3) to the other two equations, despite its somewhat lower $\bar{R}^2$. Each equation suffers from positive first-order serial correlation among residuals as indicated by the estimated value of d. This calls for further research into the behaviour of BR^d. The value of $\bar{R}^2$ attained also indicates room for further improvement. We can only add that all our trials in linear-in-variables form gave poorer results in every case.

APPENDIX G
DATA AND SOURCES

Annual data on all the variables used in our empirical analysis are given in Table G.1. The first 17 are level variables, measured in crores of rupees of the current or some base-year purchasing power, as indicated below. The next is a price index number. Variables (19) and (20) are pure numbers per year and variable (21) is only a pure number. The next six, from (21) to (27), are ratio variables, expressed in percentages. The final eight variables, from (28) to (35), are percentage rates per year.

The values of variables (13) to (17) and of the terms of the ratio variables (24) to (27) are annual averages of weekly (Friday) figures for the period 1950–1 to 1974–5. They are annual averages of 'last Friday of the month' figures for 1975–6 and 1976–7. For 1974–5, the figures are provisional. Figures for variable (18) (*WPI*) are all annual averages of weekly figures. The values of variables (5) to (12) and of the terms of (21) are annual averages of 'last Friday of the month' figures, and are provisional for the year 1976–7. The first four variables are annual flows. Comparable time series data on income variables, (1) to (4), and the *WPI* (18) have been derived by appropriate splicing and conversions of various series.

Definitions of Symbols used in Table G.1 (column-wise)

(1) y = net national income at *1960–1 market* prices
(2) Y = net national income at *current market* prices
(3) y_{fc} = net national income (at factor cost) at *1960–1* prices
(4) Y_{fc} = net national income (at factor cost) at current prices
(5) M = nominal money held by the public (narrowly defined —old definition)
(6) M/P = real money held by the public, where $P = WPI$ of column (18) ÷ 100
(7) C = currency held by the public
(8) DD = net demand deposits of banks (net demand liabilities in the case of state co-operative banks) held by the public

(9) *OD*   = 'other deposits' of the R.B.I. held by the public

(10) *TD*   = net time deposits of banks (net time liabilities in the case of state co-operative banks) held by the public

(11) *H*   = high-powered money

(12) *H**   = adjusted *H* (i.e. *H* adjusted for changes in actual statutory reserves held by scheduled commercial banks on account of changes in statutory reserve requirements)

(13) *L*   = total of demand and time liabilities of scheduled commercial banks

(14) *R*   = total reserves held by scheduled commercial banks

(15) *RR*   = required (statutory) reserves actually held by scheduled commercial banks

(16) *ER*   = excess reserves of scheduled commercial banks

(17) *BR*   = borrowed reserves (or borrowings from the R.B.I.) of scheduled commercial banks

(18) *WPI*   = Wholesale Price Index Number with base 1961–2 = 100

(19) *V*   = income velocity of money per year, computed as Y/M

(20) V_{fc} = income velocity of money per year, computed as Yf_c/M

(21) *m*   = average money multiplier, computed as M/H^*

(22) Ya/Y = percentage of agricultural income at current market prices to *Y*

(23) Za/Z = percentage of agricultural income (at factor cost) at current prices to net domestic product (at factor cost) at current prices

(24) DL/TL = percentage of demand liabilities to time liabilities of scheduled commercial banks

(25) ER/L = percentage of excess reserves to total demand and time liabilities of scheduled commercial banks

(26) Cr/L = percentage of commercial credit (advances + commercial bills purchased and discounted) to total demand and time liabilities of scheduled commercial banks

(27) $I(GS)/L$ = percentage of investment in government securities to total demand and time liabilities of scheduled commercial banks

(28) r_{12} = 12-month time-deposit rate of major scheduled

commercial banks (other than the State Bank of India), average of the rates at Bombay, Calcutta, and Madras

(29) r_{bz} = average of the bazar-bill rates at Bombay, Calcutta, and Madras. (For the period 1967-8 to 1974-5, these rates were subject to ceilings at Bombay and Calcutta. So, for this period, the rate was arrived at by using the Madras rate and a conversion factor given by the ratio of the average r_{bz} for 1966-7 to Madras rate for 1966-7)

(30) r_{adv} = weighted average of advance rates at which commercial banks make loans and advances; the proportion of the total amount loaned at a particular rate is taken as its weight. Figures for the years 1974-5 to 1976-7 are rough estimates

(31) r_{RBI} = weighted average rate at which the R.B.I. lends to banks (weighted by the proportion of the total lent at a particular rate for the years 1960-1 to 1969-70; average bank rates weighted by time for other years)

(32) r_{call} = weighted average of call money rates of scheduled commercial banks (other than the State Bank of India), the weights being proportional to the amounts accepted during the period

(33) g_y = rate of growth of y
(34) g_P = rate of growth of P
(35) g_M = rate of growth of M

TABLE G.1
DATA ON SELECTED VARIABLES

(Amount in Rs crores)

Year	y (1)	Y (2)	y_{fc} (3)	Y_{fc} (4)	M (5)
1950–1	9478	9183	9078	8796	1862
51–2	9772	9635	9279	9149	1874
52–3	10045	9380	9590	8955	1752
53–4	10688	10048	10201	9590	1765
54–5	11089	9328	10483	8818	1850
1955–6	11492	9843	10860	9302	2049
56–7	12128	11216	11461	10599	2222
57–8	12039	11329	11254	10590	2334
58–9	12945	12601	12165	11841	2394
59–60	13274	13040	12399	12181	2551
1960–1	14210	14210	13263	13263	2725
61–2	14789	15067	13729	13987	2844
62–3	15189	16059	13993	14795	3098
63–4	16134	18543	14771	16977	3475
64–5	17302	21785	15885	20001	3866
1965–6	16604	22719	15082	20637	4236
66–7	16609	26030	15217	23848	4641
67–8	17885	30478	16463	28054	5008
68–9	18556	31338	16939	28607	5428
69–70	19760	34665	18016	31606	6011
1970–1	21020	37935	19068	34412	6729
71–2	21466	40800	19323	36728	7558
72–3	21187	44990	19019	40391	8559
73–4	22098	55657	20050	50498	10058
74–5	22428	65969	20200	59417	11233
1975–6	24749	68298	21958	60596	12175
1976–7					13975

TABLE G.1—*Continued*

(*Amount in Rs crores*)

Year	M/P (6)	C (7)	DD (8)	OD (9)	TD (10)
1950–1	2083	1275	572	15	278
51–2	1987	1287	566	21	322
52–3	2193	1206	533	13	347
53–4	2111	1235	520	10	372
54–5	2375	1285	556	9	399
1955–6	2773	1432	609	8	456
56–7	2639	1561	653	8	508
57–8	2692	1609	712	13	656
58–9	2651	1674	708	12	869
59–60	2725	1814	723	14	1104
1960–1	2730	1956	751	18	1177
61–2	2844	2062	768	14	1154
62–3	2985	2235	848	15	1291
63–4	3153	2438	1012	25	1313
64–5	3161	2634	1205	27	1403
1965–6	3219	2841	1375	20	1570
66–7	3096	3028	1584	29	1821
67–8	2993	3199	1778	31	2033
68–9	3282	3436	1928	64	2366
69–70	3503	3765	2188	55	2803
1970–1	3716	4160	2514	55	3250
71–2	3953	4576	2932	50	3919
72–3	4068	4969	3532	58	4745
73–4	3975	5850	4167	41	5838
74–5	3547	6326	4856	51	6815
1975–6	3886	6554	5568	53	8128
1976–7	4374	7331	6572	72	10243

15

TABLE G.1—*Continued*

(*Amount in Rs crores*)

Year	H	H*	L	R	RR
	(11)	(12)	(13)	(14)	(15)
1950–1	1395	1386	878	95.5	35.5
51–2	1410	1401	883	94.7	35.5
52–3	1311	1303	853	85.2	33.4
53–4	1330	1323	854	76.8	32.9
54–5	1389	1381	912	86.6	35.0
1955–6	1537	1529	1017	87.2	38.6
56–7	1665	1657	1107	87.2	41.7
57–8	1753	1744	1342	117.0	48.5
58–9	1821	1815	1601	124.3	54.2
59–60	1960	1956	1834	120.6	59.2
1960–1	2126	2101	1951	140.4	83.7
61–2	2214	2208	1992	126.0	65.3
62–3	2388	2386	2197	132.7	68.8
63–4	2611	2611	2400	139.0	72.0
64–5	2827	2827	2700	159.5	81.0
1965–6	3043	3043	3058	173.0	91.7
66–7	3273	3273	3545	200.3	106.3
67–8	3472	3472	3952	224.0	118.6
68–9	3767	3767	4398	248.5	132.0
69–70	4151	4151	5092	300.0	152.8
1970–1	4577	4577	5887	347.4	176.6
71–2	5052	5052	7009	392.4	210.3
72–3	5532	5532	8509	475.4	255.3
73–4	6777	6519	10355	835.9	568.7
74–5	7244	7050	12033	843.1	555.2
1975–6	7487	7369	14190	854.9	543.4
1976–7	8589	8317	17535	1161.1	815.1

TABLE G.1—*Continued*

(*Amount in Rs crores*)

Year	ER	BR	WPI 1961-2 = 100	V (per year)	V_{fc} (per year)
	(16)	(17)	(18)	(19)	(20)
1950–1	60.0	4.5	89.4	4.93	4.72
51–2	59.2	13.9	94.3	5.14	4.88
52–3	51.8	11.2	79.9	5.35	5.11
53–4	43.9	10.5	83.6	5.69	5.43
54–5	51.6	14.9	77.9	5.04	4.77
1955–6	48.6	24.5	73.9	4.80	4.54
56–7	45.5	63.5	84.2	5.05	4.77
57–8	68.5	44.6	86.7	4.85	4.54
58–9	70.1	17.8	90.3	5.26	4.95
59–60	61.4	19.4	93.6	5.11	4.77
1960–1	56.7	43.0	99.8	5.21	4.87
61–2	50.7	21.7	100.0	5.30	4.92
62–3	63.9	19.3	103.8	5.18	4.78
63–4	67.0	22.6	110.2	5.34	4.89
64–5	78.5	38.6	122.3	5.64	5.17
1965–6	81.3	49.3	131.6	5.36	4.87
66–7	94.0	31.6	149.9	5.61	5.14
67–8	105.4	24.2	167.3	6.09	5.60
68–9	116.5	81.9	165.4	5.77	5.27
69–70	147.2	105.8	171.6	5.77	5.26
1970 1	170.8	261.4	181.1	5.64	5.11
71–2	182.1	138.4	191.2	5.40	4.86
72–3	220.1	34.7	210.4	5.26	4.72
73–4	267.2	123.1	253.0	5.53	5.02
74–5	287.9	216.9	316.7	5.87	5.29
1975–6	311.5	332.0	313.3	5.61	4.98
1976–7	346.0	873.6	319.5		

TABLE G.1—*Continued*

(Percentages, except for (21))

Year	m	Ya/Y	Za/Z	DL/TL	ER/L
	(21)	(22)	(23)	(24)	(25)
1950–1	1.343	54.5	51.2	215.1	6.84
51–2	1.338	53.0	50.3	205.7	6.70
52–3	1.345	52.8	48.9	177.7	6.07
53–4	1.334	54.2	50.7	160.7	5.14
54–5	1.340	47.6	45.3	159.0	5.66
1955–6	1.340	47.0	45.3	149.2	4.78
56–7	1.341	50.5	48.8	144.0	4.11
57–8	1.338	47.8	46.3	116.8	5.10
58–9	1.319	49.9	49.4	85.5	4.38
59–60	1.304	48.9	48.2	68.7	3.35
1960–1	1.297	49.1	51.2	68.7	2.91
61–2	1.288	47.9	50.1	74.3	2.55
62–3	1.298	46.0	48.3	73.3	2.91
63–4	1.331	46.3	48.9	89.2	2.79
64–5	1.368	48.1	50.7	95.9	2.91
1965–6	1.392	45.2	47.9	93.9	2.66
66–7	1.416	47.0	49.4	94.3	2.65
67–8	1.442	49.7	52.0	95.1	2.67
68–9	1.441	47.2	49.7	90.0	2.65
69–70	1.448	46.7	49.3	86.3	2.89
1970–1	1.470	46.0	48.7	86.3	2.90
71–2	1.496	44.3	47.3	83.7	2.60
72–3	1.547	44.2	47.1	83.0	2.59
73–4	1.543	47.9	50.7	81.9	2.58
74–5	1.593	44.8	47.4	83.2	2.39
1975–6	1.652	40.1	42.9		2.20
1976–7	1.680				1.97

TABLE G.1—*Continued*

(*Percentages*)

Year	Cr/L	$I(GS)/L$	r_{12}	r_{bz}	r_{adv}
	(26)	(27)	(28)	(29)	(30)
1950–1	52.3		1.55	10.58	4.2
51–2	61.9		1.73	10.91	4.3
52–3	58.6	35.9	2.13	11.17	4.2
53–4	57.8	37.6	2.27	11.26	4.6
54–5	60.6	37.3	2.39	11.21	4.9
1955–6	62.1	36.5	2.39	11.12	5.0
56–7	70.6	32.5	2.94	11.10	5.1
57–8	66.4	28.7	3.29	11.40	5.4
58–9	56.2	35.3	3.33	10.77	5.7
59–60	53.8	39.5	3.23	10.76	5.9
1960–1	59.5	35.3	3.31	11.57	6.0
61–2	64.2	29.4	3.97	12.72	6.2
62–3	65.2	29.0	3.99	12.82	6.7
63–4	65.3	28.8	4.00	13.33	7.6
64–5	67.0	27.1	4.79	14.07	8.3
1965–6	68.2	26.3	5.50	15.70	8.7
66–7	66.5	27.2	6.00	16.60	8.7
67–8	67.6	25.7	6.00	17.35	8.7
68–9	70.6	23.9	5.50	17.86	8.4
69–70	70.4	23.3	5.50	17.61	8.3
1970–1	73.3	21.8	6.00	19.12	9.3
71–2	69.7	21.6	6.00	19.62	9.7
72–3	63.7	23.4	6.00	18.61	9.8
73–4	63.5	22.2	6.00	20.37	10.3
74–5	65.3	21.8	7.65	20.71	13.9
1975–6	67.1	21.7	8.00	21.98	14.6
1976–7	69.6	21.2	8.00	23.40	14.9

TABLE G.1—*Continued*

(*Percentages*)

Year	r_{RBI} (31)	r_{call} (32)	g_y (33)	g_P (34)	g_M (35)
1950–1	3.0	2.46	0.30	6.31	3.46
51–2	3.2	2.67	3.10	5.55	0.61
52–3	3.5	2.81	2.79	− 15.25	− 6.49
53–4	3.5	2.81	6.40	4.60	0.73
54–5	3.5	2.94	3.75	− 6.88	4.81
1955–6	3.6	2.95	3.63	− 5.03	10.76
56–7	3.5	3.73	5.53	13.94	8.47
57–8	4.0	3.73	− 0.73	2.97	5.03
58–9	4.0	2.85	7.53	4.15	2.59
59–60	4.0	2.50	2.54	3.65	6.56
1960–1	5.1	4.27	7.05	6.62	6.79
61–2	4.6	4.19	4.07	0.20	4.57
62–3	4.8	4.03	2.70	3.80	8.91
63–4	4.8	3.98	6.22	6.17	11.99
64–5	5.0	4.25	7.24	10.98	11.22
1965–6	6.4	4.53	− 4.03	7.60	9.61
66–7	6.1	5.33	0.03	13.90	9.52
67–8	5.9	4.87	7.68	11.61	7.94
68–9	4.7	3.90	3.75	− 1.14	8.37
69–70	4.5	4.22	6.49	3.75	10.73
1970–1	5.5	6.65	6.38	5.54	11.96
71–2	6.0	4.73	2.12	5.56	12.32
72–3	6.0	3.92	− 1.30	10.04	13.24
73–4	6.8	8.33	4.30	20.25	17.43
74–5	8.3	13.53	1.49	25.18	11.68
1975–6	9.0	10.83	10.35	− 1.07	8.39
1976–7	9.0	10.77		1.98	14.78

Sources

C.S.O. 1964. *Estimates of National Income*, 1948–9 to 1962–3, February.
——. 1975. *National Accounts Statistics*, 1960–1 to 1972–3, January.
——. 1976. *National Accounts Statistics*, 1960–1 to 1974–5, October.
——. 1978. *National Accounts Statistics*, 1970–1 to 1975–6, February.
Choudhry, N. K. et al. 1974. 'Towards An Econometric Model of the Indian Economy'. Part II (Data Base of the Indian Economy), A Report submitted to the I.C.S.S.R., New Delhi (mimeo).
G.O.I. Ministry of Finance, *Economic Survey* (Annual).
R.B.I. 1964. *Supplement to Banking and Monetary Statistics of India*. Parts I and II. Bombay.
——. *Report on Currency and Finance* (annual).
——. *Reserve Bank of India Bulletin* (monthly).
——. *Statistical Tables Relating to Banks in India* (annual).
Vasudevan, A. 1978. 'Trends in Money Supply Components', Parts I, II, and III. *Financial Express*, 14, 15, and 16 Jan., Bombay.

REFERENCES

ANDO, A. and Modigliani, F. 1963. 'The "Life Cycle" Hypothesis of Saving: Aggregate Implications and Tests'. *American Economic Review* vol. 53(1), 55–84.

ASCHHEIM, J. 1961. *Techniques of Monetary Control*. Baltimore: Johns Hopkins Press.

BHATTACHARYA, B. B. 1975. *Short-term Income Determination*. Delhi: Macmillan.

BROWN, T. M. 1952. 'Habit Persistence and Lags in Consumer Behaviour'. *Econometrica* vol. 20(3), 355–71.

CAGAN, P. 1965. *Determinants and Effects of Changes in the Stock of Money, 1875–1960*. Princeton University Press.

CHANDAVARKAR, A. G. 1964. 'Some Aspects of Open Market Operations of the Reserve Bank of India'. *Reserve Bank of India Bulletin*, December 1964, 1496-1504.

CHANDLER, L. V. 1962. *Central Banking and Economic Development*. Bombay University Press.

CULBERTSON, J. M. 1960. 'Friedman on the Lag in Effect of Monetary Policy'. *Journal of Political Economy* vol. 68(6), 617–21.

DAVIS, T. E. 1952. 'The Consumption Function as a Tool for Prediction'. *Review of Economics and Statistics* vol. 34(3), 270–7.

DUESENBERRY, J. S. 1949. *Income, Saving, and the Theory of Consumer Behaviour*. Harvard University Press.

DUESENBERRY, J. S., Eckstein, O., and Fromm, G. 1960. 'A Simulation of the United States Economy in Recession'. *Econometrica* vol. 28(4), 749–809.

EVANS, M. K. 1969. *Macroeconomic Activity*. New York: Harper and Row.

FISHER, I. 1911. *The Purchasing Power of Money: Its Determination and Relation to Credit, Interest and Crises*. New York: Macmillan.

FRIEDMAN, M. 1956. 'Quantity Theory of Money—A Restatement'. In Milton Friedman (ed.) *Studies in the Quantity Theory of Money*. University of Chicago Press.

——. 1957. *A Theory of the Consumption Function*. Princeton University Press.

——. 1959. *A Program for Monetary Stability*. New York: Fordham University Press.

——. 1961. 'The Lag in Effect of Monetary Policy'. *Journal of Political Economy* vol. 69(5), 447–66.

——. 1968. 'Money: Quantity Theory'. In *International Encyclopedia of the Social Sciences*. Free Press, 432–47; reprinted in A. A. Walters (ed.) *Money and Banking*. Penguin, 1973, 36–66.

——. and SCHWARTZ, A. 1963. *A Monetary History of the United States, 1867–1960*. Princeton University Press.

GHOSH, A. 1971. *Control Techniques in Indian Monetary Management*. Calcutta: World Press.

GOODHART, C. A. E. 1975. *Money, Information and Uncertainty*. London: Macmillan.

GUPTA, S. B. 1970. 'The Portfolio Balance Theory of the Expected Rate of Change of Prices'. *Review of Economic Studies* vol. 37(2), 187–203.

——. 1974a. 'Monetary Management in India: An Evaluation'. In J. C. Sandesara (ed.) *The Indian Economy: Performance and Prospects*. Bombay University Press, 266–79.

——. 1974b. 'Credit Policy, Interest Rates, Central Banking and All That: A Comment'. *Economic and Political Weekly*, 6 July, 1071–73.

——. 1974c. 'Food-Shortage, Demand Pull, and Inflation in India'. In S. L. N. Sinha (ed.) *Inflation in India*. Bombay: Vora, 155–72.

——. 1975a. 'Inflationary Finance and Forced Saving'. Delhi School of Economics Working Paper No. 144.

——. 1975b. 'Planning Neutral Money for India'. *Indian Economic Journal* vol. 23(2), Special Number in Monetary Economics, October-December, 169–90.

——. 1976a. 'Factors Affecting Money Supply—Critical Evaluation of Reserve Bank's Analysis'. *Economic and Political Weekly*, January 4, 117–28.

——. 1976b. 'Money Supply Analysis: A Reply'. *Economic and Political Weekly*, 20 November, 1834–44.

——. 1978a. 'The Reserve Bank and a New Theory of the Trade-Off Between Credit Inflation and Under-Production'. In *Recent Developments In Monetary Theory and Policy (With Special Reference to Developing Economies)*. Papers and Proceedings of the Seminar held at Bombay, Reserve Bank of India.

——. 1978b. 'Inflation and Forced Saving (Part A)'. Delhi School of Economics Working Paper No. 144 (Revised).

JOHNSON, M. B. 1971. *Household Behaviour: Consumption, Income and Wealth*. Penguin.

KAREKEN, J. and SOLOW, R. M. 1963. 'Lags in Monetary Policy'. In Commission on Money and Credit, *Stabilization Policies*. Englewood Cliffs: Prentice-Hall.

KEYNES, J. M. 1936. *The General Theory of Employment, Interest and Money*. London: Macmillan.

LAHIRI, A. K. 1977. 'The Demand for Money'. Unpublished Ph.D. Dissertation. University of Delhi.

LAIDLER, D. E. W. 1969. *Demand for Money, Theories and Evidence*. Scranton, Pennsylvania: International Textbook Company.

MADALGI, S. S. 1976. 'Trends in Monetisation in the Indian Economy (1961–62 to 1974–75)'. *Reserve Bank Staff Occasional Papers* vol. 1(1), 46–72.

MOORE, B. J. 1968. *Introduction to The Theory of Finance*. New York: Macmillan.

MUJUMDAR, N. A. 1976. 'Money Supply Analysis—Mechanistic and Economic Explanations'. *Economic and Political Weekly*, 28 February, 371–3.

——. and PATIL, R. H. 1975. 'Impact of Domestic and External Factors on Money Supply: The 1974–75 Experience'. *Reserve Bank of India Bulletin*, June, 379–85.

MUKHERJEE, M. 1967. 'The Role of Transactions in Kind in Developing Economies'. *Review of Income and Wealth*, Series 13, 335–51.

PHILLIPS, A. W. 1958. 'The Relation Between Unemployment and the Rate of

Change of Money Wage Rates in the United Kingdom, 1861–1957'. *Economica*, New Series, vol. 29(4), 283–99.

OJHA, P. D. 1972. 'Deficit: Measurement and Its Implications for Financial Planning'. *Artha Vikas* vol. 8(1), 25–71.

PANDIT, V. N. 1977. 'Structural Basis for Macroeconomic Policy in India, 1950–51 through 1974–75', University of Manchester (mimeo).

PAREKH, H. T. 1974. 'Credit Policy, Interest Rates, Central Banking and All That'. *Economic and Political Weekly*, 25 May, 839–41.

PATINKIN, D. 1965. *Money, Interest, and Prices* 2nd ed. New York: Harper and Row.

PRASAD, K. 1969. *Role of Money Supply in a Developing Economy*. New Delhi: Allied.

RANGARAJAN, C. 1965. 'Demand for Money: Some Empirical Estimates Relating to India'. Paper presented at the 5th Indian Econometric Conference, Delhi (mimeo).

ROSA (Roosa), R. V. 1951. 'Interest Rates and the Central Bank'. In D. M. Wright and R. V. Rosa (eds.) *Money, Trade and Economic Growth: In Honor of John Henry Williams*. New York: Macmillan, 270–95.

R.B.I. 1961a. 'Analysis of Money Supply in India—I'. *Reserve Bank of India Bulletin*, July, 1045–67.

——. 1961b. 'Analysis of Money Supply in India—II', *Reserve Bank of India Bulletin*, August, 1214–19.

——. 1970. *The Reserve Bank of India: Functions and Working*. Bombay.

——. 1977. 'Money Supply: Concepts, Compilation And Analysis' (Report of the Second Working Group). *Reserve Bank of India Bulletin*, January, 70–134.

SEN, S. N. 1967. *Central Banking in Underdeveloped Money Markets* 4th ed. Calcutta: Bookland.

SHETTY, S. L., Avadhani, V. A., and Menon, K.A. 1976. 'Money Supply Analysis —Further Comments'. *Economic and Political Weekly*, 10 April, 571–4.

SINGH, B. and Kumar, R. C. 1971. 'The Relative Income Hypothesis—A Cross-Country Analysis'. *Review of Income and Wealth*, Series 17 (No. 4), 341–52.

SINGH, B., DROST, H., and KUMAR, R. C. 1978. 'An Empirical Evaluation of the Relative, the Permanent Income and the Life-Cycle Hypotheses'. *Economic Development and Cultural Change* vol. 26 (2), 281–305.

SWAMY, Gurushri. 1975. 'The Determinants of Changes in the Stock of Money in India, 1951–52—1970–71'. Unpublished Ph.D. Dissertation. University of Delhi.

TUN WAI, U. 1959–60. 'The Relation between Inflation and Economic Development: A Statistical Inductive Study'. *I.M.F. Staff Papers* vol. 7, 302–18.

TURNOVSKY, S. J. 1977. *Macroeconomic Analysis and Stabilization Policy*. Cambridge University Press.

VASUDEVAN, A. 1977. 'Demand for Money in India—A Survey of Literature'. *Reserve Bank Staff Occasional Papers* vol. 2 (1), 58–83.

INDEX